CONSIDERING THE BUSH PRESIDENCY

CONSIDERING
THE BUSH PRESIDENCY

Edited by

GARY L. GREGG II

University of Louisville

MARK J. ROZELL

The Catholic University of America

New York   Oxford
OXFORD UNIVERSITY PRESS
2004

Oxford University Press

Oxford   New York
Auckland   Bangkok   Buenos Aires   Cape Town   Chennai
Dar es Salaam   Delhi   Hong Kong   Istanbul   Karachi   Kolkata
Kuala Lumpar   Madrid   Melbourne   Mexico City   Mumbai
Nairobi   São Paulo   Shanghai   Taipei   Tokyo   Toronto

Published by Oxford University Press, Inc.
198 Madison Avenue, New York, New York, 10016
http://www.oup-usa.org

Oxford is a registered trademark of Oxford University Press

Library of Congress Cataloging-in-Publication Data
Considering the Bush presidency / edited by Gary L. Gregg II, Mark J. Rozell.
   p. cm.
   Includes bibliographical references and index.
   ISBN 0-19-516681-7 (alk. paper)—ISBN 0-19-516680-9 (pbk. : alk. paper)
   1. United States—Politics and government—2001–2. Bush, George W. (George Walker),
1946–   I. Gregg, Gary L., 1967–II. Rozell, Mark J.

E902.C66 2003
973.931′092—dc21   2003048638

Printing number: 9 8 7 6 5 4 3 2 1

Printed in the United States of America
on acid-free paper

Contents

Preface

Although barely past the midterm point, the George W. Bush presidency has already made a significant impact on the institution. Bush came to office under some of the most unusual circumstances in presidential history. He lost the popular vote to incumbent Vice President Albert Gore and then for thirty-six days the outcome of the election remained in doubt as a vote recount proceeded in Florida and the courts became involved in settling the controversy. Bush eventually won the presidency only after a highly controversial 5–4 Supreme Court decision went in his favor and stopped the recounting of ballots. Even though many Democrats were angry at the outcome and questioned its legitimacy, once the Court had spoken most of the country accepted that the election controversy was over. In a gracious speech that many observers said was better than any he had given as a candidate for the presidency, Gore dropped his legal challenges and conceded to Bush.

The president-elect thus had an abbreviated transition period during which he could pull together his White House team and map out a policy agenda. To be sure, much of that work was going on during the legal challenges in anticipation of a possible Bush victory. But the election controversy had taken considerable attention away from the transition effort and led many to believe that this distraction would harm Bush's efforts to enter the presidency "hitting the ground running." Furthermore, political observers never hesitated to point out that although Bush won the presidency, he had lost the popular vote and would be leading from a position of weakness.

When he entered office, Bush did not act like a president who needed to prove his legitimacy. He moved quickly to consolidate his power and to promote a domestic policy agenda led by large tax cuts and education reform. Having Republican control of both houses of Congress—something that was short-lived—Bush saw an opportunity to make his mark on the presidency early. The hallmark of the early months of his presidency was a tax rebate that many Democrats criticized as unneeded and ultimately bad for the economy. Bush moved with a singular focus on this issue and made the bold move of personally campaigning for the tax cut in the states of some wavering Democratic senators. Having become so personally invested in its success, Bush risked an embarrassing defeat but ultimately prevailed in achieving a $1.3 trillion tax reduction package.

During the summer of 2001, the administration's momentum stalled. The economy began to slip seriously, business scandals and bankruptcies dominated the news, the president was embattled by a controversial moral issue (stem cell research) that he did not want to be a major focus at that stage of his term, and national polls were showing some loss in his support. Then September 11, 2001, changed America and refocused the Bush presidency.

The impact of September 11 on the Bush presidency is explored in many of the essays in this book. As our lead author James Pfiffner puts it, the Bush presidency was transformed by the terrorist attacks on the United States, and it is essential to analyze the administration's record to date on that basis. Nonetheless, the tragedy of September 11 does not alone define Bush's presidency, and the contributors to this volume provide a broad-ranging overview of his leadership at home and abroad.

Bush achieved a major leadership opportunity after the GOP (Grand Old Party) victories in the 2002 midterm elections. Once again, the president personally campaigned in key states and risked the stigma of a very public defeat. When the GOP prevailed in most of the key contests in which the president had become involved, observers credited Bush and his political advisers for a brilliant strategy and the courage to use (and put at risk) the presidential image. With party control once again of both houses of Congress, the Republicans appeared poised to make major policy gains in the second half of Bush's term.

President Bush retains high levels of public support at home, yet the second half of his term is likely to be characterized by the especially troublesome issues of economic instability and war. Many observers, including a number of this volume's authors, believe that Bush met some crucial leadership challenges during the first half of his term. The ultimate success of the Bush presidency now depends on how he handles the challenges that await him as we approach the elections of 2004.

Every author has a story or two about the origins of a book. Ours is quite simple. We celebrated St. Patrick's Day 2002 together at a popular Irish pub in Washington, D.C., and began discussing the fascinating twists and turns of the incumbent administration. It became quickly evident that we shared an interest in making a contribution to the discussion about the Bush presidency within the academic community and among our students. Both of us have worked in one capacity or another with some of the very best presidential scholars, and we knew that they had important things to say about Bush's leadership. We decided to bring those scholars together for this volume.

Every author also incurs some debts during the process of developing a book. We are grateful for the assistance of our students Aaron Nathaniel Coleman and Kelly Hanlon of University of Louisville and Margaret Sammon of The Catholic University of America. Mary Ann Ealey (Catholic University) provided much-needed secretarial assistance. We also thank our colleagues who contributed to this volume with their timely and thoughtful essays on what is developing as a historic presidency.

G.L.G., Louisville, KY
M.J.R., Washington, D.C.

Contributors

James P. Pfiffner is Professor of Public Policy at George Mason University and the author or editor of ten books on the presidency and American government, including *The Strategic Presidency: Hitting the Ground Running* and *The Modern Presidency*. He has worked at the U.S. Office of Personnel Management and has been a member of the faculty at the University of California, Riverside and California State University, Fullerton. He is a member of the National Academy of Public Administration and worked on the staff of the National Commission on the Public Service (the Volcker Commission). In 1970 he received the Army Commendation Medal for Valor in Vietnam and Cambodia.

John P. Burke is Professor of Political Science at the University of Vermont. He has written numerous articles and five books, including *Bureaucratic Responsibility; How Presidents Test Reality: Decisions on Vietnam, 1954 and 1965; The Institutional Presidency: Organizing and Managing the White House from FDR to Bill Clinton; Advising Ike: The Memoirs of Attorney General Herbert Brownell;* and *Presidential Transitions: From Politics to Practice*. His book, *How Presidents Test Reality*, won the 1990 Richard Neustadt Award of the American Political Science Association for the best book on the American presidency.

Kathryn Dunn Tenpas is a guest scholar at the Brookings Institution, Associate Director of the University of Pennsylvania's Washington Semester Program, and author of *Presidents as Candidates: Inside the White House for the Presidential Campaign*.

Stephen Hess is a senior fellow at the Brookings Institution. He served on the White House staffs of Presidents Eisenhower and Nixon, and is the author of *Organizing the Presidency*, now in its third edition.

Charles E. Walcott is Professor of Political Science at Virginia Polytechnic Institute and State University. He has co-authored (with Karen M. Hult) *Governing the White House: From Hoover through LBJ* and *Governing Public Organizations* and is currently co-editor of *Congress and the Presidency*. His articles have appeared in numerous scholarly journals.

Karen M. Hult is Professor of Political Science at Virginia Polytechnic Institute and State University. She has authored *Agency Merger and Bureaucratic Redesign* and co-authored (with Charles E. Walcott) *Governing the White House: From Hoover through LBJ* and *Governing Public Organizations*. She currently serves as book review editor for the *Presidential Studies Quarterly*.

Michael A. Dimock is Research Director of the Pew Research Center for the People and the Press, and is principally responsible for the development of the center's research projects. Before joining the Pew Research Center staff, he was Professor of Political Science at North Carolina State University in Raleigh, NC.

Gary L. Gregg II holds the Mitch McConnell Chair in Leadership at the University of Louisville, where he is also Director of the McConnell Center for Political Leadership. He is the author or editor of five books, including *The Presidential Republic: Executive Representation and Deliberative Democracy, Vital Remnants: America's Founding and the Western Tradition*, and *Securing Democracy: Why We Have an Electoral College.*

Louis Fisher is a senior specialist with the Congressional Research Service of the Library of Congress, where he has worked since 1970. He served as Research Director of the House Iran-Contra Committee in 1987, writing major sections of the final report. He has written sixteen books, including *American Constitutional Law, Congressional Abdication on War and Spending, Constitutional Conflicts between Congress and the President*, and *Presidential War Power*. He has also authored over three hundred articles and has testified before congressional committees more than forty times.

Mark J. Rozell is Professor and Chair of the Department of Politics at The Catholic University of America in Washington, D.C. He is the author of numerous books and articles on the presidency, including, most recently, *Power and Prudence: The Presidency of George H.W. Bush* (with Ryan J. Barrilleaux) and *Executive Privilege: Presidential Power, Secrecy and Accountability*, now in its second edition.

Michael Nelson is Professor of Political Science at Rhodes College. He has written and edited numerous books, including *Presidents, Politics, and Policy; A Heartbeat Away; The Presidency and the Political System;* and *The Elections of 1996*. He has won several teaching and writing awards. He has published more than forty articles which have appeared in numerous scholarly journals.

Paul Kengor is Associate Professor of Political Science at Grove City College. His writings have appeared in scholarly journals, and his books include *God, Reagan, and the Soviet Empire* and *Wreath Layer or Policy Player?*

Andrew E. Busch is Associate Professor of Political Science at the University of Denver. He is author or co-author of six books on American politics, including *Horses in Midstream: U.S. Midterm Elections and Their Consequences, 1894–1998; Ronald Reagan and the Politics of Freedom;* and *The Perfect Tie: The True Story of the 2000 Presidential Election* (with James Ceaser).

CONSIDERING
THE BUSH PRESIDENCY

CHAPTER 1

Introduction

Assessing the Bush Presidency

JAMES P. PFIFFNER

George W. Bush began his presidency with as little political capital as any president since Gerald R. Ford; his opponent, Al Gore, outpolled him by more than a half-million votes in the November 2000 election. The lack of an obvious mandate did not deter the president from pursuing conservative policy priorities in the first phase of his presidency. By the end of his first six months in office, President Bush had won a major tax-cut victory and had begun to take his administration in a conservative policy direction. At the end of the summer of 2002 his poll ratings had dropped to the low fifties, and the administration was looking forward to a fall of battles with Democrats in the Senate. The second phase of the administration began with the terrorist attacks on New York and Washington, D.C., and the outpouring of public support for the president. With the war in Afghanistan going well and beginning to wind down, President Bush began the third phase of his presidency when he initiated his political campaign to convince the country that "regime change" in Iraq was essential to the security of the United States.

This chapter will examine the three phases of the first two years of President Bush's presidency: the transition and initial agenda, the war on terrorism, and the campaign for war with Iraq.

I. TRANSITION AND INITIAL AGENDA

President George W. Bush's transition into office was one of the shortest but most efficiently run in recent times. Because of the growth of the size and scope of the national government, transitions since the 1970s have been elaborately planned and bureaucratized. There never seems to be enough time to fully prepare to take over the government. Yet because of the delay in the authoritative outcome of the 2000 election, the incoming Bush administration had five fewer weeks for officially preparing to take office, about half as much time as other administrations. Surprisingly, under the circumstances, they accomplished the major tasks of the transitions—designating a White House staff, naming a cabinet, and laying the groundwork for their initial policy agenda—with dispatch.

The key to President Bush's White House staff was Vice President Richard Cheney, who was chosen to be the running mate because of his experience, competence, and relationship with the head of the ticket. Cheney was to break the mold of vice presidential unimportance in an administration. He ran the transition and dominated most of the organizational and policy deliberations early in the administration. Administration officials took pains to emphasize that all final decisions were in fact made by President Bush and that Cheney's role was merely advisory.

As chief of staff, the president chose Andrew Card, an experienced Washington insider. He had worked in the White House for Ronald Reagan and had been a deputy to John Sununu in the administration of the elder George Bush before being appointed secretary of transportation; he also ran the 2000 Republican National Convention for Bush. While Card was the key to managing the White House, the dominant person, short of the President, was clearly Vice President Cheney, whose national experience far outmatched that of President Bush. Cheney put together an impressive staff of his own, including his own national security aides and a domestic policy staff. Because of Cheney's prominence in the administration, White House officials were careful to emphasize his subordinate position to the president. According to Cheney's counselor, Mary Matalin, "The vice president has no personal or political agenda other than advising President Bush."[1]

After Cheney and Card, the two key aides to Bush were his political strategist, Karl Rove, and his counselor, Karen Hughes. Hughes had been Bush's closest aide while he was governor of Texas and throughout his campaign for the presidency. When he reached the White House, Bush said, "I want you in every meeting where major decisions are made."[2] She played important roles in creating a sense of order in the White House and crafting Bush's public image. She was in charge of forty-two staffers involved in communications or press issues. The president lost an important adviser when she left the administration in the summer of 2002, though she continued to advise the president from her home in Texas.

Karl Rove had been Bush's top campaign strategist, and in the White House played the role of senior political adviser, directing the offices of Political Affairs and Public Liaison. While not as close to Bush as Hughes, Rove played the important roles of concentrating on political strategy and tending to Bush's links to the conservative wing of the Republican Party. At the senior level was the Rove-led "Strategery Group" (named for a humorous television skit on Bush diction) of the top domestic and national security aides. He was also in charge of the Office of Communications, which had a two- to three-week time horizon, and the Press Office with a twenty-four- to forty-eight-hour time horizon.[3]

Bush's national security assistant, Condoleezza Rice, was a veteran aide to Brent Scowcroft in the administration of the first President Bush and top national security adviser to candidate Bush during the 2000 presidential campaign, where she earned his respect and trust. She was, at forty-six, the youngest person to direct national security as well as the first woman in the post. Rice's initial move was to restructure the National Security Council (NSC) and cut its staff by a third. Rice would focus on advising the president, but—just as her mentor, Scowcroft—she did not plan to dominate the national security policy-making process. In the Bush administration it would be difficult for *anyone* to dominate the policy process, with such formidable principals as Dick Cheney, Secretary of Defense Donald Rumsfeld, and Secretary of State Colin Powell, each with their own sizable staffs, on the National Security Council.

The Bush cabinet selection committee consisted of only four people: the president-elect, Dick Cheney, transition director Clay Johnson, and Andrew Card. Great pains were taken to keep cabinet choices secret until immediately before their announcement.[4]

Without echoing President Clinton's promise to appoint a cabinet that "looks like America," Bush recruited a cabinet equally diverse by contemporary standards. Bush appointed four women (Elaine Chao at Labor, Ann Veneman at Agriculture, Gale Norton at Interior, and Christine Whitman at the Environmental Protection Agency—designated as part of the cabinet), two African Americans (Colin Powell at State and Roderick Paige at Education), one Arab American (Spencer Abraham at Energy), one Hispanic (Mel Martinez at Housing and Urban Development), and two Asian Americans (Chao and Norman Mineta at Transportation, also a Democrat who had been secretary of commerce in the Clinton administration). Only six of the fifteen were white males. The diversity of the cabinet reflected both the increasingly qualified pool of minorities in the United States and the signal that Bush wanted to send to draw minority voters from the Democratic to the Republican Party.

Despite Bush's care in recruiting an experienced and well-credentialed cabinet, he was not about to reverse the trend of the past four decades of power gravitating to the White House. All of the policy priorities of the early administration were dominated by White House staffers rather than led from the cabinet. The administration began with monthly cabinet meetings and frequent contact between cabinet members and the White House staff, but that did not translate into policy clout.

During the presidential campaign of 2000, candidate Bush set a moderate tone by asserting that he was a "compassionate conservative" and advocating educational proposals that often appealed to Democratic voters. He promised to "change the tone" in Washington by taking a bipartisan approach to governing, as he had in Texas. While arguing for more defense spending and a national missile defense, privatization of part of Social Security, and a large tax cut, the emphasis was not on the more conservative aspects of his policy agenda.

In his first weeks in office he followed up on his promise to change the tone in Washington by meeting with a large number of members of Congress, many of them Democrats. He even attended caucus meetings of the Democrats in the House and the Senate to show that he was willing to communicate with the opposition. In his initial policy agenda, however, he pursued a conservative agenda that pleased his Republican base in the House of Representatives and the electorate.[5] His first executive order reversed U.S. policy and shut off U.S. funds to international family planning programs that allowed abortions. He also suspended, and later canceled, Department of Labor ergonomic regulations designed to reduce harm from repetitive-motion injuries.

In January 2001 Republicans controlled both houses of Congress and the presidency for the first time since the beginning of the Eisenhower administration, but their control of Congress was tenuous. The Senate was split 50–50, and Republican control depended on the tie-breaking vote of the vice president. The partisan split in the House in the first session of the 107th Congress was 222 to 211 (with two Independents), and the defection of a handful of Republican votes could defeat Republican measures.

President Bush's first and largest legislative initiative was to propose a large tax cut, as he had promised in the campaign. The administration's proposal was for a $1.6 trillion cut over ten years that included reducing the top brackets, eliminating the estate tax, reducing the marriage penalty, and increasing child credits. Democrats argued that most of the benefits would go to the relatively well off and that the overall size of the reduction in revenues would threaten the projected surpluses; they favored a smaller cut that was targeted at lower income levels. The House passed Bush's plan, but the Senate held out for a smaller cut. After negotiations, the Senate went along with the House to vote for a $1.35 trillion cut, an important policy victory for the president.

In another of Bush's top priorities he established by executive action a White House Office of Faith-Based and Community Initiatives to facilitate the use of federal funds for social purposes to be administered by faith-based organizations. He proposed privatizing part of the Social Security system by setting aside a portion of contributions to the system for private investment in personal retirement accounts. Although much of his education agenda was endorsed by Democrats, Bush favored the creation of vouchers allowing public funds to be used by parents to send their children to private schools. A version of his education plan, without vouchers, was passed by Congress in the late fall of 2001.

In the late spring of 2001 the president had won an important victory in his large tax cut and was turning to his other priorities when his political power was dealt a blow. Senator James Jeffords, a third-term Republican from Vermont, had been a moderate but loyal Republican, but he had felt increasingly out of place in the conservative Republican Party of the 1990s. He felt particularly strongly about special education policy, and felt that his priorities were being ignored by Republican conservatives in Congress. He decided that he no longer felt welcome in the Republican Party and, after voting for the Bush tax cut, switched his affiliation to Independent and caucused with the Democrats in the Senate. He said that the Republican Party was moving away from the traditional values of "the Party of Lincoln," specifically, "moderation, tolerance, fiscal responsibility."[6]

Thus in the middle of the first session of the 107th Congress, party control of the Senate shifted from the Republicans to the Democrats. With the 50–50 split after the election, the Republicans could count on a tie-breaking vote from the vice president. But with the Democrats controlling fifty-one votes to the Republicans' forty-nine, control of the Senate agenda, along with chairmanships of all the committees, went to the Democrats, who would not be as sympathetic to President Bush's priorities.

At 180 days in office President Bush enjoyed public approval of 57 percent—not bad, but lower than the postwar presidents except for Bill Clinton, at 45 percent. In late summer President Bush won three victories in the House—on his comprehensive energy plan, the Faith-Based Initiative, and on a patients' bill of rights. But victories in the Senate were going to be much more difficult with the new Democratic majority.

Thus in the summer of 2001 the Bush administration began to recalibrate its policy priorities to adjust to Democratic control in the Senate and looked forward to some difficult policy battles in the fall. Then came the terrorist attacks that transformed the Bush presidency and the nation's priorities.

II. THE BUSH PRESIDENCY TRANSFORMED

At 8:48 A.M. on September 11, 2001, American Airlines Flight 11 crashed into the north tower of the World Trade Center; at 9:03 A.M. United Airline Flight 175 slammed into the south tower; at 9:45 A.M. American Airlines Flight 77 hit the Pentagon; by 10:30 A.M. both towers had collapsed and the west section of the Pentagon was in flames. More than 3,000 people died in the attacks: almost all were Americans, along with several hundred citizens of more than fifty other nations. Thus were world history, international relations, American politics, and the Bush presidency transformed within minutes. A surge of public unity gave President Bush unprecedented public support; a compliant Congress voted support for his administration's war on terrorism; and early successes in the war in Afghanistan bolstered the President's popularity.

The first and most important political effect of the terrorist bombings of September 11 was a huge jump in public approval of President Bush. In the September 7–10 Gallup poll, public approval of the President stood at 51 percent; the next poll, on September 14–15, registered 86 percent approval—a 35 percent jump virtually overnight. It is common for presidents to enjoy increased public approval whenever there is a crisis involving U.S. national security, called by political scientists a "rally event." But the magnitude of sudden change in public opinion was unprecedented; for instance, the Vietnam peace agreement in 1973 caused a sixteen-point jump, and the Truman

Doctrine and the Cuban Missile Crisis each caused a twelve-point jump.[7] Interestingly, the increased public approval for the president was accompanied by jumps in approval for the federal government in general and for Congress. For the remainder of 2001 public approval of President Bush averaged 87 percent, whereas his approval for the first several months of his presidency averaged 56 percent.

The sustained historically high public approval ratings of President Bush reflected public confidence in the way he and Congress handled the U.S. reaction to the terrorist bombings. In an address to a joint session of Congress on September 20, President Bush declared, "Tonight we are a country awakened to a danger and called to defend freedom. . . . Whether we bring our enemies to justice, or bring justice to our enemies, justice will be done" (White House transcript 2001). Congress responded quickly with virtually unanimous support for measures designed to support what the President called a war on terrorism. Congress quickly passed a bill providing $40 billion in emergency appropriations for military action, beefing up domestic security, and rebuilding New York City.

The administration also asked for and got sweeping authority to pursue an international war on terrorism. On September 14 Congress passed a joint resolution giving President Bush broad discretion in his direction of the military response to the terrorist attacks. Section 2(a) of the resolution provided:

> That the President is authorized to use all necessary and appropriate force against those nations, organizations, or persons he determines planned, authorized, committed, or aided the terrorist attacks that occurred on September 11, 2001, or harbored such organizations or persons, in order to prevent any future acts of international terrorism against the United States by such nations, organizations or persons.

The grant of power was sweeping in that it allowed the president to decide as "he determines" which "nations, organizations, or persons" United States forces may attack.

On September 12, the day after the attacks, the Central Intelligence Agency (CIA) and military leaders briefed the president on plans that had been under way to deal with Al Qaeda and current military options. President Bush then made the key initial decisions of the war after meeting on September 15 at Camp David with his war council, who presented a range of options for pursuing the war. The key elements of his decision were that the initial military actions would be limited to Afghanistan and that the war would begin with a massive air campaign before ground forces were introduced in large numbers.[8] On October 7 airstrikes began on Taliban forces in Kabul, Kandahar, and Jalalabad. U.S ground forces cooperating with the Northern Alliance began attacking Taliban forces, with the tide turning in favor of the United States in mid-November, with Kabul falling to the Northern Alliance on November 13. In early December allied forces took control of Kandahar, and a coalition of Afghan forces took official control of the country by the end of the year.

Congress also passed antiterrorism measures proposed by Attorney General John Ashcroft with broad, bipartisan support. The legislation which was passed by Congress in mid-October and signed by the president later in the month was titled the "Uniting and Strengthening America by Providing Appropriate Tools Required to Intercept and Obstruct Terrorism Act of 2001," or more briefly the "U.S.A. Patriot Act." The bill broadened the definition of who might be considered a terrorist and gave the attorney general expanded powers to deal with suspected terrorists. If the attorney general had "reasonable grounds to believe" that certain foreigners might be terrorists, the Justice Department could detain them indefinitely. Congress also passed provisions expanding government powers on wire tapping, computer surveillance, and money laundering. Attorney General Ashcroft also issued an order allowing officials to listen in on attorney-client communications for suspects who might be terrorists. Under the new legal powers, government authorities had detained more than one thousand people by November 2001. Many of these people were confined secretly for indefinite periods without being charged with crimes.[9]

The Bush administration was even more disciplined and loyal than before the attacks. There had been relatively little of the infighting, backbiting, and leaks in the Bush White House that were common to most other administrations, including his father's. In part, this was because White House staffers genuinely liked the president, but it was also a consequence of Bush's high premium on loyalty and the willingness of his top staffers to aggressively enforce discipline. Similarly, in the cabinet, there was usually not much room between what the president thought and his cabinet secretaries' public positions. One senior Bush aide put it this way: "This is not a presidency under which there's a lot of freelancing within the cabinet. It's a very tight team, very regimented, very tight message discipline, and I think the cabinet officers realize a large part of their job is to be shields."[10]

The shift of the presidency to a war footing also changed the agenda and importance of the cabinet and White House advisers. The turnaround in the reputations of the secretaries of state and defense was most striking. Secretary of Defense Rumsfeld in the spring of 2001 was leading a reevaluation of U.S. national security forces and contemplating major changes in the role and size of the Army. But he was running into flak from top military leaders for his top-down approach and from Congress for insufficient consultation. There was even public speculation that he would leave the administration at the end of its first year in office. But once the war in Afghanistan began, Rumsfeld became the clear leader of U.S. military forces and the preeminent spokesman for the military actions of the administration.

In his first six months in office Secretary of State Colin Powell had lost a number of minor skirmishes within the administration over foreign policy (on relations with North Korea, U.S. commitments in the Balkans, the

Kyoto global warming agreement, and abandoning the antiballistic missile [ABM] treaty) and was seen as being marginalized by his foes within the administration. Immediately after the terrorist attacks, Powell became the architect of the coalition of allies that joined the war effort by providing overflight rights, bases, troops, or public support. He soon came to be seen as the main spokesman for the president in foreign policy matters. Vice President Cheney continued to play a crucial role in the operations of the White House, though much of the time he was "at an undisclosed location" for security purposes.

III. THE POLITICAL CAMPAIGN FOR WAR WITH IRAQ

A. The Shift from the War on Terrorism to War with Iraq

After the attacks on the United States by Al Qaeda, President Bush did an effective job in uniting the country, mobilizing the military for retaliation, and laying the groundwork for organizing the government to ensure homeland security. The initial stages of the U.S. military response in Afghanistan were effective, and the international community was successfully courted to secure its support for U.S. actions against terrorists.

The military mission in Afghanistan, however, did "creep" in its scope. It began as an attempt to capture or kill the planners of the terrorist attacks on the United States, particularly Osama bin Laden and his Al Qaeda organization of terrorists. But the U.S. military mission soon grew to the military defeat of the Taliban regime that controlled Afghanistan, and with the help of local warlords of the Northern Alliance, the mission was successful in defeating them militarily and driving much of the Taliban regime into the mountains or out of the country.

But with the defeat of the Taliban came the need to create a national government for Afghanistan, and the resulting coalition of Afghan forces met with some success, with the United States providing aid and military training while its own forces continued to operate in the country in search of Al Qaeda remnants. But the new government was not immediately successful in uniting the country, and it was subject to armed attack from rival internal forces. U.S. forces faced difficulties in their search for terrorists and killed a number of Afghan civilians because of poor intelligence.[11]

In the summer of 2002 the United States was faced with winding down its military mission in Afghanistan and providing for the permanence of its new government. Thus "mission creep" in Afghanistan was the reality that faced President Bush who had previously derided nation building as a goal of U.S. foreign policy. But there was a logic and necessity to the expansion of the U.S. responsibilities in its war against the terrorists, Al Qaeda, and the Taliban. Each became a logical outcome of the other, and U.S. security could not be protected without the progression.

However, before the war in Afghanistan was finished, President Bush decided to undertake a campaign to convince Americans that major threats to U.S. security existed in the world and that "regime change" in Iraq was essential to U.S. security. His first major shift in focus came in his State of the Union address in January 2002, when he denounced an "axis of evil" that comprised North Korea, Iran, and Iraq. U.S. foreign and military policy were to be focused on the mitigation of danger to the United States from these "rogue states." While the hostile reaction of these states to Bush's rhetorical attack was predictable, the United States took no immediate action with respect to North Korea and Iran.

In contrast to the lack of major initiatives to follow up on the verbal attacks on North Korea and Iran, the spring and summer of 2002 saw the Bush administration prepare for a major war with Iraq in order to effect a regime change by deposing Saddam Hussein from power. In a speech at West Point in June 2002, President Bush declared that the growing threat to the United States from terrorism and rogue states made it necessary to consider preemptive military strikes in defense of the United States against these threats. The United States must "be ready for preemptive action when necessary to defend our liberty," Bush declared. "The war on terror will not be won on the defensive. We must take the battle to the enemy, disrupt its plans, and confront the worst threats before they emerge. . . . The only path to safety is the path of action. And this nation will act."[12] Though Bush did not directly say that his remarks were directed at Saddam Hussein and Iraq, that was the subtext that everyone understood.

B. Arguments for and against War with Iraq

Few in the United States questioned that Saddam Hussein was a tyrant who deserved to be overthrown. The international case against Saddam was strong. He fought a long, bloody war with Iran; he invaded Kuwait and threatened Saudi Arabia in 1991; he brutally suppressed his own people and used poison gas against the Kurds in northern Iraq; he fired Scud missiles into Israel during the Gulf war; he stockpiled and developed chemical and biological weapons and attempted to develop nuclear weapons; and he was an implacable enemy of the United States, which defeated him in the Gulf war in 1991. He consistently refused to comply with the provisions for United Nations' inspection of his weapons facilities that he agreed to at the end of the Gulf war.

President Bush's national security assistant, Condoleezza Rice, summarized the administration's case for war in August 2002, "This is an evil man who, left to his own devices, will wreak havoc again on his own population, his neighbors and, if he gets weapons of mass destruction and the means to deliver them, on all of us. There is a very powerful moral case for regime change. We certainly do not have the luxury of doing nothing."[13] Vice President Cheney also argued for a U.S. attack on Iraq in a speech to the Veterans of Foreign Wars on August 26, 2002:

Deliverable weapons of mass destruction in the hands of a terror network or a murderous dictator, or the two working together, constitutes as grave a threat as can be imagined. . . . The risks of inaction are far greater than the risk of action. . . . Armed with an arsenal of these weapons of terror and a seat atop 10 percent of the world's oil reserves, Saddam Hussein could then be expected to seek domination of the entire Middle East, take control of a great portion of the world's energy supplies, directly threaten America's friends throughout the region, and subject the United States or any other nation to nuclear blackmail.[14]

The administration was also convinced that there was a connection between the terrorists and the Iraq government in the form of a meeting in April 2001 in the Czech Republic between Mohamed Atta, the leader of the terrorist attack in the United States, and an Iraqi diplomat. The argument that there was not a tight link between Saddam and the war on terrorism was made by Brent Scowcroft, national security adviser to President Ford and the first President Bush and a close friend to the latter. Scowcroft wrote an op-ed piece in August 2002 arguing against a U.S. attack on Iraq: ". . . there is scant evidence to tie Saddam to terrorist organizations, and even less to the Sept. 11 attacks. Indeed Saddam's goals have little in common with the terrorists who threaten us, and there is little incentive for him to make common cause with them."[15]

Thus the moral case that Saddam was a tyrant who ought to be overthrown was a strong one that was accepted by many countries in Europe and some in the Middle East. But the moral case against Saddam was not universally accepted as sufficient justification for initiating a U.S. war against Iraq.

The arguments for a preemptive attack by the United States on Iraq were compelling to the administration and its supporters. But critics of a U.S. preemptive war made a number of points against a U.S. attack. As Henry Kissinger (who supported the administration's argument for regime change) pointed out, a preemptive U.S. attack would undermine conventions of international law centuries old. The Treaty of Westphalia of 1648 "established the principle" that nations are not justified in interfering in the internal affairs of other nations. Contemporary international law justifies war in response to attack, but does not provide for preemptive wars in many circumstances.[16]

This argument was also made, surprisingly, by Representative Dick Armey, Republican Majority Leader of the House of Representatives, in early August of 2002. "I don't believe that America will justifiably make an unprovoked attack on another nation. It would not be consistent with what we have been as a nation or what we should be as a nation."[17]

Besides the argument that there was not a sufficient *casus belli* to justify war, the main objections to war were prudential. That is, even though Saddam's regime deserved to be toppled, it would be unwise for the United States to do it through force. After talk of war with Iraq became serious in the White House, leaks began to flow out of the Pentagon that some in the military did not think that a war would be as easily winnable as some in the White House thought. One line of thinking held that the United States should not undertake another war while troops were still in Afghanistan dealing with the remnants of Al Qaeda and trying to support the new Afghan government (the "one war at a time" objection). Another argument was that the war on terrorism should be our first priority. In Brent Scowcroft's judgment, "Our pre-eminent security priority—underscored repeatedly by the president—is the war on terrorism. An attack on Iraq at this time would seriously jeopardize, if not destroy, the global counterterrorist campaign we have undertaken."[18]

Proponents of war with Iraq argued that terrorists are stateless people who are willing to die for their cause; thus they are undeterrable. The "impossibility of deterrence" argument for war with Iraq was based on the premise that Saddam would likely attack the United States as soon as he had the means to do it, and he would probably share his weapons with Al Qaeda. According to Henry Kissinger, "The terrorist threat transcends the nation-state. . . . This is why policies that deterred the Soviet Union for 50 years are unlikely to work against Iraq's capacity to cooperate with terrorist groups. . . . And the terrorists have no national base to protect."[19]

But skeptics of arguments for a war with Iraq pointed out that Saddam was a tyrant who gained great benefits from his control of Iraq, and that fear of losing his power, his country, and even his life were sufficient deterrents to keep him in check for reasons that terrorists did not share. These reasons should deter him from any obvious aid to terrorists who might attack the United States. In the words of journalist Thomas L. Friedman, Saddam could be deterred *"because he loves life more than he hates us."* Terrorists are undeterrables because they *"hate us more than they love their own lives,* and therefore cannot be deterred" (italics in original).[20] During the Gulf war Saddam had chemical and biological weapons mounted on Scud missiles, but he did not use them against U.S. bases or Israel for fear of massive retaliation.[21]

Some proponents of war argued that in addition to removing Saddam from power, a U.S. invasion of Iraq could establish a democratic regime that might transform the Arab states of the Middle East. Paul D. Wolfowitz, deputy secretary of defense, who had advocated a U.S. attack on Iraq since the immediate aftermath of the terrorist attacks on the United States, said: "I don't think it's unreasonable to think that Iraq, properly managed—and it's going to take a lot of attention, and the stakes are enormous, much higher than Afghanistan—that it really could turn out to be, I hesitate to say it, the first Arab democracy, or at least the first one except for Lebanon's brief history."[22] Advocates of regime change in Iraq, Robert Kagan and William Kristol, argued: "A devastating knockout blow against Saddam Hussein, followed by an American-sponsored effort to rebuild Iraq and put it on a path toward democratic governance, would have a seismic impact on the Arab world—for the better. The Arab world may take a long time coming to terms with the West, but that process will be hastened by the defeat of the leading anti-western Arab tyrant."[23]

While no one doubted the ability of the United States to prevail in a war with Iraq, critics of the administration's war plans were dubious about the ease with which the war might proceed. If Saddam learned any tactical lessons from the Gulf war and the war in Afghanistan, he might very well refuse to mass his troops in the open and withdraw them to urban centers, particularly Baghdad, and engage U.S. troops in urban guerilla warfare. This possibility would put U.S. troops at a disadvantage and take away much of U.S. technological superiority. With Saddam's military assets located close to civilian housing, U.S. precision bombing would still not be able to avoid civilian casualties.

Even if a U.S. invasion were successful in toppling Saddam, it was not clear that any alternative acceptable government would emerge, and U.S. forces might have to stay in Iraq to stabilize the country and eventually be perceived as an occupying force that would antagonize Arabs in and out of Iraq. James A. Baker III, secretary of state in the administration of George H.W. Bush warned, "If we are to change the regime in Iraq, we will have to occupy the country militarily. The costs of doing so, politically, economically and in terms of casualties, could be great. . . . It cannot be done on the cheap. It will require substantial forces and substantial time to put those forces in place to move. . . . We will face the problem of how long to occupy and administer a big, fractious country and what type of government or administration should follow."[24]

In addition to the reservations of active duty professional military in the Pentagon, others with combat experience expressed reservations about war with Iraq. Republican Senator Chuck Hagel of Nebraska, a decorated Vietnam war veteran, said: "Many of those who want to rush this country into war and think it would be so quick and easy don't know anything about war. They come at it from an intellectual perspective versus having sat in jungles or foxholes and watched their friends get their heads blown off. I try to speak for those ghosts of the past a little bit."[25] Retired General Anthony Zinni, senior advisor to Secretary of State Powell and former chief of the U.S. Central Command (which includes the Middle East), said: "We need to quit making enemies that we don't need to make enemies out of. . . . It's pretty interesting that all the generals see it the same way and all the others who have never fired a shot and are not to go to war see it another way."[26]

James Webb, Vietnam veteran and assistant secretary of defense and secretary of the Navy in the Reagan administration argued that war with Iraq was ill-considered:

> Meanwhile, American military leaders have been trying to bring a wider focus to the band of neoconservatives that began beating the war drums on Iraq before the dust had even settled on the World Trade Center. Despite

the efforts of the necons to shut them up or dismiss them as unqualified to deal in policy issues, these leaders, both active-duty and retired, have been nearly unanimous in their concerns. Is there an absolutely vital national interest that should lead us from containment to unilateral war and a long-term occupation of Iraq? . . . The issue before us is not simply whether the United States should end the regime of Saddam Hussein, but whether we as a nation are prepared to physically occupy territory in the Middle East for the next 30 to 50 years.[27]

Echoing another president from Texas, Lyndon Johnson, George Bush dismissed the concerns of the professional military: "There's a lot of nervous nellies at the Pentagon."[28]

C. Persuading Congress and the United Nations

In August 2002 the Bush administration argued that the 1991 resolution authorizing the first President Bush's decision to initiate the Gulf war extended to his son's initiating war with Iraq in 2002 or 2003. Although the president said that he would consult with members of Congress before going to war, he did not admit that he needed the approval of Congress or a declaration of war. A senior administration official said, "We don't want to be in the legal position of asking Congress to authorize the use of force when the president already has that full authority. We don't want, in getting a resolution, to have conceded that one was constitutionally necessary."[29] White House Counsel Alberto R. Gonzales and deputy, Timothy E. Flanigan, were in charge of the administration's legal case.

The administration had planned to begin an intensive political campaign in September 2002 to convince Congress and the country that war with Iraq was necessary. Plans had been made in the summer of 2002, long before the president's vacation at his home in Texas in August. Rather than directly meeting objections to the war plans in the summer as leaks from the Pentagon and op-ed pieces raised cautionary concerns, the administration preferred to wait until September to take its case to the American people. "From a marketing point of view you don't introduce new products in August," explained chief of staff Andrew Card.[30] Despite White House plans to wait until September, the rising frequency of voices critical of Bush war plans (some from members of his father's administration) prompted Vice President Cheney to deliver a strong speech defending the administration's plans on August 26 to a Veterans of Foreign Wars convention in Nashville. "This nation will not live at the mercy of terrorists or terror regimes," declared Cheney.[31]

In September, President Bush changed the administration's argument and said that he would seek congressional approval of a resolution to support his taking the nation into war and that he would take his case to the United Nations. Briefing congressional leaders at White House on September 4, Bush said: "I also made it very clear that we look forward to an open dialogue with Congress. . . ."[32]

The administration's arguments for the necessity of war to achieve regime change in Iraq were made in several forums over the next month. They included a presidential address to the nation on the anniversary of the September 11 terrorist attacks, a speech to the General Assembly of the United Nations the next day, the release of a new national security doctrine, and a presidential address to the nation.

In his speech to the United Nations on September 12, the president framed the issue as one that tests the credibility of the UN and the need for its many resolutions to be enforced. Citing "flagrant violations" by Saddam Hussein of UN resolutions, Bush declared that "we have been more than patient. . . . The conduct of the Iraqi regime is a threat to the authority of the United Nations and a threat to peace." Arguing that the United Nations cannot afford to be "irrelevant," he urged the passage of a tough resolution that would threaten Saddam with military action if he did not give up his weapons of mass destruction. "We cannot stand by and do nothing while dangers gather. We must stand up for our security and for the permanent rights and the hopes of mankind."[33]

Shortly after Bush's UN speech, the administration released a new national security doctrine for the United States that justified preemptive military strikes by the United States.[34] The long document began with statement that "The United States possesses unprecedented—and unequaled—strength and influence in the world."[35] It asserted that the United States "will not hesitate to act alone, if necessary, to exercise our right to self defense by acting preemptively against . . . rogue states and terrorists."[36] Since traditional deterrence does not work against stateless terrorists, "the overlap between states that sponsor terror and those that pursue WMD [weapons of mass destruction] compels us to action." It concluded that the danger of inaction while enemies build their forces was greater than the danger of attacking enemies preemptively.[37]

In anticipation of the congressional vote on a resolution authorizing war with Iraq, the President made a speech to the nation from Cincinnati on October 7, 2002, in which he explained the need for the authorization to take military action:

> Some citizens wonder, 'After 11 years of living with this problem, why do we need to confront it now?' And there's a reason. We have experienced the horror of September the 11th. We have seen that those who hate America are willing to crash airplanes into buildings full of innocent people. Our enemies would be no less willing, in fact they would be eager, to use biological or chemical or a nuclear weapon. Knowing these realities, America must not ignore the threat gathering against us. Facing clear evidence of peril, we cannot wait for the final proof, the smoking gun that could come in the form of a mushroom cloud.[38]

The president made the case that America was vulnerable to terrorist attack and that a hostile regime in Iraq might be willing to share its CBN [chemical, biological, nuclear] technology with terrorists. Thus the United States had to act preemptively to prevent this from happening.

But not everyone agreed that the threat from Saddam was as immediate as the president argued. In a letter to Senator Bob Graham (D-Fla.), chair of the Intelligence Committee, CIA Director George J. Tenet said that, in the judgment of the CIA, the probability of Saddam initiating an attack on the United States "in the foreseeable future, given the conditions we understand now, the likelihood I think would be low." But if faced with a "use or lose" situation, Saddam would likely use his weapons. "Baghdad for now appears to be drawing a line short of conducting terrorist attacks with conventional or C.B.W. [chemical and biological weapons] against the United States. . . . Should Saddam conclude that a U.S.-led attack could no longer be deterred, he probably would become much less constrained in adopting terrorist actions."[39]

Critics of the administration's war plans argued that a U.S. attack would likely precipitate the use of the chemical and biological weapons that the United States feared. They also felt that the negative consequences of a U.S. invasion of Iraq would outweigh the benefits of stopping Saddam's efforts to obtain nuclear weapons. But President Bush's arguments were sufficient to persuade a majority of Congress to vote for an authorizing resolution.

The final resolution, which was passed by the House on October 10 and by the Senate on October 11, was very similar to the draft resolution proposed by the White House. After detailing Iraq's refusal to comply with UN resolutions on weapons inspections and noting that members of Al Qaeda were in Iraq, the resolution stated: "The president is authorized to use the armed forces of the United States as he determines to be necessary and appropriate, in order to: (1) defend the national security of the United States against the continuing threat posed by Iraq; and (2) enforce all relevant United Nations Security Council resolutions regarding Iraq." It also required the president to notify the Speaker of the House and the President Pro Tempore of the Senate "no later than 48 hours after exercising" his authority and present the reasons for his actions.[40]

While there was a debate in Congress and statements by those supporting and opposing the resolution, there was never much doubt about the outcome, and the debate lacked the drama of the deliberation in 1991 over the Gulf war resolution. A number of Democrats voted for the resolution from fear that a negative vote could be used against them in the upcoming elections. The Democratic leadership, Majority Leader of the Senate Tom Daschle and House Minority Leader Richard Gephardt voted for the measure. The resolution passed in the house by 296 to 133, with 6 Republicans and 126 Democrats (and one Independent) voting against it. In the Senate the resolution passed 77 to 23, with 21 Democrats, 1 Republican, and 1 Independent voting against it. The president had managed to persuade former critics of war with Iraq—Senators Hagel, Lugar, and Kerry and Representative Richard Armey—to vote for the resolution.

As the administration was convincing Congress to give the president authority to attack Iraq, U.S. diplomats were hard at work building a coalition to convince the UN Security Council to pass a new resolution on Iraq. While in the summer the administration had not intended to go to the United Nations, sustained arguments from Secretary of State Powell and Britain's Prime Minister Tony Blair convinced the president that the United States would be in a stronger position if it had international support. Intense negotiations took place throughout the month of October and early November 2002 to bring around the members of the UN Security Council. The United States backed off its insistence that a new resolution was not needed and agreed to French insistence that if Saddam did not comply with the inspection regime, the Security Council would meet again to "consider" options. At the last minute France, Russia, China, and Syria went along with the rest of the Council on a strongly worded resolution. Resolution 1441 gave Iraq one week to promise to comply with it and until February 21, 2003, at the latest for the UN inspectors to report back on Iraq's compliance.

The UN weapons inspectors searched Iraq with seeming carte blanche and surprise visits to sites of possible weapons manufacture, but by late January 2003 they had found no "smoking gun." Chief UN inspector, Hans Blix, said that he needed more time to do a thorough job. The U.S. began to deploy troops to the Middle East in preparation for war with Iraq, with troop strength approaching one-hundred-fifty thousand in the region by late February. As the initial reporting date for the UN inspectors (January 27, 2003) approached, the Bush administration became increasingly impatient with the inability of the UN inspection team to locate evidence of Iraq's weapons of mass destruction. The administration argued that Iraq's formal account of its weapons program was false and that it constituted a breach of United Nations Security Council Resolution 1441.

While the United States, with the support of Britain's Tony Blair, was progressively moving toward war, Germany, France, and Russia expressed strong reservations. They argued that the inspectors needed more time to thoroughly determine whether Iraq had weapons of mass destruction and that any military attack should be delayed. France declared that it would veto any UN Security Council resolution authorizing war with Iraq, and the United States decided that it would not seek one. By early March it was clear that, barring a sudden capitulation by Saddam, the United States and Britain were going to attack in order to remove him from power.

On March 17 President Bush ceased diplomatic efforts to resolve the crisis and announced that Saddam had forty-eight hours to leave Iraq, or the United States would attack. On March 19 the CIA had intelligence about the location where Saddam was spending the night, and at 7:12 P.M. Eastern time President Bush gave the order for a U.S. bombing and missile attack on Saddam's bunker in an effort to kill Saddam before the war started. The next day it appeared that Saddam had survived, and U.S. ground forces began their attack on Iraq and the drive to Baghdad.

CONCLUSION

In sum, the first two years of George W. Bush's term were remarkable. He quickly overcame the deficit of having won five hundred thirty-nine thousand fewer votes than Al Gore in the 2000 election and set out on a concerted conservative agenda. Though not successful across the board with all of his policy priorities, he was able to push his most important initiative— a $1.35 trillion tax cut over ten years—through the closely split, Republican-controlled Congress. He also won approval for a large new federal role in education, with federal funding linked to student performance on tests.

After the terrorist attacks on New York and Washington, he reassured the nation and won significant new power to pursue terrorist suspects within the United States. Though he did not capture Osama bin Laden, he led an effective war effort in Afghanistan that overthrew the Taliban regime, scattered Al Qaeda, and undermined the Al Qaeda's infrastructure. In the summer and fall of 2002 he used the powers of the presidency to convince the Congress, despite the serious reservations of much of the foreign policy establishment and the professional military, to grant him sweeping authority to take the nation to war at his own discretion. In a historic departure from U.S. tradition, he revised formal U.S. national security doctrine to allow for wars of preemption.

In the congressional elections of 2002 the Republicans recaptured control of the Senate and increased their margin in the House. This was only the second time since 1934 that the president's party gained seats in the House in a mid-term election. The election was an important victory for the Republicans because it gave them control of both houses of Congress along with the presidency. Additionally, the election was perceived to be a personal victory for President Bush who had traveled ten thousand miles in the last five days before the election, and who was given credit for making the difference in several key races.

Despite widespread international opposition to war with Iraq, with many NATO allies among those opposed, President Bush was able to use the military, economic, and diplomatic power of the United States to win unanimous UN Security Council approval of a resolution that threatened Saddam Hussein with military action if he refused to comply. When the UN Security Council was unwilling to vote for military action against Iraq, the United States, Britain, and Australia, with some international support, began the war to end the reign of Saddam in Iraq.

All in all, President Bush's successful pursuit of his major objectives during his first two years in office was nothing short of remarkable. Judging whether his objectives were well-conceived would have to await the outcome of the war with Iraq and its aftermath.

NOTES

1. Eric Schmitt, "Cheney Assembles Formidable Team," *New York Times*, 3 February 2001, pp. 1, A8.

2. Mike Allen, "Hughes Keeps White House in Line," *Washington Post*, 19 March 2001, pp. 1, A6.

3. Dana Milbank, "Serious 'Strategery,' " *Washington Post*, 27 April 2001, pp. 1, A5.

4. Mike Allen and Dana Milbank, "Cabinet Chosen Quietly, Quickly," *Washington Post*, 7 January 2001, pp. 1, A6.

5. Gloria Borger, "Pleased as Punch," *U.S. News and World Report*, 9 April 2001, 35; David Broder, "No Moderate in GOP Clothing," *Washington Post*, 18 April 2001, p. A21; Dan Balz, "Bush Protects His Right Flank," *Washington Post*, 12 February 2001, p. 1, A13; Adam Clymer, "Not So Fast," *New York Times*, 1 April 2001, p. E1; Bob Herbert, "The Mask Comes Off," *New York Times*, 26 March 2001, p. A23.

6. *New York Times*, 25 July 2002, p. A19.

7. John Mueller, *War, Presidents and Public Opinion* (New York: John Wiley, 1973); Barbara Hinckley and Paul Brace, *Follow the Leader: Opinion Polls and the Modern Presidency* (New York: Basic Books, 1992).

8. James Carney and John F. Dickerson, "Inside the War Roomm" *Time*, 31 December 2001.

9. Matthew Purdy, "Bush's New Rules to Fight Terror Transform the Legal Landscape," *New York Times*, 25 November 2001, pp. 1, B4.

10. Richard L. Berke, "This Time, Dissent Stops at the White House Door," *New York Times*, 16 December 2001, p. wk3.

11. Dexter Filkins, "Flaws in U.S. Air War Left Hundreds of Civilians Dead," *New York Times*, 21 July 2002, p. 1.

12. Robert G. Kaiser, "The Long and Short of It," *Washington Post*, 8 September 2002, pp. B1, B2.

13. Glenn Kessler, "Rice Lays Out Case for War in Iraq," *Washington Post*, 16 August 2002, pp. 1, A20.

14. Dana Milbank, "Cheney Says Iraqi Strike Is Justified," *Washington Post*, 27 August 2002, pp. 1, A8.

15. Brent Scowcroft, "Don't Attack Saddam," *Wall Street Journal*, 15 August 2002, p. A12.

16. Henry A. Kissinger, "Our Intervention in Iraq," *Washington Post*, 12 August 2002, p. A15.

17. Eric Schmitt, "House G.O.P. Leader Warns against Iraq Attack," *New York Times*, 9 August 2002, p. A6.

18. Brent Scowcroft, "Don't Attack Saddam," *Wall Street Journal*, 15 August 2002, p. A12.

19. Henry A. Kissinger, "Our Intervention in Iraq," *Washington Post*, 12 August 2002, p. A15.

20. Thomas L. Friedman, "Iraq, Upside Down," *New York Times*, 18 September 2002, p. A31.

21. Graham T. Allison, "The View from Baghdad." *Washington Post*, 31 July 2002, p. A19.

22. Bill Keller, "The Sunshine Warrior," *New York Times Magazine*, 22 September 2002, 48–55.

23. Ivo H. Daadler, and James M. Lindsay, "It's Hawk vs. Hawk in the Bush Administration," *Washington Post*, 27 October 2002, p. B3.

24. James A. Baker III, "The Right Way to Change a Regime," *New York Times*, 25 August 2002, p. wk9.

25. Associated Press, *New York Times*, 26 August 2002, p. 1.

26. "Powell Aide Disputes Views on Iraq," *Washington Post*, 28 August 2002, p. A16.

27. James Webb, "Heading for Trouble," *Washington Post*, 4 September 2002, p. A21.

28. Steven R. Weisman, "History Lessons for Wartime Presidents and Their Generals," *New York Times*, 15 September 2001, p. wk14.

29. Mike Allen and Juliet Eilperin, "Bush Aides Say Iraq War Needs No Hill Vote," *Washington Post*, 26 August 2002, pp. A1, A12.

30. Elizabeth Bumiller, "President to Seek Congress's Assent over Iraq Action," *New York Times*, 5 September 2002, pp. 1, A10.

31. Glenn Kessler and Peter Slevin, "Cheney Is Fulcrum of Foreign Policy," *Washington Post*, 13 October 2002, pp. 1, A16.

32. Bumiller, "President to Seek Congress's Assent over Iraq Action."

33. George W. Bush, *Washington Post*, 13 September 2002b, p. A31.

34. George W. Bush, *The National Security Strategy of the United States of America*. Washington, D.C.: The White House, 2002a. Available from whitehouse.gov/nsc/print/nssall.html.

35. *Ibid*, Part I, p. 3.

36. *Ibid*, Part VIII, p. 23; Part V, p. 9.

37. *Ibid*, Part V, p. 11.

38. George W. Bush, *Washington Post*, 8 October 2002, p. A20.

39. Central Intelligence Agency, Letter printed in the *New York Times*, 9 October 2002, p. A12.

40. United States Congress, "Authorization for the Use of Military Force against Iraq," printed in *New York Times*, 12 October 2001, p. A12.

SOURCES CONSULTED

Allen, Mike. "Airport Bill Approach Could Be Repeated." *Washington Post*, 19 November 2001, p. A2.

Allen, Mike, and Eric Pianin. 2001. "Ridge Carries Message on Anthrax." *Washington Post*, 25 October 2001, p. A4.

Barnes, James A. 2001. "Is Bush Poisoning His Well?" *National Journal*, 2001, 1120.

Berke, Richard L. "Bush Shapes His Presidency with Sharp Eye on Father's." *New York Times*, 28 March 2001a, pp. 1, A13.

———. In the White House, a Sense of What History Can Teach. *New York Times*, 9 January 2001b, pp. 1, A18.

———. "Jokes Remain, but Many Say Bush Is Showing Signs of War's Burden." *New York Times*, 9 December 2001c, p. B7.

Bumiller, Elisabeth. "Bush Aides Set Strategy to Sell Policy on Iraq." *New York Times*, 7 September 2002a, p. 1.

———. "For a President at War, Refuge at Camp David." *New York Times*, 5 November 2001b, pp. 1, B6.

Bumiller, Elisabeth, and David E. Sanger. "Taking Command in Crisis, Bush Wields New Powers." *New York Times*, 1 January 2002, pp. 1, A10.

Burke, John P. *Presidential Transitions*. Boulder, Colo.: Lynne Rienner, 2000.

Carney, James, and John F. Dickerson. "Inside the War Room." *Time*, 7 January 2002.

Central Intelligence Agency (CIA). Letter reprinted. *New York Times*, 9 October 2002, p. A12.

Dahl, Robert. "The Myth of Presidential Mandate." *Political Science Quarterly*, Fall (1990).

Fineman, Howard. "Bush's Next Challenge: Dodging No. 41's Fate." *Newsweek*, 31 December 2001—7 January 2002.

Goldstein, Amy, and Eric Pianin. *Washington Post*, pp. 1, A6.

Greenstein, Fred I. "The Presidential Leadership of George Bush: A Pre- and Post-9/11 Comparison."

Harris, John, and Dan Balz. "A Question of Capital." *Washington Post*, 29 April 2001, pp. 1, A6.

Hoagland, Jim. "The Danger of Bush's Unilateralism." *Washington Post*, 29 July 2001, p. B7.

Jones, Charles O. *The Presidency in a Separated System*. Washington, D.C.: Brookings, 1994.

Kahn, Joseph. "House Supports Trade Authority Sought by Bush." *New York Times*, 7 December 2001, pp. 1, A22.

Lewis, Anthony. "Mr. Bush's New World Order." *New York Times*, 13 October 2001, p. A23.

Lewis, Neil A. 2001b. "Ashcroft Defends Antiterror Plan; Says Criticism May Aid U.S. Foes." *New York Times*, 7 December 2001, pp. 1, B6.

Morin, Richard, and Claudia Deane. "Most Americans Back U.S. Tactics." *Washington Post*, 29 November 2001, pp. 1, A12.

Nakashima, Ellen, and Dana Milbank. "Bush Cabinet Takes Back Seat in Driving Policy." *Washington Post*, 2001, pp. 1, A12.

Pfiffner, James P. *The Modern Presidency*. Bedford, N.Y.: St. Martin's Press, 2000.

———. "The President and Congress at the Turn of the Century: Structural Sources of Conflict." In *Rivals for Power: Presidential-Congressional Relations*. Edited by J. A. Thurber. Lanham, Md.: Rowman & Littlefield, 2002a.

———. "The Transformation of the Bush Presidency." In *Understanding the Presidency*. 3rd ed. Edited by J. P. Pfiffner and R. H. Davidson. New York: Longman, 2002b.

Pianin, Eric. "EPA Chief Lobbied on Warming before Bush's Emissions Switch." *Washington Post*, 14 March 2001, p. 1, A6.

Reid, T. R. "Europeans Reluctant to Send Terror Suspects to U.S." *Washington Post*, 29 November 2001, p. A3.

Ricks, Thomas E. "Rumsfeld Warned Not to Cut Size of Army." *Washington Post*, 3 August 2001, p. A8.

Sanger, David E. "Bush Offers Arms Talks to China as U.S. Pulls out of ABM Treaty." *New York Times*, 14 December 2001, pp. 1, A12.

Sanger, David E., and Patrick E. Tyler. "Wartime Forges a United Front for Bush Aides." *New York Times*, 23 December 2001, pp. 1, B4.

Shanker, Thom. "White House Says the U.S. Is Not a Loner, Just Choosy." *New York Times*, 31 July 2001, pp. 1, A10.

Sipress, Alan. "Aggravated Allies Waiting for U.S. to Change Its Tunes." *Washington Post*, 22 April 2001, p. A4.

Smith, Dita. "Going It Alone." *Washington Post*, 4 August 2001, p. A15.

United States Congress. Resolution. *New York Times*, 12 October 2002, p. A12.

CHAPTER 2

The Bush Transition

JOHN P. BURKE

Since the advent of the modern presidency under Franklin Delano Roosevelt (FDR), the actions that presidents-elect undertake before Inauguration Day have been seen by scholars, journalists, other observers, and even by presidents themselves as critical in determining their successes—and failures—once in office. A successful transition enables a new administration to "hit the ground running." By contrast, mistakes during the transition can lead them to "hit the ground stumbling," creating an inauspicious debut from which it can be difficult to recover.[1]

For FDR, his transition to office was a crucial time for assembling his "Brain Trust" of close advisers and crafting a number of the policy proposals that he hoped would lead the country out of the Depression. After Inauguration Day, this effort set the stage for his landmark "one hundred days," during which Congress quickly passed much of what he wanted into law. Almost forty years later in 1980, Ronald Reagan and his advisers also experienced a successful transition to office, one that facilitated their ambitious first-year program of tax and budget cuts and the rebuilding of the American military.

Other presidents-elect have been less successful. Internal feuding among staff plagued Jimmy Carter's transition to office in 1976. Carter also failed to develop a coherent policy agenda, which soon generated opposition in Congress. In 1992, Bill Clinton used the time before he took office to plan his program of economic recovery and deficit reduction. But he failed to recognize the need to plan more effectively for his White House staff and to develop orderly procedures and processes for policy deliberations. Years later, he would reflect that choosing a number of important White House staff positions only days before he was inaugurated was the "biggest mistake" of his first term.[2]

George W. Bush's transition to office had the potential for a disaster in the making, given that the election outcome was not settled until December 13 (following the Supreme Court's decision to halt the Florida vote recount and, shortly thereafter, Al Gore's concession speech). In the interim, roughly half the time of the normal Election Day to Inauguration Day transition period had passed. Bush, moreover, faced a potential crisis of legitimacy: he was the first president-elect to receive fewer popular votes than his opponent since Benjamin Harrison in 1888, and he was the first president since Rutherford B. Hayes in 1876 to attain an electoral vote majority based on contested results.

Yet a disaster did not occur. In fact, Bush and his advisers quickly announced key appointments, in many cases doing so earlier than their Clinton counterparts eight years before. By Inauguration Day, the top levels of the White House staff were in place and the cabinet was awaiting confirmation. During the early months of the new administration, few mistakes or missteps occurred that could be traced to a faulty transition. Bush avoided the problems that had beset Carter and Clinton, and it was a transition to office that resembled the successful Reagan effort in 1980. In some respects, it was even a smoother transition than the "friendly takeover" of George H. W. Bush in 1988.

Questions about the legitimacy of Bush's presidency were also quickly pushed aside. He pursued an ambitious political agenda, resembling that of a new president who had been elected with a substantial popular and electoral vote margin. His domestic proposals certainly exceeded those of his own father, and his approval ratings were higher than those of Bill Clinton at comparable points in their early presidencies.[3]

STARTING EARLY: BEFORE ELECTION DAY

The reality of the Bush transition was that it was well under way even as the uncertainty over who won Florida dragged on. In fact, the planning for a Bush presidency had actually commenced in the spring of 1999, when Bush asked Clay Johnson (a friend since prep school and Yale, who was then serving as his gubernatorial chief of staff) to take on the job. "I would like you to figure out what we need to do starting the day after the election," Bush told him. "Come up with a plan—talk to people who have done this before, read what you can get your hands on, confer with people, pick their brains and come up with a plan."[4]

Bush's preparation was early but not unique among his recent predecessors. Jimmy Carter's effort began in the spring of 1976, when he asked a young aide, Jack Watson, to begin planning for his presidency. Although some prior presidential candidates had done some preparation before Election Day, Carter was the first to invest significant staff resources and money in the effort. The practice of significant pre-election planning continued under Reagan, the first President Bush, and Clinton.

Although George W. Bush broke the record for beginning early, an early start was not the only important feature of his pre-election effort. Bush's selection of Johnson to undertake the task was also important. As a longtime friend and associate of Bush, Johnson knew his principal. Questions about how Bush made decisions, delegated authority, dealt with staff, digested information, and organized his workday were familiar territory for Johnson— so, too, what he valued in appointees.

Johnson was also a member of the Bush inner circle. This close association brought an element of trust with others in the Bush team and among the campaign staff: groups that might otherwise be concerned about who had the candidate's ear presidency-wise or that might have a hand in future spoils after Election Day. By contrast, in both the Carter and Clinton transitions mistrust quickly emerged between those involved in pre-election planning and in the campaign. Those tensions, in turn, would spill over after Election Day, with negative consequences for both transitions.

Johnson, moreover, proceeded with discretion. There was little media attention about his work until shortly before Election Day. Again, the Bush pre-election effort was in contrast to 1976 and 1992, when newspaper stories reported on the operations of the pre-election planners, much to the consternation of their campaign war rooms.

As part of his work, Johnson contacted a range of former George H. W. Bush and Ronald Reagan administration officials. As he later reflected: "[I met with] a number of people to understand what some of the big issues are in a transition and how do you try to deal with them, how do you try to prevent the problems from rearing their ugly head and take advantage of the opportunities that you have during the seventy-some days of a typical transition."[5] James A. Baker III (a former secretary of state and treasury) and George Shultz (a former secretary of state, treasury, labor, and Office of Management and Budget [OMB] director) were particularly influential sources of advice:

> But most importantly [it was meetings] with Jim Baker and George Shultz . . . it was ten key things to be looking for in setting up a White House; and also the kinds of people to be looking for in a secretary of state or a secretary of defense. Qualities to look for and how they all relate to each other and the role of cabinet secretaries versus the [national] security adviser.[6]

Johnson was also in close contact with Chase Untermeyer, who had been the elder Bush's pre-election planner in 1988 and then had served as head of the White House personnel office (Untermeyer had also helped in George W. Bush's transition to the Texas governorship), and with C. Boyden Gray, another key member of the the elder Bush's inner circle who had served as legal counsel for the 1988 transition, then as White House legal counsel. The positions both had occupied—director of White House personnel and White House legal counsel—are critical to the appointment process of a new administration.

Johnson learned the lessons of prior transitions in order to prevent the repetition of past mistakes. By June 2000, he recognized that a successful Bush transition would necessitate:

- picking a chief of staff early
- trying to identify cabinet secretaries by mid-December, but also recognizing that it is more important to select senior White House staff by this time

- proceeding with hiring based on the new administration's policy priorities
- identifying the qualities needed for key positions and identifying prospective candidates before opening up discussions with particular individuals, especially in order to counterbalance the political pressure to make certain appointments
- developing a clear set of policy goals to avoid having these goals set by others.
- recognizing that Congress and career executives pay attention to how a new administration reaches out to and communicates with them
- also recognizing that the public is attentive to how the president-elect acts prior to Inauguration Day, as this will begin to indicate what kind of president he will be.[7]

Even though he was still campaigning for the presidency, George W. Bush heeded Johnson's counsel. The selection of Andrew Card as chief of staff was settled before Election Day. In addition, a decision was made over the summer of 2000 that Bush's running mate, Richard Cheney, would serve as the transition's director, presuming a Bush victory on Election Day. Both Card and Cheney came well-equipped for the task at hand. Both had served in key White House positions, both had headed cabinet departments, and both had been in charge of outgoing transitions for the administrations in which they served (Cheney for Ford in 1976, Card for the elder Bush in 1992). Clay Johnson's appointment as executive director of the Bush transition rounded out the team. All told, it was an impressive lineup. Their collective knowledge and experience surpassed their counterparts in earlier transitions: Jack Watson and Hamilton Jordan in 1976, Ed Meese in 1980, Robert Teeter and Craig Fuller in 1988, and Warren Christopher and Vernon Jordan in 1992.

Card's selection as chief of staff before Election Day was especially crucial. As Johnson later recalled:

> One of the primary things we did in the transition—and has borne fruit during the first 100 days—we got the president to do what most people running for the presidency do not want to do [and that is] to decide who their chief of staff is to be and ask him to be the chief of staff before the election. So that Andy Card had been asked and accepted and was on the ground prior to the election and beginning to have conversations with the president . . . doing what is very hard to do when you are fighting for your political life. And then also think beyond that about what you want the White House to be, who you want, have conversations with your chief to staff to be, and to think about who you want in this position and that position.[8]

Johnson also undertook a number of steps before Election Day to prepare for the task ahead:

1. Setting up a Web site for prospective job seekers that would go on-line after Election Day. It would pay off later in Johnson's view: "We received probably 97, 95 percent, or something, of all of our requests on line. . . . It made a huge difference. We [were] in the people-picking business not in the data-entry business."[9]

2. Establishing a budget for the transition. The estimate was $8.5 million, about what the Clinton transition had spent in 1992. This was $4 million over the federal allocation, so efforts were also undertaken to prepare a direct mail campaign to Bush donors to cover the additional costs.

3. Drafting letters and e-mails that might be used after Election Day to contact supporters, job seekers, members of Congress and others, especially concerning how to apply for jobs or make recommendations.[10]

WAITING FOR FLORIDA: A TRANSITION NOT QUITE A TRANSITION

Following Election Day, Bush and his team were in the unprecedented position of continuing a number of transition-related activities, but proceeding with some circumspection until the matter of Florida's electoral vote was settled. Throughout the period, Bush led—although with narrow margins—in Florida's popular vote count. But the Bush team carefully avoided the presumption that Bush was indeed the president-elect, lest it politically backfire. At the same time, they also recognized that some transition planning needed to proceed lest valuable time be lost.

The time frame allowed Bush and his associates to further narrow their list of choices, especially for cabinet positions. Some names had surfaced before Election Day (some two hundred or so by Clay Johnson's recollection). The next few weeks allowed them to further narrow their list of potential nominees; this effort proved useful, according to Johnson, because once Florida was settled, "We were able to get into the meat of some of these [cabinet] secretary decisions because there was something on the blackboard; there was not an empty blackboard."[11]

Card was also at work organizing and staffing the Bush White House. According to Johnson, Card was "busy with people about their interests and what kind of role they might want to have in the White House. He was also thinking about how he wanted to structure the presidency. And so he was doing that during Florida."[12]

Following Bush's "certification" as the winner of the Florida vote (by a margin of 253 votes) on Sunday, November 26, by the Florida secretary of state's office, the Bush transition became more open about its efforts and took on more the appearance of a traditional transition. The legal challenges raised by the Gore camp would continue. But certification did offer an opportunity for the Bush camp to move forward and also to more firmly entrench the perception of Bush as the presumptive president-elect.

Still, an element of caution prevailed. In the view of one Bush adviser: "What you're balancing here is a very imperative need to move forward with the process of governing while avoiding any sense of presumption. . . . We're dealing with an extraordinary set of circumstances that have not been dealt with in this country in more than a century. So you have to move at a pace and with a demeanor that is different from all recent transitions."[13]

At 9:00 P.M. on that Sunday evening, Bush addressed the nation from the state capitol in Austin. "Now that the votes are counted, it is time for the votes to count," Bush stated. Pledging to "work to unite our great land," Bush noted that "the election was close but tonight after a count, a recount, and yet another recount, Secretary Cheney and I are honored to have won the state of Florida, which gives us the needed electoral votes to win the election." Bush also added, "I respectfully ask" that Gore reconsider further contesting the Florida results.

Bush took the opportunity to more firmly establish his position as president-elect, adding that he would begin "preparing to serve as president." He announced that Cheney would direct the transition's operation in Washington and that Andrew Card had been selected as his chief of staff (both, of course, were already well at work at their designated tasks). Cheney, he said, had asked to "work with President Clinton's administration to open a transition office in Washington." Bush also briefly sketched out a legislative agenda including education reform, Social Security reform, Medicare reform and a prescription drug benefit, and lower taxes.

Cheney's efforts, the next day, to move transition operations into the federal facility designated for that purpose and to receive federal funding were quickly denied by the General Services Administration, which oversees transition operations. But the Bush transition proceeded nonetheless. On Tuesday, November 28, Bush held a well-publicized meeting with Andrew Card on transition planning, while Cheney, appearing on NBC's *Today Show*, emphasized that the Bush team is "rapidly running out of time to put together that new administration."

Up to this point, the Bush effort had been directed out of Austin. But by Wednesday, November 29, Cheney had secured a lease on a building in McLean, Virginia, that would serve as a privately funded, temporary transition headquarters. By midday Thursday, fifteen paid staffers were at work, plus some fifty volunteers.[14] Ten of those staff members, including Clay Johnson, had flown up quickly from Austin. On December 3, it was announced that Karl Rove, Bush's chief political adviser and strategist, would be joining them. On December 4, the transition Web site (www.bush cheneytransition.com) was up and running, with job information and downloadable personnel forms.

The transition proceeded on course but with little of the panoply associated with prior transitions. As one account noted, Bush and Cheney "accelerated and formalized" their transition efforts, but "they did so in muted tones, without any sense of political revelry."[15] Reports indicated that Bush had made some cabinet selections and had developed a short list for other posts, and that Cheney had been contacting prospective appointees for interviews and background materials.

Clay Johnson would later recall that the effort had been more cautious: Bush and Cheney "began to have conversations . . . about cabinet secretaries. We didn't approach anybody, but we began to get the [pre-election] lists of 10 or 15 people down to one or two, so that when it became official, we would agree that we were going to try to get this person in first for an interview and talk to them. We were going to do some background checking or whatever."[16]

One selection was clear, and that was that Colin Powell would be secretary of state. Powell, however, demurred from a public announcement of his selection until the legal challenges in Florida ended. But he did agree to meet with Bush at the latter's ranch in Texas in late November, during which both national security policy and possible appointments were reported to be the subject of their conversations. During the visit, Bush took the opportunity to emphasize to the press that his transition was well underway: "Dick [Cheney] has opened up our office there in Washington, D.C.—we're open for business. Andy [Card] has been spending time with me and getting our White House team in place." As for Powell and other nominees: "We'll make those announcements at the appropriate time." Press spokesman Ari Fleischer was asked whether the visit was designed to create and "aura of inevitability"; Fleischer responded that it would be more appropriate to term it an "aura of responsibility."[17]

AFTER DECEMBER 13: A TRANSITION UNFOLDS

Picking a Cabinet

Following Gore's concession (the day after the Supreme Court's decision that ended continuation of the Florida recount), the Bush transition quickly moved to fill cabinet and White House positions. Bush was clearly not in a position to match the pace of cabinet nominations set by his predecessors (although in the end he got very close). In 1976, the first Carter nominee was unveiled on December 3 and the last on December 23. In 1980, the first Reagan nominee was announced on December 11, with all but one named by December 23 (the last nominee—secretary of education—came on January 6). In 1988, the elder George Bush announced James A. Baker III's nomination to be secretary of state two days after the election, with all but one named by December 24 (the last nominee—secretary of energy—came on January 12).[18] In 1992, Clinton announced his first appointments on December 10 and his last on December 24.[19] Seen from another perspective, however, Bush rolled out his cabinet picks in three weeks from the time his "official" transition started on December 13, rather than the eight to ten weeks it took his predecessors since Carter.

The first Bush nominee, made on December 16, came as no surprise: Colin Powell as secretary of state. The last three announcements were made on January 2 (thus he finished ahead of Reagan and the first President Bush but behind Carter and Clinton).[20] Although Bush had made no public pronouncements about picking a cabinet that "looked like America," as Bill Clinton had proclaimed eight years before, the Bush team was notable for its diversity: two African Americans (Colin Powell at State and Roderick Paige at Education), one Hispanic male (Mel Martinez at Housing and Urban Development [HUD]), one Hispanic female (Linda Chavez, the initial nominee at Labor), one Asian American male (Norman Mineta at Transportation, also a Democrat), one Arab American (Spencer Abraham at Energy), and three women (Ann Veneman at Agriculture, Gale Norton at Interior, plus Chavez at Labor).[21] From a political perspective, it was a mix of moderate and conservative Republicans (with the exception of Mineta, a Democrat), several seasoned corporate executives, and a number of Washington insiders (ten of the fourteen had prior experience in the federal government), as well as outsiders with a strong connection to Bush and allegiance to the Bush policy agenda. It was clearly not the "coalition government" some Democrats had pushed for in the aftermath of the divided election. It was also a cabinet appointment process that had comparably few leaks and a number of surprise nominations.

The nominations of Ashcroft and Norton raised some controversy, although both were eventually confirmed by the Senate. The one major stumble was Bush's nomination of Linda Chavez as labor secretary, which ran into trouble over her assistance to an illegal immigrant. Yet it was quickly over and done with (within fifty-five hours from the time the accusations against her surfaced). Unlike the prolonged battle over the nomination of John Tower as secretary of defense that had plagued his father's first months in office, Bush quickly dumped Chavez and announced a replacement, Elaine Chao, an Asian American and the wife of Sen. Mitch McConnell (R-Ky.).

The Bush transition also took quick steps to bring its nominees up to speed. Beginning with the Carter transition, extensive efforts have been made to set up teams for each cabinet department in order to gather information, prepare new cabinet officers, establish new priorities, and set new agendas. The track record of these operations has often been mixed; a number of the Reagan cabinet members, in particular, found them not particularly useful. The Bush transition was aware of these part efforts and put in place on December 15 a much smaller operation: groups of six to eight (under the direction of Bush's chief domestic policy aide, Josh Bolten), rather than the forty or fifty persons sometimes assigned to each department in past transitions. But the Bush transition also created a larger set of "transition advisory teams": 474 persons who would provide input to the process but not be directly involved with the outgoing Clinton departments.[22]

The selection of Cheney to head the postelection transition and Clay Johnson to serve as its executive director (with major duties in the appointment process) also avoided a major problem that beset Clinton's transition into office. In 1992, Clinton named Warren Christopher (a prominent Los Angeles lawyer who had served in the Kennedy, Johnson, and Carter administrations) as transition director and Governor Richard Riley of South Carolina as the head of its appointment talent search. Yet both were soon tapped to head cabinet-level departments—Christopher as secretary of state and Riley as secretary of education—leading them to focus a good part of their attention on preparing for their confirmation hearings and assuming their offices after Inauguration Day. With Cheney and Johnson occupying key positions in Bush's 2000 transition, by contrast, their efforts focused on the job at hand. Cheney needed little preparation to assume the vice presidency, while Johnson's position neatly tracked into his postinaugural duties as director of the White House personnel office.

Organizing a White House Staff

As noted earlier, Andrew Card's acceptance of Bush's offer to serve as chief of staff was made before Election Day, which gave him the longest period for any chief-of-staff designate to begin assembling a White House staff. By contrast, Clinton's first chief of staff—Thomas "Mac" McLarty—was settled on December 12, halfway through the 1992 transition.

Card used the period from Election Day through mid-December profitably, and by December 17, the first set of appointments were unveiled: (National Security Council (NSC) assistant Condoleezza Rice, White House legal counsel Alberto Gonzales, and Karen Hughes, "counselor" to the president. Bush's first three staff selections, after choosing Card, were two women (one of whom was an African American) and a Hispanic man. Other key appointments quickly followed. Mitchell Daniels was tapped to head the Office of Management and Budget (OMB) on December 23. Ari Fleischer was officially designated press secretary on December 28, and two of Card's deputy chiefs of staff, Joseph Hagin and Joshua Bolten, were designated the same day. The next day, Clay Johnson's appointment as White House personnel director was made public. On January 3, 2001, Bush's director of the National Economic Council, Lawrence Lindsey, was named, followed the next day by Nicholas Calio as legislative affairs director, and the day after that with Margaret LaMontagne Spelling's appointment as director of the Domestic Policy Council. By January 9, most other major White House positions had been filled.

Although a number of the top-level White House staff members had worked for Bush in Austin and many were involved in the campaign (more than eighty percent were either paid or volunteer campaign workers, by one measure),[23] Bush also could draw on a pool of talent that he had come to know who also had prior White House experience: Card, Rice, Bolten, Hagin, Daniels, Lindsey, and Calio, to name just a few. Calio, his deputy Jack Howard, and Hector Irastorza, director of Management and Administration, had even held the same positions in George H. W. Bush's staff. Bush was thus able to meld loyalty, personal connection, and adherence to his policy agenda with "inside the Washington Beltway" experience. The temptation that "political outsiders" face in assuming office—bringing novice loyalists from back home into the White House—was not a problem for Bush. An unusually high number of his loyalists had already worked in the White House before; according to one analysis, 38 percent had served in the his father's White House.[24]

What was unique about the Bush staff was its organization at the very top. Karen Hughes's position as "counselor to the president" signaled both her stature within the Bush inner circle and a recognition of the importance of communicating the message of this White House. She was given responsibility for the White House Press, Communications, Media Affairs, and Speechwriting offices, and would likely be an important player in melding these functions with the Bush legislative agenda.

The other major staff appointment—that of longtime political and campaign adviser Karl Rove—was not announced until January 4. According to Rove, however, the decision had been made three weeks earlier but had been delayed until the cabinet was named: "We wanted to set the tone and make it clear he [Bush] wanted to bring in a lot of different faces."[25] Rove's duties as "senior adviser" (like Hughes's "counselor," another unique title) were broadly political, with special emphasis on developing better strategic efforts for the Bush policy initiatives. Rove was given authority over the White House Political Affairs Office, Public Liaison Office, and a newly created Office of Strategic Initiatives, which would handle long-term planning. In organizational terms, it was the first White House staff structure in which those political units were directed by a top-level aide other than the chief of staff.

That the Bush White House would have three central figures—Card, Hughes, and Rove—was not unique. In some ways it resembled the James Baker—Ed Meese—Michael Deaver "troika" of the first Reagan administration; indeed, media reports quickly began to speculate about its operations with that past arrangement in mind. The other analogy was Bush's own gubernatorial "iron triangle" of Joseph Allbaugh (his chief of staff before Johnson), Hughes, and Rove, with the new arrangement now dubbed a "platinum triangle": "Rove will govern strategic and political decision, Hughes will create the public face of the White House, and Card will handle day-to-day operations."[26]

But as a White House staff structure, the tripartite arrangement was different from both Bush's own past practice and that of the Reagan troika. In the Reagan White House, Ed Meese controlled the cabinet councils and policy development, while Jim Baker was in charge of the remainder of the White House units, including Political Affairs, Legislative Affairs, Speechwriting, and Communications. Deaver, moreover, was clearly subordinate to and closely allied with Baker.

For the Bush principals, while the division of labor was different (Card controlled policy in ways that Baker did not) the arrangement posed some challenges. Would Card be bypassed and weakened as chief of staff if it were perceived that Hughes and Rove had the president's ear? Rove was quick to point out that Card would be "first among equals."[27] In Clay Johnson's view, it was not a triumvirate of the sort that existed in the early Reagan White House: "Andy is the chief of staff, and if Karl and Karen and Clay and Al and so forth aren't working, aren't being orchestrated well, it's Andy who needs to step in and do something different. But I wouldn't describe it as a triumvirate."[28]

Nor were the three the only centers of power in the Bush administration. A strong and talent-filled cabinet had been selected (especially in the areas of foreign and defense policy) and Vice President Cheney became a central player in an array of policy areas and in the White House's dealings with Congress. Moreover, within the White House there were other key players, a fact that the Bush camp quickly emphasized to defuse the troika analogy: "The White House power structure will be much broader than three people, Bush advisers are quick to note. Policy head Josh Bolten, a deputy chief of staff, has developed a close relationship with Bush and will have an important voice in administration's decision."[29] Bolten, of course, worked for Card, as did the other White House staffers who would provide substantive domestic and economic policy advice.

The appointments of Rove as senior adviser to the president and Karen Hughes as counselor to the president found places in administration for two long time Bush aides and may have also reflecetd some lessons learned from George H. W. Bush's presidency. Both participants and observers of the elder Bush's White House have noted that too much was delegated to the chief of staff alone and that its Communications and Political Affairs units were poorly organized and utilized. Those errors were not repeated. Card himself, in fact, was cognizant (from his own experience as deputy chief of staff) that "marketing and selling" as well as strategic planning were weak points in the elder Bush's White House.[30]

Overall, George W. Bush's White House staff valued loyalty, cohesiveness, and teamwork. James Barnes of the *National Journal* later observed that while "the Clinton White House was more of a coalition—with aides from all parts of the Democratic Party," the Bush White House was more cohesive. "Because so many people on the Bush White House staff worked together either on the campaign or, even before that, in Austin, they've not only demonstrated their fidelity to Bush, they've operated as a team and formed bonds with each other, which may diminish prospects for internecine warfare."[31] Loyalty, cohesiveness, and teamwork were also values embraced if not demanded by George W. Bush. "Bush insists that loyalty can flower in an institution known for distractions and back-stabbing," one transition adviser noted at the time.[32] In Karl Rove's view, Bush's own role in the appointment process was a key factor: "Bush has tended to surround himself with people he's taken the measure of."[33]

CRAFTING A POLICY AGENDA AND BUILDING BRIDGES

Transitions are also times when campaign themes are prioritized and translated into a legislative agenda. For Reagan in 1980 and Clinton in 1992, the period was especially critical in developing their respective economic and fiscal proposals. For Carter in 1976, it was the time when his energy plan was developed, but it was also a period when priorities failed to be established, leading to a "laundry list" of legislative proposals once he was in office. Crafting a policy agenda during the transition is especially crucial in order to take advantage of whatever "honeymoon" period a new president might enjoy in dealing with Congress.

Bush and his associates used the transition to focus on a limited number of policy proposals that Bush had made during the campaign: tax cuts, education reform, faith-based initiatives, defense modernization and Social Security reform. In so doing, Bush drew not just on the experience of his predecessors, but also on how he dealt with the Texas state legislature on becoming governor: stick with a limited number of proposals that had been the centerpiece of the campaign.

Rove's efforts during this period were especially important, and he drew on the lessons of the 1980 Reagan transition, particularly its efforts to develop a long-range strategic plan. According to one account, Rove was placed in charge of

> drawing up a detailed action plan for the first 180 days of the Bush Administration. Rove's task: to take items in the agenda Bush campaigned on, turn them into pieces of actual legislation, and then choreograph their rollout for maximum political benefit. The best antidote to the public's lingering qualms about Bush's legitimacy, says an adviser, is to "show that we're very busy doing things that real people want. We have to get some things done—fast. . . . Rove has laid out a plan—in a series of memos and calendars—for the boss's first four weeks.[34]

According to Rove, the impetus for the effort came from Bush shortly after Gore conceded. At a meeting with his top aides, Bush told them:

> I want to have a plan for how we begin the administration for at least the first six weeks, but I'd like to extend it as long as possible. . . . I saw what happened to my dad, who got elected and came in and then said, What do we do? . . . I saw what happened to Clinton who campaigned on a number of issues, and then came in and immediately began—got enmeshed in an entirely different set of issues. . . . I want a plan that will describe from the moment I say "So help me God" what it is we're going to do, based on fulfilling the things we did in the campaign.

In fact, in Rove's view, work was already well under way:

> We had a lot of people who, after the election and during the 36 days from hell, were in Austin and were not fully occupied, and so we put then to work basically researching the first 100 days or the first year actually, but in particular the first 100 days of every President, sort of [to] see how they had done it, what was important, and what was the framing and the flow of it, what were the successes and failures.[35]

From mid-December through January, Bush also undertook a number of public relations efforts to emphasize his policy agenda. These included meetings with Federal Reserve Chairman Alan Greenspan, with educators and school officials to sell them on his reform and school voucher plan, with African American religious leaders to explain his faith-based initiatives program, and with business executives and Republican governors to sell his tax-cut plan.

The transition is also a time when bridges can be built with the Congress and a political coalition assembled. As Washington newcomers, Carter and his "Georgia mafia" had difficulty understanding and dealing with members of Congress, most notably, incoming House Speaker Tip O'Neill (D-Mass.). Clinton's efforts were compromised by his handling of the gays in the military issue. Bush's situation was unusually precarious: the partisan battle over Florida might have poisoned the atmosphere for future bipartisan cooperation. Bush, however, held an unprecedented number of meetings with both Democratic and Republican members of Congress. Many of them were targeted at members on the key committees that had jurisdiction over his policy initiatives.

CONCLUSION

Despite the unusual circumstances surrounding his election to the presidency and the delays it generated, the Bush transition from its beginnings in 1999 through his inauguration as president, served his subsequent administration well. As an activity in itself, it was at least successful—perhaps even more successful—than the Reagan transition in 1980, which is generally regarded as the benchmark for a successful effort among recent transitions.

That Bush and his advisers sought to push his tax-cut plan immediately and were prepared to do so paid off enormously. Whether the plan was wise or not is another matter, but had the Bush administration delayed until the summer of 2001, when the prospects of deficits were more clearly mounting, or after September 11, the prospect of passage would have been slimmer. In the spring of 2001, Bush controlled the political agenda: the issue was not Bush's plan versus Gore's more limited targeted proposals, but how much in across-the-board reductions that Congress would approve.

Yet even well-organized and executed transitions are not guarantors of future success. Other initiatives would take more time or stall. His education reforms would pass in February 2002, but without a voucher plan to allow parents to transfer students from failing public schools to private ones. Social Security privatization was sent off to a blue ribbon commission for further study, but as the stock market weakened, it was a proposal that remained on the back burner. A prescription drug plan for senior citizens and a patients' bill of rights were caught up in partisan wrangling in Congress. A White House Office of Faith-Based and Community Initiatives was created by executive order on January 29, as were centers in five federal departments that would analyze regulatory barriers. However, the compromise bill before the Congress by the end of 2002 was a far cry from Bush's initial proposal.

Other issues would crop up that had not been anticipated or were not of Bush's making: an energy crisis in California that forced the creation of a task force under Vice President Cheney's direction; a variety of last-minute executive orders and regulatory rules—many of them politically controversial—put in place by the outgoing Clinton administration that had to be dealt with; a campaign finance reform proposal pushed by Senator John McCain (R-Ariz.); and the moral and political complexities of federal rules dealing with stem cell research. The economic downturn especially affected the Bush policy agenda: projected surpluses began to vanish and policy choices were harder than had been expected or prepared for. In May 2002, the defection of Senator James Jeffords of Vermont from the GOP (Grand Old Party) caucus dealt Bush a particularly hard blow as control of the Senate passed to the Democrats.

But all of this paled in comparison to the effects of September 11. It marked a new and unpredictable era in world affairs and a transformation in the American national experience. It marked, in many ways, a new Bush presidency. That Bush rose to the challenge is clear. That his White House and cabinet adapted to changing circumstances and a new agenda is also apparent. In assuming office, Bush and his associates drew well on the lessons of their immediate predecessors. In the aftermath of September 11, had the success of their own transition positioned them to respond to the gravest challenge facing a modern presidency?

NOTES

1. For a fuller analysis of presidential transitions from Carter through Clinton, see John P. Burke, *Presidential Transitions: From Politics to Practice* (Boulder, Colo.: Lynne Rienner, 2000). For earlier twentieth-century transitions, see Lauren Henry, *Presidential Transitions*, (Washington, D.C.: Brookings Institution, 1960). Other sources on transitions include Carl Brauer, *Presidential Transitions: Eisenhower through Reagan* (New York: Oxford University Press, 1986); James P. Pfiffner, *The Strategic Presidency: Hitting the Ground Running* (Lawrence, Kans.: University Press of Kansas, 1996); Charles O. Jones, *Passages to the Presidency: From Campaigning to Governing* (Wash-

ington, D.C.: Brookings Institution, 1998); Alvin Felzenberg, ed., *The Keys to a Successful Transition* (Washington, D.C.: Heritage Foundation, 2000); David Abshire, ed., *Report to the President-Elect 2000: Triumphs and Tragedies of the Modern Presidency* (Washington, D.C.: Center for the Study of the Presidency, 2000); and Martha Joynt Kumar and Terry Sullivan, eds., *The White House World: Transitions, Organization, and Office Operations* (College Station, Tex., Texas A&M University Press, 2003).

2. Elizabeth Drew, *Whatever It Takes* (New York: Viking Books, 1997), 257.

3. From February through early September, Clinton's Gallup poll "presidential approval" rating was at its highest (59 percent) in early March, and at its lowest (37 percent) in early June. For Bush, the highest rating was 62 percent in late April and the lowest was 51 percent, right before September 11. Although the surveys for each were undertaken on different dates, Bush's approval ratings were all higher than Clinton's.

4. James Bennet, "The Bush Years: CEO, USA," *New York Times Magazine*, 14 January 2001.

5. Clay Johnson, "Bush Transition to the Presidency: Planning and Implementation" (panel discussion, American Enterprise Institute, Washington, D.C., 11 December 2001).

6. Clay Johnson, telephone interview, 20 September 2001.

7. These items are adapted from two sources: Dana Milbank, "Tome for the Holidays: A Transition Reading List," *Washington Post*, 19 December 2000, and Clay Johnson, "The 2000–01 Presidential Transition: Planning, Goals and Reality," *PS: Political Science and Politics* 34 (2002), 51.

8. Clay Johnson, "President Bush's First 100 Days," (panel discussion, Kennedy School of Government, Harvard University, 2 May 2001).

9. Johnson, "Bush Transition to the Presidency."

10. Clay Johnson, "The 2000–01 Presidential Transition," 52.

11. Johnson, "Bush Transition to the Presidency."

12. Johnson interview.

13. Frank Bruni, "Quietly But Confidently, Bush Pushes Ahead," *New York Times*, 28 November 2000.

14. Kevin Merida, "From the Ground Up," *Washington Post*, 1 December 2000.

15. Bruni, "Quietly But Confidently, Bush Pushes Ahead."

16. Johnson, "Bush Transition to the Presidency."

17. Mike Allen, "Powell Meets with Bush, Cheney in Texas," *Washington Post*, 30 November 2000.

18. Former Senator John Tower's nomination as Secretary of Defense was rejected by the Senate on March 9, 1989. Rep. Richard Cheney (R-Wyo.) was quickly tapped to replace him on March 10.

19. The last appointment made, that of Zoe Baird for Attorney General quickly ran into controversy concerning her employment of an undocumented alien and her husband as household help and her failure to pay their Social Security taxes. Baird's replacement, Kimba Wood, had a similar problem. It was not until February 11 that Janet Reno's nomination to the post was made public.

20. In the interim the following nominations were announced: December 20, Paul O'Neill (Treasury), Donald Evans (Commerce), Mel Martinez (Housing and Urban Development [HUD]), and Ann Veneman (Agriculture); December 22, John Ashcroft (Attorney General), Donald Rumsfeld (Defense); December 29, Tommy Thompson (Health and Human Services [HHS]), Roderick Paige (Education), Gale

Norton (Interior), and Anthony Principi (Veterans Affairs); January 2, Spencer Abraham (Energy), Norman Mineta (Transportation), and Linda Chavez (Labor). On January 11, Chavez's replacement, Elaine Chao, was announced.

21. Former New Jersey Governor Christie Todd Whitman, Bush's choice to head the Environmental Protection Agency, was also given "cabinet rank."

22. Mike Allen, "Bush Enlists Cast of 474 Insiders," *Washington Post*, 1 January 2001. The transition announced the creation of the larger advisory teams on December 29.

23. James A. Barnes, "Bush's Insiders," *National Journal*, 23 June 2001, 1868.

24. Barnes, "Bush's Insiders," 1869. For further analysis of the backgrounds of Bush White House appointees and their effect, see Martha Joynt Kumar, "Recruiting and Organizing the White House Staff," *PS: Political Science and Politics* 35 (2002), 35–40.

25. Dana Milbank, "Bush Names Rove Political Strategist," *Washington Post*, 5 January 2001.

26. Milbank, "Bush Names Rove Political Strategist."

27. Ibid.

28. Johnson, "Bush Transition to the Presidency."

29. Milbank, "Bush Names Rove Political Strategist."

30. Andrew Card, Jr., telephone interview, September 17, 1998.

31. Barnes, "Bush's Insiders," 1869.

32. Mike Allen, "A Team Built on Conservative Discipline," *Washington Post*, 3 January 2001.

33. Barnes, "Bush's Insiders," 1869.

34. James Carney and John F. Dickerson, "Rolling Back Clinton," *Time*, 29 January 2001.

35. Karl Rove, "A Discussion with Karl Rove," (panel discussion, American Enterprise Institute, Washington, D.C., 11 December 2001).

CHAPTER 3

Organizing the Bush Presidency

Assessing Its Early Performance

KATHRYN DUNN TENPAS
STEPHEN HESS

When the disputed election of 2000 ended with the Supreme Court's decision on December 12, it effectively shortened the presidential transition to less than fifty days and complicated the incoming administration's personnel problems. Chief among George W. Bush's immediate hiring decisions was the choice of senior White House staff, those advisers with whom he would have the most day-to-day contact. Selecting an ideal White House staff is confounded by a host of factors: satisfying the president-elect's personal preferences, honoring political obligations, finding experts with the appropriate ideological hue, and achieving diversity goals. While these were his initial goals, the terrorist attacks of September 11, 2001, required instant adjustments that resulted in structural, procedural, and staff changes.

This chapter examines Bush's first crack at assembling his White House and assesses its early performance, as well as the staff and structural changes made in the wake of the terrorist attacks. In an effort to gain perspective on the Bush record, we compare his staff to the initial staffs of his three immediate predecessors—Bill Clinton, George H. W. Bush, and Ronald Reagan. More specifically, we examine appointments to the Executive Office of the President (EOP), including such senior staff members as the national security adviser and the director of the Office of Management and Budget.

The conventional wisdom was that President Bush hired an older, wiser set of advisers than President Clinton, who had rewarded "the kids"—hardworking, youthful campaign staffers.[1] Furthermore, while Clinton worked hard to assemble a team that "looked like America," Bush hired establishment Republicans, particularly those with a conservative bent. However, staff biographies published in *National Journal* reveal remarkable similarity between the two administrations.[2] Adding Presidents George H. W. Bush

This essay is a revised and updated version of a paper that originally appeared in *Presidential Studies Quarterly*, 32, No. 3, September 2002, pp. 577–585.

and Ronald Reagan into the comparison provides a long-term look at presidents' initial staffing, revealing additional similarities as well as important differences.

As with every new administration, personnel changes are bound to occur as campaign aides realize that governing is not all it is cracked up to be, staff members burn out on the long hours and low pay, and some seek more prestigious positions in the executive branch. In an effort to put the Bush experience in context, we examined staff turnover of the "A" team and compared turnover rates to his four predecessors.[3] Though there is not complete uniformity among the turnover rates, the Reagan administration stands out for the highest amount of overall change within the "A" team, while George H. W. Bush's administration has the lowest.

The first part of this chapter discusses presidents' first attempts to staff the White House from 1981 through 2001 and demonstrates key demographic characteristics as well as personnel turnover within the first eighteen months. The second part identifies the unique features of President Bush's staffing organization as well as recent structural additions. The third part reviews the personnel picture at midpoint in the president's term, again compared to his predecessors. We conclude with an evaluative discussion of the Bush operation, addressing various missteps and putting them in perspective.

HITTING THE GROUND RUNNING

Seeking to avoid the missteps of the early Clinton administration as well as skepticism surrounding his ability to govern, President-elect Bush "hit the ground running."[4] Clinton had not chosen his White House staff until a week before his inauguration. But by January 4 Bush had nearly completed the selection of his senior aides.[5] As he made his choices public, pundits were quick to highlight distinctions between the Clinton and Bush staffs, with Bush's people clearly getting higher grades. The *National Journal*, for instance, characterized the Bush team as "one of the most experienced senior staffs in modern memory."[6] Interestingly, as Table 3.1 illustrates, the characteristics of these staffs—age, gender, ethnicity—were remarkably similar.

The average age of incoming staffers has remained steady since 1981. For all the raves about "seasoned veterans" and critiques of Clinton's youthful staff, the average age of Bush's "A" team was identical to Clinton's. Articles written in the early days of the Clinton administration portrayed his aides as "star struck young staffers" and compared the atmosphere to that of a college dormitory. The title of one op-ed piece—"Home Alone 3: The White House; Where Are the Grown-ups?"—captures the sentiment among many observers.[7] Yet for the past twenty years the average age of presidents' closest advisers has hovered in the mid-forties, a particularly productive and energetic period in the lives of many executives.

Despite opposition cries that the Bush White House is nothing but "a bunch of white males," the numbers indicate that the president appointed

TABLE 3.1 Staff Characteristics, "A" Team: The Executive Office of the President (EOP)

Executive Office of the President	Reagan 1981 (N = 61)	George H. W. Bush 1989 (N = 58)	Clinton 1993 (N = 72)	George W. Bush 2001 (N = 65)
Average age	45	44	45	45
% Women	5	14	29	28
% Minorities	3	7	8	11
% Home state	26	9	10	29
Most common job experience	Executive branch	Executive branch	Capitol Hill	Presidential campaign

Source: Periodic editions of "Decisionmakers" in National Journal (April 25, 1981, p. 678; June 10, 1989, p. 1405; June 19, 1993, p. 1457; and June 23, 2001, p. 1866) (see n. 1). Tables prepared with the assistance of Daniel Reilly.

women and minorities in numbers that more closely resembled the composition of Clinton's White House than that of the elder Bush. Significantly, President Bush appointed women to more influential positions than any prior president. The Bush inner circle included Karen Hughes, counselor to the president, ("the most powerful woman ever to work on a White House staff"[8]), national security assistant Condoleezza Rice, and Margaret Spelling (née La Montagne), Assistant to the President for Domestic Policy.

President Bush's minority appointments are substantially greater than all three predecessors and, at the highest echelons, include Rice and Alberto Gonzales, counsel to the president. The expanded role of Hispanics reflects the president's Texas roots as well as the growing influence of this sector of the population.

Surrounding oneself with a home state "mafia," as the press sometimes charges, may be viewed as a president choosing loyalty over ability. But for two-term governors of the nation's two largest states, it is hardly surprising that Reagan and Bush turned to the talent pools of California and Texas for executives. The first President Bush, lacking a true home state (Connecticut, Maine, or Texas), had a low percentage of home state appointments. And despite the public impression of Washington being overrun by Arkansans when Clinton was president, Arkansas is a very small state, which was reflected in the low number of appointments.

Finally, in terms of prior experience, the Bush administration turned most often to his campaign, reflecting that there had been less "ad hocery" than in many campaign organizations. As the well-financed front-runner, he had the luxury of picking experts who could move into the White House with him. The Clinton administration was the only one in which working in the executive branch was not among the top two occupations, a phenomenon explained by the twelve-year dearth of Democratic presidents. This resulted in a smaller talent pool of former White House staff members. Working within these constraints, Clinton recruited from the halls of Congress, where Democratic aides and advisers bided their time between presidential elections.

What is most surprising in this longitudinal comparison is that much of conventional wisdom is wrong. The Clinton administration was not run by youngsters and the Bush administration was not hostile to appointing minorities and women. The realities of White House staffing defy popular myth.

INAUGURAL INNOVATIONS

Although President Bush's staff possessed qualities similar to those of his predecessors, he imposed his own ideas about running a White House by making structural changes within the EOP, reflecting his administration's priorities, goals, and general approach to governing. He began his term by adding two new units: the Office of Strategic Initiatives (OSI) and the Office of Faith-Based and Community Initiatives (OFBCI). He bolstered the Office of the Vice President, and his cabinet was given both standard and non-traditional functions.[9] The events of September 11, 2001, additionally imposed various structural and procedural changes that affected cabinet and White House staff. Each innovation represented a break with the Clinton presidency, although in some cases there were roots in prior administrations.

The OSI, led by Bush confidant Karl Rove, was designed to think ahead and devise long-term political strategy. "It is an effort to solve the problem that consistently dogs White House staffs: the pressure to respond to unexpected events and to react to daily news cycles, which causes presidential advisers to lose sight of the big picture."[10] The equivalent during the Reagan administration could have been the Office of Planning and Evaluation, led by Richard Beal, a colleague of pollster Richard Wirthlin. It is hardly unusual for presidents to create offices designed to ensure their political longevity. For instance, Reagan's Office of Political Affairs, initially led by Lyn Nofziger, was charged with maintaining and expanding his electoral coalition, but was not afforded the opportunity to devise long-term strategy.

The unique feature of the OSI was that the president's leading political adviser was in charge. George H. W. Bush relied on the strategic advice of Lee Atwater, but did not provide him with a White House perch. Atwater resided at the Republican National Committee until health problems forced him to resign. After Atwater's death, the absence of political insight and strategy became a serious weakness in the administration and reelection campaign. President Clinton used outside consultants James Carville, Paul Begala, Mandy Grunwald, and pollster Stanley Greenberg until the disastrous 1994 midterm elections. Subsequently, Dick Morris provided strategic input while running a consulting firm in which he offered advice to politicians of all stripes. The Bush administration clearly took a different approach by thoroughly integrating Rove into the White House chain of command. Unlike Atwater, "Rove is not content to be seen as a political operative. . . . Rove is as comfortable weighing in on trade-promotion authority as he is discussing the electoral map. . . . No other aide has Rove's singular influence on both politics and policy."[11] The criticism of Rove is that he has over-politicized policy decisions, minimizing the input of policy expertise and maximizing the political "bang for the buck." Observers raised particular concerns over his input regarding agricultural subsidies, steel tariffs, and the pre-election saber-rattling against Iraq.

But the president's success in the 2002 midterm elections, securing Republican majorities in the House and the Senate, proved Rove's worth as a political operative. Along with Ken Mehlman, the Director of the Office of Political Affairs, Rove's OSI played an integral role in devising campaign strategy, from recruiting top-notch candidates to planning the President's appearances and fund-raising activities. Looking ahead to 2004, Karl Rove will continue to strategize and analyze the political landscape with an eye on securing the president's reelection.

Another Bush innovation, the White House OFBCI, was established by executive order. It was meant to demonstrate President Bush's commitment to "compassionate conservatism" by reaching out to faith-based and community organizations in an effort to help the needy. The initial focus of the office was the promotion of H.R. 7, a legislative initiative that sought to ease government restrictions on religious organizations so that faith-based groups could more easily provide government services, such as day care and alcohol rehabilitation. Though Republicans and Democrats alike began to question the constitutionality of financially assisting religious institutions that provide government services, the House passed the president's initiative with an anemic victory. After September 11, the Senate version, which was fundamentally different than H.R. 7, was relegated to the sidelines and OFBCI pursued the less controversial component of its agenda—tax incentives for charitable giving (the CARE Act, S.1924).

In the aftermath of numerous staff resignations (all senior staff members but one left the OFBCI within roughly one year of its creation) and recognizing the uphill battle in the Senate, the OFBCI shifted gears and assumed a more political role in anticipation of the midterm elections. By making appearances in key congressional districts and holding seminars to publicize and explain how faith-based groups can apply for government grants, the office transformed its role from a policy-based office to a political outreach. One report suggested that the office deliberately targeted heavily black audiences to boost support for GOP candidates in midterm elections.[12] Since the CARE Act was unlikely to garner sufficient support in the Senate, the shift to outreach was the only viable approach to promoting the faith-based initiative. Of course, numerous presidents have created offices solely for the sake of pursuing a single policy (Clinton for the Y2K problem, for example), but the shifting focus of the OFBCI, however, reveals the risks associated with relying on legislative success to define the office.

Aside from structural innovations, President Bush expanded the influence of some positions, most notably the vice president. The stature of vice presidents has risen markedly since Jimmy Carter selected Walter Mondale in 1976, and Al Gore was clearly the most engaged vice president of the twentieth century. But Cheney's vast Washington experience, as well as his formidable role in the transition, catapulted the vice presidency to new heights. The vice president's initial activities included devising energy policy, diplomacy and congressional lobbying. In the aftermath of September 11, while intermittently placed in an "undisclosed location" for security reasons, the vice president continued to play an integral role in the administration. Cheney created the initial plan to set up the Office of Homeland Security. At the same time, his aides were fully integrated into the president's senior staff, what some describe as a "seamless operation."[13] His chief of staff attended "most of the A-level meetings" at the White House, and two of his aides—Mary Matalin and I. Lewis Libby—also were titled assistant to the president.[14]

In the aftermath of September 11, the administration shifted its focus to Saddam Hussein and conflict in Iraq—a shift that Cheney is thought to have precipitated. "Cheney and his small but powerful staff have emerged as the fulcrum of Bush's foreign policy. . . . Cheney's impact on the Iraq debate— or his influence on the president—cannot be overstated."[15] Unlike his predecessors, Vice President Cheney was not assigned a particular project (e.g., global warming, reinventing government), but rather has broad-ranging influence on all manner of issues.

President Bush's reputation as one who likes to delegate authority, along with the impressive résumés of some cabinet members, led observers to expect the cabinet to play an enhanced role in the administration. According to one early forecast, "With their golden resumes, long years of public service, strong personalities and close ties to Mr. Bush, Vice President-elect Cheney, and the Republican establishment-in-waiting, the men and women of the emerging cabinet can be expected to exert just as much influence over the administration as the staff in the White House exerts, if not more."[16] The supposition was that these department heads would need little direction from the White House, particularly on day-to-day matters. But students of American politics remembered Jimmy Carter's failed attempt to form a "cabinet government" and how his White House staff rejected this approach in favor of centralizing control, maintaining the authority to rein in cabinet members when necessary.

Though this centripetal force is quite powerful, September 11 enhanced the power of key Cabinet members in the Bush administration. Just days before the September 11 attack, *TIME* magazine published an article declaring Secretary of State Colin Powell the "odd man out." Then the events on that fateful day strengthened the role of Powell and a number of other cabinet secretaries, particularly Attorney General Ashcroft and Secretary of Defense Rumsfeld. Indeed, any department with important homeland security concerns instantly moved up a notch on the power ladder in Washington. Just as scholars have noted the presence of an "inner" and "outer" cabinet in which the original departments (State, War, Treasury, and Justice) dominate the president's time and attention, the terrorist attacks created a somewhat expanded inner cabinet. The tendency for certain members, given their prior relationship with the president or the relevance of their department, to exert more influence than others resulted in a variation on the "inner" and "outer" cabinet model. The "war cabinet"—the foremost cabinet innovation to deal with terrorism—"composed of top national security officials from the White House, CIA, State Department, and Pentagon has become the main decision-making body determining how the United States will frame its response to the September 11th attacks."[17]

There is considerable conflict within the war cabinet, however, although it was not acknowledged by the administration until Bob Woodward's book, "Bush at War," was published in the fall of 2002. Especially in internal debates on the U.S. position on Iraq, Woodward juxtaposes Powell, the cautious diplomat seeking a United Nations solution, against Cheney and Rumsfeld, who favor bold action, with Rice portrayed as a calming influence. Bush told Woodward:

> I've grown very comfortable with them as human beings and as people that were capable of handling their responsibilities. And therefore I—and when they give advice, I trust their judgement. Now sometimes the advice isn't always the same, in which case my job—look the job is to grind through these problems and grind through scenarios, and hopefully reach a consensus of six or seven smart people, which makes my job easy.

Later he added, "If everybody had the same opinion and the same prejudices and the same belief structure, it would be a dull administration. I would not get the best advice."[18]

After September 11, Bush's organizational challenge was how to respond to the urgent need for homeland security. He had to choose between two basic approaches: the department model, a single operating agency with overall responsibility for preventing, protecting against, and responding to terrorist attacks, or the National Security Council (NSC) model, a White House office responsible for coordinating the various operating agencies and getting them to work as a team.[19] In an effort to maximize presidential control, Bush opted for the NSC model and chose a good friend, Governor Tom Ridge of Pennsylvania, to be his homeland security adviser. But with no authority over the operating units, Ridge's chances of success, observers calculated, would depend importantly on his perceived clout with the president and his personal leadership skills. At the same time, many in Congress were pushing a bill to create a new cabinet department whose secretary would be confirmed by the Senate and who would be expected to testify before congressional committees, ultimately resulting in an entity with far more accountability to Congress.[20]

The most important test of whether the NSC model under Ridge's leadership was effective came in December, when he proposed to the president a new agency merging those parts of government with responsibilities for protecting U.S. borders, such as the Coast Guard and the Customs Service. What happened next, according to the *Washington Post*, was that the proposal was leaked to the press and "the bureaucracies erupted . . . scuttling the border proposal." The lesson learned by Bush's team was that "ideas introduced piecemeal will be killed piecemeal."[21] Such unexpected controversy precipitated the formation of a top-secret White House operation that eventually produced a surprising mega-proposal.

Reversing course, the president on June 6, 2002, asked Congress to join him in creating a Department of Homeland Security with 169,154 employees and a budget of $37.5 billion. The major pieces of the new department— the third largest unit of the federal government—would be the Coast Guard, Transportation Security Administration, Immigration and Naturalization Service, Customs Service, Secret Service, and the Federal Emergency Management Agency. Bush would continue to have a cabinet-level Homeland Security Council and a homeland security adviser in the White House, both created by executive order.[22] After months of congressional bickering (particularly over the provision dealing with federal employee policy), and a lame-duck session, the president signed a bill to establish the Department of Homeland Security in November 2002, and named Ridge its secretary.

Though clearly an accomplishment for the Bush team, the road ahead for the new department is likely to be a rocky one. Paul Light, an expert on government organization, compared the task ahead for Ridge to "the most difficult bureaucratic reorganization since the Roman Empire tried to take over the administration of Egypt." Of the twenty-two agencies involved, some had important functions unrelated to protecting against terrorism, such as the Coast Guard, while the major intelligence agencies, Federal Bureau of Investigation (FBI) and the Central Intelligence Agency (CIA) and CIA, remained outside the new department's jurisdiction. Moreover, noted Light, "It would be difficult to coordinate 22 separate agencies under the best of circumstances, but there is great unevenness among these 22. Several are damaged goods . . . and there is huge variation in the quality of the technology in the different agencies. The basic organizational systems will have to be reconciled."[23] As this new department embarks on this Herculean task, cracks are likely to emerge and the president's team must be prepared both to quell criticism and public fear while proposing meaningful solutions.

Though on a much smaller scale, President Bush created another White House office in January 2002 (Executive Order 13254) in response to his State of the Union challenge to the American people to commit themselves to 4,000 hours of public service. The President established the U.S.A. Freedom Corps, with a council similar to the Homeland Security Council, and gave an assistant, John Bridgeland, instructions to coordinate other government agencies in the volunteer business, such as the Peace Corps, AmeriCorps, and Senior Corps. This new entity has remained in the background since its inception, though this should not be surprising given the "war on terror," a focus on midterm elections, and debate over the Department of Homeland Security.

Aside from these more ambitious innovations, the events of September 11 clearly altered "business as usual" in the White House. In the immediate aftermath, most aides, whether in the Offices of Communications, Public Liaison, Political Affairs, or Faith-Based and Community Initiatives, assumed responsibilities pertaining to the attack and recovery.[24] Deputy Chief of Staff Josh Bolten was put in charge of the Domestic Consequences Principals Committee, assessing the impact of the attacks on domestic policy. Presidential confidant Karen Hughes created a special White House–based public relations operation, the White House Coalition Information Center, aimed at winning international support, particularly in the Islamic world, for the antiterrorist campaign.[25] This office eventually became a fully staffed, permanent entity called the Office of Global Communications. Directed by Bush aide Tucker Eskew, the office's mission was to coordinate the administration's foreign policy message and supervise America's image abroad. The office works most directly with the State department and its public diplomacy efforts.[26]

While it is important to identify new features of an incoming administration, it is equally important to note the volatility of these innovations. If they fail to live up to expectations—or worse, if they create new problems—innovations must be quickly discarded. Presidents are rightly cautious when it comes to adding or subtracting White House offices and responsibilities. Unfortunately, they are often less adept at correcting their own mistakes.

TURNOVER AT THE TOP

Just as the ability to "hit the ground running" is one measure by which to judge the effectiveness of a president-elect's transition, so too should personnel turnover be considered among the criteria for effective early actions by a president.[27] Clearly a president wants to start his administration with a staff of the proper people in the proper jobs in the proper organizational structure for a sufficient time to give him the best shot at accomplishing his goals. Staff stability and continuity are important features, but a president must also demonstrate that he is prepared to fire staff that fail to meet expectations. At the same time, while some turnover is inevitable and even a healthy sign, too much turnover can be disruptive, leading to all sorts of inefficiencies.

To measure turnover rate, we turn again to the "A" Team of Presidents Reagan, Clinton, and the two Bushes as designated by the *National Journal* at the beginning of their presidencies, then compare 2 years later whether these people have remained in the same position. If not, we determine whether they moved to another job within the EOP, or within the executive branch, or if they have left the government altogether. The results are in Table 3.2.

Clearly turnover is by no means a uniform process—there are no easily recognized patterns based on party affiliation or transition performance, and there is much variation. Staff turnover ranges from a high of 55 percent for Reagan to a low of 27 percent for President George W. Bush. The Reagan turnover can be partially explained by the mini-exodus within the NSC. Upon the controversial departure of National Security Assistant Richard V. Allen, six other NSC staffers followed suit.[28] The low turnover of both Bush presidencies may be partly explained by the emphasis placed on loyalty when recruiting. While some turnover is expected, some departures clearly have greater impact than others. A closer look at President George W. Bush's staff reveals this fact and, in the process, illustrates the various reasons that staff members depart.

The first senior departure was John J. DiIulio, Jr., a Democrat and professor at the University of Pennsylvania, who was the director of the White House OFBCI. As previously noted, his office had not succeeded in getting legislation through Congress and was encumbered by a variety of controversies. DiIulio had been hired because of his expertise rather than loyalty and long service to the president. He had indicated that he only planned to stay for six months and left in August 2001. It is doubtful that any of Bush's inner circle asked him to stay.

This was hardly the case with Karen Hughes. When she announced that she was leaving in August 2002, Chief of Staff Andrew Card woefully told a reporter that "she's irreplaceable."[29] "My family and I made a tough decision," she said. "As I told the President, 'Mr. President, I love you but my family and I want to live in Texas.' " Given her long years of service to the president, this type of departure no doubt created a considerable void. Sur-

TABLE 3.2 24-Month "A" Team Turnover: The Executive Office of the President (EOP)

President	% Changed Jobs	% Within EOP	% Other Gov't. Jobs	% Left Gov't.
Reagan ($N = 60$)	55	13	12	30
George H. W. Bush ($N = 57$)	28	4	8	16
Clinton ($N = 71$)	40	14	10	16
George W. Bush ($N = 64$)	27	5	7	15

Sources: Based upon a comparison of the 1981, 1989, 1993 and 2001 National Journal "Decisionmakers" editions to the 1982, 1990, 1994 and 2002 U.S. Government Manuals and Federal Yellow Books (see n. 2). Due to the fact that publication deadlines for the manual and yellow book occurred before the 2-year mark, turnover data for all Presidents was supplemented by relevant primary sources. Table prepared with the assistance of Daniel Reilly and Elizabeth Redman.

prisingly, there were no public signs of disorganization, nor was there an ensuing staff exodus and/or overhaul of the Office of Communications.

Aside from these highly visible aides, others left the White House because of more prestigious offers. Mark McClellan, who handled health issues as a member of the president's Council of Economic Advisors, was nominated by the president to be commissioner of the Food and Drug Administration. Similarly, Sean O'Keefe, deputy director of the Office of Management and Budget, left to be administrator of the National Aeronautics and Space Administration (NASA).

Additional reasons for staff changes may be a presidential request, monetary concerns, or involuntary departure. John Bridgeland was moved from the Office of Domestic Affairs to run the U.S.A. Freedom Corps for President Bush. The departure of White House deputy counsel Timothy Flanigan was motivated by financial concerns. According to news reports, Flanigan was "soon to make serious money in the private world." He has fourteen kids to feed.[30] In the wake of successful midterm elections and in an effort to refresh his economic team, the president asked for the resignation of Treasury Secretary Robert O'Neill and his top economic aide, Larry Lindsey.[31] One news analyst contends that President Bush's willingness to fire two aides indicates the "danger a lumbering economy poses to Bush's reelection prospects."[32] Regardless, it suggests a certain toughness in dealing with perceived staffing problems that has eluded some past presidents.

Bush's low turnover rate, a good sign of an efficient operation, again reflects the same set of circumstances that had produced an exceptional transition—long-standing relationships, persons coming from service in a large state government, reliance on others with previous high-level federal experience, and others coming from a presidential campaign in which the frontrunner candidate could be choosy. In addition, the extraordinary events of September 11 may have had a unique impact on staff members, as the gravity of the "war on terror" instilled a renewed sense of dedication and loyalty. Short of conducting periodic interviews with the president's advisers, it is difficult to fully account for staff tenure, though anecdotal evidence provides important insight into this phenomenon.

ASSESSING THE BUSH TEAM: EARLY MISSTEPS

Mistakes are endemic to the start of any administration. A lethal combination of early arrogance and euphoria often derail best intentions. George W. Bush's first stumble was over the nomination of Linda Chavez to be labor secretary. Some blamed the debacle on a lax vetting process, but Chavez withdrew quickly and a less controversial successor was named and confirmed without incident. Having recovered from this mishap, a blast of criticism erupted over the delayed stock divestitures of senior staff and cabinet members, especially the holdings of treasury secretary Paul O'Neill. The heat was turned up even more when Karl Rove met with lobbyists for Intel, a company in which he owned stock, thereby opening the door to political opponents who promptly demanded an investigation. These missteps resulted in bad publicity that may have distracted White House officials but did not prove disabling.

In fact, these missteps pale in comparison with the shock waves following Senator Jim Jeffords' summer of 2001 defection from the Republican Party, causing the party's loss of majority status in the Senate, jeopardizing the president's legislative agenda, and, for the first time, casting serious doubt on the performance of the White House staff. Why didn't they know about Jeffords' apparent dissatisfaction? If they did know, why didn't they do something?

Aside from these more visible missteps, there have been various incidents that have distracted the Bush team. Among the most visible points of criticism were Vice President Cheney's reluctance to turn over energy-related documents to the General Accounting Office (GAO) and the ensuing legal battle, Attorney General Ashcroft's post-September 11 policies that have been portrayed as infringing on civil liberties, the shift away from domestic policy achievements, the eruption of corporate scandal and the congressionally motivated response, the transformation of the U.S. budget from surplus to deficit status, and the perception of the Bush team as favoring industry over the environment. Of course, no administration is beyond criticism, but the Bush team does its very best to defuse these critics. Given its approval ratings, their efforts can be deemed a success.

In addition, the Bush team has endured a steady but relatively silent stream of criticism from the press in regard to the administration's high level of secrecy: "The men and women who cover this White House believe they are being not only used, but also disrespected—and prevented from doing their jobs properly."[33] While the relationship between president and press has always been a tense one, the danger of this "undue" level of secrecy and concomitant withholding of information may backfire if the White House should ever reach a point where some goodwill within the media is needed.

How quickly such missteps faded in one's memory after the impressive Republican performance in the midterm elections. As we enter 2003, it is not clear that the staff and structural innovations designed to meet the challenges of "America's New War" can achieve the necessary level of integration and cooperation, but public approval ratings indicate that the perception of the Bush administration is certainly a positive one. How long this support lasts is anyone's best guess, but the instability within the economy coupled with the fallout from the conflict with Iraq could turn President Bush's numbers upside-down. Current White House staffers are all too aware of the elder Bush's last two years in office and the precipitous decline in his approval ratings. Nevertheless, the Bush team appears to have established an advisory system reflective of a unique balance between White House staff and cabinet input—a system that fits the needs of today's crisis atmosphere—with a new cabinet department taking shape in Bush's third year in office. The president will have to respond to cracks that appear in his administrative structures and personnel weaknesses and departures, but he deserves credit for diminishing the intense public fear in the aftermath of September 11 by responding in a manner that suited the needs of the country.

In the end, it is impossible for any administration to be mistake free. Stumbling is inevitable. Still, President Bush benefited from his predecessors' mistakes. His transition and first days seemed like a cakewalk compared to the unrelenting criticism faced by President Clinton. Assembling a staff of seasoned veterans in less than fifty days is no small feat. Avoiding all manner of mistakes is well beyond the realities of doing governance in Washington.

NOTES

1. See George Stephanopoulous, *All Too Human* (New York: Little, Brown, 1999); Fiona Houston, "Youth Actively Served by Junior Clinton Aides," *New York Times*, 28 March 1993.

2. This analysis reflects a comparison of the Executive Office of the President in the "Decisionmakers" editions of the *National Journal* for the years 1981, 1989, 1993, and 2001. All editions were composed by a different set of reporters with some overlap. Reporters utilized titles, perceptions of influence, and their general experiences having covered the White House to compile these listings of top staffers. Unlike the *Congressional Directory*, which also provides a listing of staff members in the Executive Office of the President, the *National Journal* is particularly valuable because it includes biographies of individual staff members. Both sources, however, roughly parallel one another, with the *Congressional Directory* including a greater number of lower-level aides. (See Martha Kumar, "Recruiting and Organizing the White House staff. *PS* 35, no. 1 (XXXX): 35–40.) Note that these figures vary from those published in *Presidential Studies Quarterly* (2002), as there was a discrepancy between the hard copy of the 1989 *National Journal* "*Decisionmakers*" edition and the Lexis-Nexis version. The discrepancies did not, however, make a substantive difference.

3. In order to calculate turnover, we compared the incoming "A" team (as documented by the *National Journal*) to the successive editions of the *U.S. Government Manual*'s listing of White House staff, the *Federal Yellow Book* and relevant news articles. The *U.S. Government Manuals* included the following editions: 7/1/1982, 7/1/1990, 7/1/1994, and 6/1/2002. The *Federal Yellow Books* included the following editions: 12/1982, 10/18/1990, 10/13/1994, and 9/04/2002. Taken together, these three sources provide the most accurate figures on White House staff tenure. The *Federal Yellow Book* is a directory of the federal departments and agencies. The listings include the EOP, the departments, and the independent agencies. According to the senior editor of the *Yellow Book*, if a person is not in the book "they are not in the senior levels of the federal government." The authors are deeply indebted to the staff of Leadership Directories, Inc., for their generous support.

4. This phrase is borrowed from presidential scholar James Pfiffner, *The Strategic Presidency: Hitting the Ground Running* (Lawrence: University Press of Kansas, 1996).

5. While President Bush was quick to name senior aides, filling top federal posts proved far more problematic. The Brookings Institution's Presidential Appointee Initiative (PAI) revealed that twenty-two months into the administration, many key federal vacancies remained (e.g., Housing and Urban Development [HUD] Assistant Secretary for Policy Development and Equal Opportunity, Deputy Administrator of the Federal Aviation Administration [FAA]). On average, Bush appointees were confirmed 8.5 months after the inauguration compared to 2.3 months during JFK's administration. (Information obtained in personal communication with Paul Light, Director of the PAI, and from an article by Christopher Lee, "Bush Slow to Fill Top Federal Posts, *Washington Post*, 18 October 2002, p. A35.)

6. Alexis Simendinger, "Stepping into Power," *National Journal*, 4 January 2001, 246.

7. Charles Krauthammer, "Home Alone 3: The White House; Where Are the Grown-ups?" *Washington Post*, 14 May 1993, p. A31.

8. Geraldine Baum and Elizabeth Mehren, "She Has the President's Ear, as a Loyalist and Alter Ego," *Los Angeles Times*, 1 April 2001, p. A1.

9. Ellen Nakashima and Dana Milbank, "Bush Cabinet Takes Back Seat in Driving Policy," *Washington Post*, 5 September 2001, p. A1.

10. Dana Milbank, "Serious 'Strategery'; As Rove Launches Elaborate Political Effort, Some See a Nascent Clintonian 'War Room,' " *Washington Post*, 22 April 2001, p. A1.

11. Matt Bai, "Rove's Way," *New York Times Magazine*, 20 October 2002, 59.

12. Thomas B. Edsall and Alan Cooperman, "GOP Using Faith Initiative to Woo Voters," *Washington Post*, 15 September 2002, p. A5.

13. Carl Cannon, "The Point Man," *National Journal*, 12 October 2002, 2958.

14. James Barnes, "The Imperial Vice Presidency," *National Journal*, 17 March 2001, 814.

15. Glenn Kessler and Peter Slevin, "Cheney Is Fulcrum of Foreign Policy," *Washington Post*, 13 October 2002, p. A16.

16. Joseph Kahn, "Bush's Selections Signal a Widening of Cabinet's Role," *New York Times*, 31 December 2001.

17. Mike Allen and Alan Sipress, "Attacks Refocus White House on How to Fight Terrorism," *Washington Post*, 26 September 2001, p. A3.

18. Bob Woodward, " A Struggle for the President's Heart and Mind," *Washington Post*, 17 November 2002, p. A1.

19. See chapter 7, "Organizing for Success," in Michael E. O'Hanlon and others, *Protecting the American Homeland: A Preliminary Analysis* (Washington, D.C.:Brookings, 2002), 99–124.

20. For an account of the strained relations between Ridge and Congress during this period, see Adriel Bettelheim, "Turf Wars Take Toll on Ridge," *CQ Weekly*, 27 April 2002, 1071–72.

21. David Von Drehle and Mike Allen, "Bush Plan's Underground Architects," *Washington Post*, 9 June 2002, p. A1.

22. See "Special Report: Homeland Security," *CQ Weekly*, 8 June 2002, 1498–1508.

23. David Broder, "Why is This Man Smiling?" *Washington Post*, 1 December 2002 p. B7.

24. Dana Milbank, "White House Staff Switches Gears," *Washington Post*, 17 September 2001, p. A25.

25. Karen DeYoung, "Bush to Create Formal Office to Shape U.S. Image Abroad," *Washington Post*, 30 July 2002, p. A1.

26. Scott Lindlaw, "White House Ramping Up a Little-Known Office to Buff America's Image Abroad," Associated Press, 30 July 2002.

27. For a longitudinal look at turnover among presidential advisors, see Matthew J. Dickinson and Kathryn Dunn Tenpas, "Explaining Increasing Turnover Rates among Presidential Advisors, 1929–1997," *Journal of Politics* 64, no. 2 (2002), 434–48.

28. Martin Schram, "Continued Hostilities Cost Allen His Job," *Washington Post*, 5 January 1982, p. A4.

29. Ron Suskind, "Mrs. Hughes Takes Her Leave," *Esquire*, July 2002; see www.esquire.com/features/articles/2002/020701_mfe_hughes_1.html.

30. Al Kamen, "Now Where Were We?" *Washington Post*, 18 November 2002, p. A19.

31. Note that unlike National Economic Director Lindsey, cabinet secretaries are not included in our analysis of the "A" team. For a news analysis of these departures, see Mike Allen and Jonathan Weisman, "Treasury Chief, Key Economic Aide Resign as Jobless Rate Hits 6 Percent," *Washington Post*, 7 December 2002, p. A1, and Dana Milbank, "With '04 in Mind, Bush Team Saw Economic, Political Peril," *Washington Post*, 7 December 2002, p. A1.

32. Milbank, "With '04 in Mind. . . . "

33. Carl M. Cannon, "Goodbye to Goodwill," *National Journal*, 13 July 2002, 2090.

CHAPTER 4

The Bush Staff and Cabinet System

CHARLES E. WALCOTT AND KAREN M. HULT

Throughout most of the modern era of the presidency, a lively debate has raged over the optimal size and organization of the president's staff, and its proper relationship to the cabinet and the rest of the executive branch. To a considerable extent, this has been a partisan argument. Democrats, beginning in the days of Franklin Delano Roosevelt (FDR) and Harry Truman, developed a tradition of "spokes of the wheel" White House organization. This meant a relatively nonhierarchical senior staff, with no formal chief of staff standing between top aides and the president. The top assistants themselves tended to be generalists. Democratic White Houses tended to avoid specialized job definitions, taking pride instead in the flexibility and versatility of individual staff members, and the consequent adaptability of the White House to a constantly changing environment. Democratic presidents from FDR through Jimmy Carter opted for a version of this organizational model, at least at the outset of their administrations. In areas other than national security, at least, this model has also stressed the importance of "cabinet government," in the form of strong cabinet secretaries with easy access to the president.

Republicans, by contrast, have a tradition of more hierarchical White Houses that stems originally from the organizational philosophy of Dwight Eisenhower. In this version, the president is assisted and protected by a strong chief of staff, who monitors access on the part not only of White House advisers, but of all or most cabinet secretaries as well. Republican White Houses have tended toward specialized offices and advisers, coordinated by the chief of staff and an extensive "staffing" system consisting mainly of memos on paper and coordinated by a staff secretary who reports to the chief of staff. This approach seeks to attain the kind of "multiple advocacy" that decision-making scholars have recommended, without the hit-or-miss quality of a more informal advisory system.[1]

Republicans also have shown a notable tendency toward centralizing policy initiative in staffs lodged in the White House (or the Executive Office of the President [EOP]), overseen by groups of cabinet members, and guided by a top White House official at the head of the staff. This strategy first manifested itself when Richard Nixon created the Domestic Council to oversee policy development and, eventually, implementation as well. Nixon and Gerald Ford extended this model to include coordination of economic policy, with Ford's Economic Policy Board still seen as a highly successful undertaking. These proved valuable, and have become a regular feature of administrations of both parties. Combined with the well-established National Security Council, such policy staffs make the White House the focal point for integrating and overseeing department and agency proposals and actions. Thus, the White House and the cabinet can for many purposes be viewed, as we do here, as elements of a single presidential decision-making system.

Over time, Democrats' faith in their version of White House organization has faded. It was Lyndon Johnson who created the first domestic policy staff, albeit one not formally connected to the cabinet. Jimmy Carter finally abandoned the "spokes of the wheel" when he named his top generalist adviser, Hamilton Jordan, chief of staff. But the final nail in the coffin for the Democrats' ideal was Bill Clinton's experiment with a "weak" chief of staff, in the person of his long-time friend Mack McLarty. Clinton's attempt to recapture the free-wheeling dynamism associated with Roosevelt, Truman, and Kennedy resulted instead in a chaotic period marked by overlong meetings, indecisiveness, and a string of embarrassing gaffes, most of which traced to shoddy staff work. Indeed, journalistic critics memorably dubbed the first eighteen months of the Clinton presidency a "madhouse."

Although the Clinton White House subsequently came under the more competent management of strong chiefs of staff, beginning with Leon Panetta, and in other ways reflected elements of the erstwhile-Republican model (e.g., policy councils in both domestic and economic policy areas, as well as, of course, in national security), a consensus emerged among journalists, politicians, academics, and White House veterans that a corner had been turned, and even the residual Democratic organizational model had shown itself inadequate to the challenges of the contemporary presidency. With that judgment widely shared, the Eisenhower model, as embellished especially by Nixon, had become by consensus the "standard model" of the institutional presidency. Thus, as the election of 2000 impended, the Washington establishment was at pains to avoid a repetition of the early days of Clinton. Think tanks ranging, left to right, from the Brookings Institution through the American Enterprise Institute to the Heritage Foundation were among the organizations sponsoring seminars on transitions and White House organization, producing books and articles, and even writing briefing books for the new denizens of the White House, whoever they might prove to be.[2] The thrust of much of the advice: hew to the standard model.

GEORGE W. BUSH AND THE STANDARD MODEL

As fate would have it, the selection of George W. Bush as the forty-third president made much of this effort and advice unnecessary. The new president, son of the forty-first president, was no stranger to the White House, having worked there during his father's term. Even more important, Bush and his advisers knew well the dangers of populating the top ranks of the White House and the executive branch with people of limited Washington experience, as Clinton had done to some extent. Instead, Bush looked to Republican administrations of the past for both top staffers and key cabinet members. Of course, he had already begun at the top, with Vice President Dick Cheney, who had launched his White House career on Nixon's staff and had been, in effect, chief of staff to Gerald Ford.

Troika

The central inspiration for the new President Bush was not his father's administration, however, nor was it Gerald Ford's. Both of those had been organized along Nixonian lines, with a chief of staff (or, in Ford's euphemism, a "staff director") presiding over White House organization and processes and active principally in the realms of domestic policy and electoral politics. Bush knew whom he wanted for chief of staff. He tapped Andrew Card, who had been deputy chief of staff under George H. W. Bush, had been active in the campaign and transition, and was well known and respected in Washington. In the latter respect, especially, the younger Bush diverged from his father, who had brought a relative Washington novice, John Sununu, a former New Hampshire governor, into the White House as chief.

Yet the new president also had two long-time, indispensable aides whom he wished to place on a par with anyone else in the White House. The first was Karl Rove, the political strategist who had guided George W. Bush's political career and presidential campaign. Second was Karen Hughes, his campaign press secretary and all-around press and public relations adviser. It would not do to require either Rove or Hughes to report to Bush through a chief of staff. So the two were installed as counselors to the president, essentially Card's equals in the White House hierarchy. The resulting configuration at the top, a three-way sharing of power and responsibilities, was most reminiscent of the "troika" of advisors that had overseen Reagan's White House during his first term. There, James Baker, the chief of staff, managed the White House decision-making process (and, crucially, staffed the policy-making "cabinet councils"), while Edwin Meese had a domestic policy portfolio and Michael Deaver, formally Baker's assistant, had responsibility for presenting the public face of the president.

Under George W. Bush, the emphasis at the top was decidedly different. The two counselors, Hughes and Rove, together shared responsibility for the political and public relations aspects of the presidency. Neither, at the outset, was necessarily seen as a force on the policy side—although since the White House is famously the intersection of politics and policy, some impact from the two was inevitable. Still, the contrast to Baker and Meese, both of whom were powerful policy players, could hardly have been sharper.

In effect, Hughes had a portfolio much like Deaver's, while Rove and Card shared Baker's job in its political and management aspects, respectively. There was no Meese at the top—nobody principally dedicated to the substance of domestic or economic policy. Even when Rove, early on, launched an Office of Strategic Initiatives that verged into domestic policy territory, the focus was on the politics, not the substance, of policy. Thus, the Bush White House, in any administration the key point for integrating politics and policy, showed a pronounced tilt at the top toward politics.

Policy Councils

As already noted, an area of White House organization where the Democrats and Republicans have not diverged a great deal has been the use of policy councils—essentially committees comprised of top executive branch officials, supported by a presidential adviser and a significant staff housed in the Executive Office of the President—to oversee major areas of public policy. This organizational approach has become not only prevalent, but also increasingly important in recent administrations. Complex new issues, like "intermestic" economic policy or "nation building" abroad, defy traditional categories and established definitions of bureaucratic competence. As a result, the task of weaving multiple, sometimes novel, policy streams and organizations together has become more urgent. Here, Bush mostly replicated Clinton's organizational scheme, indicating how thoroughly institutionalized this aspect of the presidency has become.

The National Security Council (NSC), created by Congress during the Truman administration, has served as the central point of integration of military, diplomatic, and related concerns. Its staff and the head of that staff, the national security assistant,[3] have been important actors in national security policy since the days of Kennedy. Then, McGeorge Bundy first defined the role of the dominant national security assistant, whose influence would rival or exceed that of the secretaries of state and defense. That this was not a partisan approach was demonstrated under Nixon and Ford, when Henry Kissinger was even more the fulcrum of national security policy, even to the point of holding simultaneously, at least for a time, the jobs of national security assistant and secretary of state.

Since the heydays of Kissinger and Zbigniew Brzezinski, under Carter, the role of the national security assistant has shrunk somewhat. More recent national security assistants have been primarily process managers, serving the president by coordinating the policy-planning process and supervising the implementation of policy. In effect, national security assistants have worked as chiefs of staff for the foreign and defense policy side of the presidency, although this has not precluded chiefs of staff from becoming involved in national security themselves.[4] Perhaps the paragon of this kind of national security assistant was Brent Scowcroft, who served under Gerald Ford and George H. W. Bush. Here, the younger Bush followed suit, tapping Condoleezza Rice, a well-regarded academic who had served on the NSC staff under Scowcroft and the elder Bush. Rice's mandate was not to dominate the advising process, but, with her staff, to coordinate and integrate it, presenting a full range of information and options for presidential decision.

Bush likewise followed precedent, especially that of his immediate predecessor, in keeping the National Economic Council (NEC). He appointed Lawrence B. Lindsey to be director of the EOP-based staff of the council, whose members include various department and agency heads. Created in 1993 by executive order, the NEC's principal functions are " to coordinate policy-making for domestic and international economic issues, to coordinate economic policy advice for the President, to ensure that policy decisions and programs are consistent with the President's economic goals, and to monitor implementation of the President's economic policy agenda."[5] The key area in which this council goes beyond most of the arrangements in previous administrations is its capacity to integrate both domestic and international economics, thus spanning the increasingly critical "intermestic" issues that partake of the character of both.

Finally, in domestic (i.e., not national security, not economic) policy, Bush again continued in the well-established pattern of using the "cabinet council" structure as a device to integrate and supervise diverse policy threads. The council itself is comprised of the heads of relevant departments and agencies. The council and its staff, headed initially by Assistant to the President Margaret LaMontagne and her top aide, John Bridgeland, were designed to oversee policy planning and implementation in major policy areas, while coordinating with the specialized White House policy bodies dedicated to drug control, AIDS policy, and faith-based initiatives (discussed later in this chapter). At the outset, the domestic policy staff was tasked with translating Bush's "compassionate conservative" policy agenda, including such issues as education reform, into legislation.[6]

The Institutionalized White House

The standard model prescribes not only a chief of staff and a systematic decision process, but also an array of offices that have become, since the Nixon administration, a stable and predictable aspect of the White House. Subordinate to and reporting to the chief of staff, these units serve, ideally, to extend the reach of the president beyond what any one person can manage. In addition, they maintain orderly processes within the White House itself. The predictability of this array is attested to by the fact that one of the contributions of the Pew-funded White House 2001 Project was to prepare extensive "briefing books" on seven of these units that either provide support services to the president or facilitate presidential outreach: chief of staff, counsel to the president, Communications, Press, Personnel, Staff Secretary, and Management and Administration.[7] Needless to say, the Bush White

House produced its version of these offices, along with such other standard units as Legislative Affairs, Speech Writing, and Public (interest group) Liaison—in addition to an equally predictable range of policy staff, notably those in national security, domestic, and economic policy. Chief of Staff Card maintained control over this array with the assistance of two deputies. The heads of the policy staffs reported to Card through one deputy, while almost all of the remaining elements of the White House reported through another.[8] This meant that office heads had to go through Card to get themselves or their views to the President. As mentioned earlier, however, Card's purview did not extend to Hughes and Rove, and Bush was soon to create another unit that reported directly to him.

Bush had learned the lesson of Clinton's early struggles. His White House not only formally reflected the standard model—as, for the most part, had Clinton's—but it was, from the start, "well-disciplined, tightly organized, and extremely efficient. It had a hierarchical structure with clearly differentiated lines of authority compared to Clinton's more informal, flatter, and fluid operation."[9] George W. Bush, the first president possessing an MBA, had created a White House modeled on traditional business organization, and dedicated to an orderly, businesslike approach to the presidency. Indeed, it was typically characterized as "a corporate hierarchy, [with] clearly defined responsibilities and a central role for longtime loyalists to shape and communicate an agenda for a time of peace and prosperity."[10]

Bush Elaborates the Standard Model

Every president since Herbert Hoover has placed some new element in the White House. Usually, this reflects a particular policy interest of the president. Dwight Eisenhower, for instance, added staff for working on arms control and the planning of the interstate highway system. Kennedy had White House units dedicated to the arts and to the problem of mental retardation. For Bill Clinton, at the outset, the issue was health care. George W. Bush was no exception. During the campaign he had stressed his intention to use the federal government to stimulate greater involvement by the "faith-based community" of religiously affiliated organizations in carrying out the functions of social welfare policy. To that end, President Bush created the Office of Faith-Based and Community Initiatives, whose first director, University of Pennsylvania political scientist John DiIulio, Jr., though a Democrat, had been an adviser to Bush during the campaign. In announcing this initiative, Bush noted that DiIulio would report directly to him, and praised his new aide extravagantly as one who "has a servant's heart on the issue that we will confront."[11]

While the faith-based initiatives represented Bush's primary innovative *policy* use of the White House, he also relied on another kind of innovation used by recent presidents, in the White House presence of his vice president, Dick Cheney. As a former White House aide, and later secretary of defense, Cheney's credentials as a top administration adviser were indisputable. Cheney's relative prominence was consistent with a trend in the modern vice presidency, dating at least from Walter Mondale's prominent role in the Carter administration as a political and policy adviser, and continuing through the work of Al Gore on environmental issues and government reform under Clinton. Cheney was invited to attend such meetings as he chose, and was immediately placed in charge of the administration's review of national energy policy. In light of his credentials, he also was clearly expected to play a role in national security policy.

THE BUSH WHITE HOUSE IN ACTION:
BEFORE THE ATTACKS

It is generally accepted that the terrorist attacks of September 11, 2001, "transformed" the Bush White House. Before turning to that, however, it is useful to briefly recall the White House prior to any transformation. As suggested earlier, the most common media image of the Bush administration was of a "corporate" operation, with clear task definitions and lines of authority, in which the president, acting essentially as a chief executive officer, delegated freely to his more experienced subordinates. So well managed and controlled was this operation that the most frequently voiced complaint was that it was actually *too* disciplined and rigidly programmed—perhaps, some suggested, in order to compensate for the limitations of the leader at the top. Concerned especially with domestic and economic issues, such as education, faith-based initiatives, and the successful push for tax cuts, the Bush White House emphasized what aides wryly labeled " 'strategery,' the deliberative focus on long-term initiatives with slow roll-outs and elaborate communications planning."[12] In other words, the Bush White House was working largely as planned.

If there was a flaw in the formula, it appeared connected to the virtues of a disciplined, tight ship. Administration aides were accused of lack of openness, unwillingness to consult, and, on occasion, arrogance. Moreover, such behavior was directed even toward some who should have been their allies—especially those in Congress. It was in part this perception of the White House that provoked Senator James Jeffords of Vermont to bolt the Republican party in mid-2001. That move shifted control of the Senate to the Democrats, since Jeffords, now an Independent, chose to caucus with the Democrats, and stalled the Bush agenda in Congress. Jeffords's specific complaints centered on what he considered heavy-handed White House retaliation after he became one of three GOP (Grand Old Party) Senators to vote to scale back the Bush tax-cut proposal. Although the White House denied the charges, there seemed to be something to them. For instance, a "well-connected GOP source" was quoted as placing responsibility on Card, Rove, and congressional liaison head Nicholas Calio.[13]

The evident White House attitude toward other constituencies reflected similar problems. Vice President Cheney's energy task force, criticized for talking mainly with energy producers in formulating its recommendations, refused to allow public or congressional scrutiny of its proceedings. This led to lawsuits against the task force by, for example, Judicial Watch, a conservative "legal watchdog" group, and the General Accounting Office, an arm of Congress.[14] At the same time, the White House moved to place sensitive records from prior administrations off-limits to journalists and scholars.[15]

The centerpiece faith-based policy initiative also took a major hit when John DiIulio became the first senior staff member to resign, in August 2001. In part, the resignation stemmed from the difficulties in Congress that legislation embodying the faith-based principles had experienced. Jeffords's defection had helped make the Senate, in particular, a challenge. Yet DiIulio himself had been part of the problem, with respect to both some of his tactical choices and the perception that "he lacked necessary political ease and skills."[16]

For his part, DiIulio, in an *Esquire* magazine interview with journalist Ron Suskind, focused responsibility on the White House itself. Although avoiding fixing blame on Rove, whose political strategizing brought him into debates over the direction of policy, DiIulio did lament what he viewed as excessive concern for pleasing certain key Republican constituencies, especially the religious right. More damning, perhaps, he rendered an overall judgment that the early Bush White House was too dominated by strategic political thinking, leading to an indifference to policy details in the name of getting legislation, any legislation, passed. Rove and his "Mayberry Machiavellis," DiIulio opined, "consistently talked and acted as if the height of political sophistication consisted in reducing every issue to its simplest black-and-white term for public consumption, then steering . . . proposals as far right as possible."[17] Although DiIulio later retracted these remarks and apologized, they nonetheless seem to point to a built-in bias of the Bush version of the troika system, where concern for politics and public image was not effectively balanced by attention to the substance of policy.[18]

At the same time, "despite a disciplined public affairs operation and tighter lips than most of its predecessors," the Bush administration "had trouble singing from the same foreign policy hymnal," and it struggled to keep the resulting internal conflict out of the public eye.[19] Having assembled "one of the most experienced national security teams in the history of the presidency,"[20] the President soon saw press reports that commented on the "two competing foreign policy camps" within his administration.[21] One side, anchored at the Pentagon, prominently featured Secretary of Defense Donald Rumsfeld, Deputy Secretary Paul D. Wolfowitz, and, by most accounts, Vice President Cheney. On the other side was Secretary of State Colin Powell. The position of NSA Condoleezza Rice often was less clear, although both sides claimed her allegiance. For the most part, the conflict pitted the more conservative Defense Department against the more moderate State

Department, the former urging a more "unilateralist" foreign policy and the latter arguing the benefits of continued multilateralism. Ideological differences emerged on a variety of issues, ranging from missile defense to U.S. relations with North Korea and Russia to Middle East peace negotiations to UN sanctions policy in Iraq.

Clearly, such diversity of views is among the desirable features of multiple advocacy. President Bush, too, apparently prefers to listen to differing perspectives as he makes decisions.[22] Yet, the conflicts among national security officials often became public, in part due to key players' links to conservative writers and think tanks outside the administration, as well as to former President Bush and his national security assistant, Brent Scowcroft.[23] Evidently, too, the ideological divide permeated the higher levels of both departments as well as the vice president's staff, expanding the numbers of potential "anonymous" sources. By early September, *Time* picked the most likely loser in many of these struggles, with a cover that pointedly inquired: "Where Have You Gone, Colin Powell?"[24]

Nonetheless, despite the inevitable internal disagreements and external criticism, the Bush White House remained a relatively calm and corporate place during its first eight months, especially when compared to the gaffe- and scandal-plagued beginning that his predecessor had endured. Then, on September 11, everything changed.

SEPTEMBER 11, 2001

In the immediate aftermath of the attacks on the World Trade Center and the Pentagon, the White House went onto a war footing. No longer entirely hierarchical and controlled, the White House suddenly became what analyst Paul Light called "an organized anarchy or an organized adhocracy . . . [T]here's more dotted lines here than on a dress pattern."[25] Decision making, at least in national security and related areas, was hurried, often the product of ad hoc meetings that brought together diverse White House offices and executive agencies "in a collection of interwoven coalitions handling shared tasks."[26] The National Security Council began to meet daily, supplemented by a "war cabinet" of top White House officials, including Card, Cheney, and Rice, as well as Secretary of State Powell, Defense Secretary Rumsfeld, Secretary of the Treasury Paul O'Neill, and CIA chief George Tenet, among others, often including the principals' deputies.[27] At the same time, Deputy Chief of Staff Joshua Bolten chaired a "domestic consequences" group that met daily "to deal with fallout from the attacks on the home front."[28] Notably absent from the war cabinet, although still close to Bush, were Hughes and Rove. The focus of the administration had shifted irreversibly from domestic and economic concerns to national security and the President's "War on Terror."

Nevertheless, the more routine functions of the White House, such as scheduling the President's appearances and writing his speeches, remained essential. This became clear when the nation was reassured by the "eloquent meditation on grief and resolution" authored by White House speechwriter Michael Gerson, which the President delivered at the National Cathedral.[29] Even more impressively, the full White House speech and support system, including Gerson, Hughes, and Rove, went into action in choosing a site for the delivery (Congress) and preparing a powerful and well-received televised address that some viewed as a turning point, establishing when George W. Bush truly grew into the presidency.[30]

Homeland Security

The initial, relatively frantic "adhocracy" was a response to a terrorist event. Terrorism directed at Americans, however, clearly is a long-term problem, not a single event. Critically needed, then, was a structural response. In early October, this was forthcoming, when the President named then-Pennsylvania Governor Tom Ridge to head a newly created White House Office of Homeland Security (OHS). This unit was created by Executive Order 13228, signed on October 8, 2001—less than one month after the attacks. In many respects, the cabinet council structure of the office was "modeled after the current iteration of the National Security Council (NSC) and the Assistant to the President for National Security Affairs."[31] Like the NSC, the OHS was designed as a coordinating body whose director is a top presidential adviser and whose staff is located in the Executive Office. Overseeing the operation was a Homeland Security Council, comprised of top cabinet members and agency heads, and including Chief of Staff Andrew Card.[32] The coordinating responsibilities envisioned for the unit were daunting: over forty agencies were involved in aspects of homeland security as defined by the president, not to mention the critical roles played by state and local governmental bodies. Moreover, as critics were quick to point out, Ridge was not given much in the way of resources. He had only a small staff and, perhaps most important, no statutory authority to tell agencies to do or not do anything, and no control over their budgets. He would have to rely almost entirely on support from the president to have any chance of success.

For the most part, it did not work. Virtually all assessments of OHS have concluded that, crippled from the start, there simply was no way for Ridge to succeed in the short run. He "lacked the necessary clout to move the bureaucratic behemoth at anything but a snails' pace,"[33] and in the face of the threat of terrorism, that was not enough. Thus, by June 2002, President Bush had abandoned his initial resistance to the idea of elevating Homeland Security to the status of a cabinet department. After months of wrangling with the Senate over his proposal to weaken civil service protections for employees of the new department (on the grounds that on matters of spying and terror, senior managers could not afford to battle "red tape"), and in the aftermath of the 2002 election, which returned control of the Senate to the GOP, Bush got his department. He nominated Tom Ridge to be the first Secretary of Homeland Security.

The War on Terrorism

At the same time, national security policy making remained in high gear. In *Bush at War*, for instance, Bob Woodward provides details on forty-two NSC and sixteen principals' meetings held between September 11 and November 13. Certainly at the outset, whatever public conflicts there had been among senior foreign policy advisers were set aside, even as they continued to give President Bush sometimes contrasting assessments of appropriate U.S. responses.[34]

As the U.S. attacks on Afghanistan receded and life returned generally to the "new normal," however, differences among national security advisers (and their external advocates) again became public fodder.[35] The administration's war against terrorism, itself "all consuming" in geographical scope and demands for resources, soon was joined by myriad other foreign policy issues.[36] After several Palestinian suicide bombings took place in May 2002, for example, the administration turned its attention to the Middle East.[37] Yet it took several weeks of reportedly fierce internal debate before the president publicly committed the United States to support the establishment of a Palestinian state within three years. Even after that, Secretary of Defense Rumsfeld was characterized as seeming "deeply equivocal about a Palestinian state."[38] Meanwhile, media reports appeared that the Joint Chiefs of Staff disagreed with civilian officials at the Pentagon about appropriate U.S. actions to remove Saddam Hussein from power in Iraq.[39] In addition, debate continued among advocates of disarmament and of regime change in Iraq.[40]

Morton Abramowitz, who served as an assistant secretary of state under Ronald Reagan, observed that by the summer of 2002, the Bush administration's "foreign policy wars" once more were mostly over ideology. Moreover, "the differences between the top team seem to stretch over major issues—from Iraq to Afghanistan to China, from the Arab-Israeli issue to North Korea, from alliance management to public diplomacy."[41]

Much like several months before as well, many presumed that Secretary of State Powell typically was the loser in such battles.[42] Yet, after several months of intra-administration debate and weeks of diplomacy, Powell evidently "carried the day" when the U.N. Security Council agreed on a resolution to resume inspections for weapons of mass destruction in Iraq.[43] Whether that ultimately stops the United States from going to war, of course, remains to be seen.

The First Top-Level Departure

Counselor Karen Hughes left the White House in July 2002, by most accounts because her son and husband wanted to return home to Texas.[44] Her title, "Counselor to the President," was retired.

Once Hughes announced her departure in April, speculation immediately started about the nature of the "seismic shift" predicted to take place in the distribution of influence in the White House.[45] Dan Bartlett, the White House communications director who had served as Hughes's assistant, "took over the 45-person press, speechwriting and message-development operation" she had directed.[46] Bartlett's power, along with that of press secretary Ari Fleischer and head writer Michael Gerson, likely increased. Yet, most in Washington believed that Karl Rove, "the feared and canny political advisor who tends to the president's conservative base, [would] fill the void left by the more moderate Ms. Hughes."[47] Even Chief of Staff Card voiced concern that with Hughes gone, he would need to find others who could effectively balance Rove's tendency to "swing a sharp sword of partisanship on matters of policy and politics."[48]

Precisely how the internal staff dynamics have played out since Hughes left is difficult to determine, since most in the Bush White House refuse to discuss such issues, especially when they concern Karl Rove.[49] Moreover, even before Hughes's departure, reports circulated about Rove's increasing involvement in policy issues. Allegedly "expanding his White House portfolio by inserting himself into the debate over how to deal with the Middle East, trade, terrorism, Latin America, and other foreign policy matters," Rove's fingerprints were detected on, for example, President Bush's decision to support protection for farmers and steelworkers and the administration's withholding of funding for the United Nations Population Fund.[50]

For her part, Hughes reportedly "still talks to Mr. Bush two or three times a week, if not more, and she is in daily contact with some of the most important officials in the West Wing." She also campaigned extensively for Republican candidates during the fall of 2002, traveled with the president to an economic conference in Mexico, wrote Bush's speech on the anniversary of the September 11 attacks, and confers on other important speeches.[51]

Persisting Economic Problems

Even as the administration struggled to cope with homeland security and foreign policy challenges, it confronted serious economic problems, both at home and abroad. The U.S. economy threatened to plunge back into recession, the dangers of international financial contagion (including serious debt problems in Argentina and an economic boycott in oil-rich Venezuela), and the continuing effects of major business scandals, and stock market losses combined to create considerable political and economic uncertainty. At the same time, relatively few had favorable views of Bush's economic and financial advisers.

Congressional Republicans rather handily survived the fall elections that many had worried might reflect the public's economic concerns.[52] Yet, especially in a White House looking toward the 2004 reelection campaign, concern focused anew on underscoring the President's commitment to addressing ongoing economic weaknesses and to pushing hard for a new round of tax cuts. Among the results were the dismissals in early December 2002 of both Treasury Secretary Paul O'Neill and the assistant to the president for economic policy, Lawrence Lindsey. Both were faulted for their weak presentations of administration policy.[53] Within days, the president nominated railroad executive John Snow to fill the Treasury post. Then, despite public criticism from advocates of supply-side economics, Stephen Friedman, former chairman of Goldman Sachs, was named as Lindsey's replacement.[54]

Of course, whether this—or any other—administration can do much to revive the increasingly complex and volatile national and global economies remains an open question. At the very least, the new appointments create an opportunity for dialogue within the administration, pitting traditional budget balancers against supply-side tax cutters. Thus, on the economic side, the structures for soliciting and integrating diverse perspectives will be critical to the administration's efforts.

CONCLUSION

The Bush administration's adoption of the standard model of White House structural design was not surprising. But, as each presidency demonstrates anew, effective organization can facilitate the pursuit of presidential objectives, but it guarantees nothing more. Each administration adapts the inherited structures to the president's purposes and style, and to the political, policy, and security environments that the administration and the country face. That perhaps has never been clearer than in the first two years of the presidency of George W. Bush. His tightly structured, domestically oriented White House operation underwent a transformation almost as sharp as the country's reaction in the aftermath of the terrorist attacks of September 11, 2001. Suddenly national security was the all-consuming issue, and the White House cabinet policy-councils charged with coping with it became the focus of the presidency. To its credit, the Bush White House showed a capacity to reorient and restructure swiftly in the face of this imperative.

Yet, even in the midst of this crisis, the ordinary functioning of the White House, as evidenced by the successful speechwriting operation, was crucial. Moreover, when the immediate crisis abated, the initial tendencies of the White House remained. These included the strong focus on the political side of the politics-policy relationship, enhanced as the influence of Karl Rove grew and the midterm election of 2002 became a focus of strategy. Similarly, the relative weakness of the economic team demanded, and got, attention in the aftermath of the successful election outcome. Throughout, the discipline and relative opaqueness of much of the White House and policy councils' operations continued to both impress and frustrate outside commentators. Leaks generally were few in number and controlled, overt dissent was unusual, and the capacity to stay "on message" was striking.

Nonetheless, in spite of these more closed features, the Bush White House has never seemed in danger of sliding into the kind of paranoia that

Charles Cameron has suggested might be the fate of an ideological White House in a highly polarized partisan environment, facing a resistant Congress and a reluctant bureaucracy. There is little evidence so far of " 'the OliverNorth/Gordon Liddy problem': rogue operations . . . and vindictive actions directed at 'enemies' without and within."[55] Instead, the structures of the Bush White House and the policy councils that link cabinet and White House officials appear to have been able to provoke and manage healthy policy debates while maintaining a generally positive relationship with the media, the public, and the Washington establishment. The crisis that bonded Americans across party lines may have taken some of the edge off of the partisanship, at least temporarily, and the 2002 election seemingly handed the president a Congress with which he can work.

The Bush White House has been relatively successful so far. The standard model evidently has worked well, vindicating those who have urged its adoption by all incoming administrations. Moreover, the "political" tilt at the top of this White House has so far produced considerable political success for the President. Still, the halfway point is too early for any final judgment. Given the global and domestic challenges ahead, the Bush system surely will be tested in the future as it has been in the past.

NOTES

1. See Alexander L. George, "The Case for Multiple Advocacy in Making Foreign Policy," *American Political Science Review* 66 (1972): 751–85.

2. Among the others who participated were the Center for the Study of the Presidency and the James Baker Institute. A representative sampling of the kind of advice that was proffered can be found in the volume collecting the works of the White House 2001 Project, funded by the Pew Charitable Trusts, and involving both Brookings and the American Enterprise Institute (AEI). See Martha Joynt Kumar and Terry Sullivan, eds., *The White House World: Transitions, Organization, and Office Operations* (College Station, Tex.: Texas A&M University Press, 2003).

3. The official title of the position is assistant to the president for national security affairs—hence "national security assistant, "or "NSA." More commonly, this official is referred to as the president's "national security adviser."

4. See David B. Cohen, Chris J. Dolan, and Jerel A. Rosati, "A Place at the Table: The Emerging Policy Roles of the White House Chief of Staff," *Congress and the Presidency* 29 (Autumn 2002): 119–50.

5. Description of the National Economic Council available at http://www.whitehouse.gov/nec/. See also Kenneth I. Juster and Simon Lazarus, *Making Economic Policy: An Assessment of the National Economic Council* (Washington, D.C.: Brookings Institution Press, 1997).

6. Dana Milbank, "A Hard-Nosed Litigator Becomes Bush's Policy Point Man," *Washington Post*, 30 April 2002, p. A17.

7. See Kumar and Sullivan, *The White House World*.

8. John F. Harris and Dan Balz, "A Question of Capital," *Washington Post*, 29 April 2001, p. A6.

9. George C. Edwards III and Stephen J. Wayne, *Presidential Leadership: Politics and Policy Making*, 6th ed. (Belmont, Calif.: Wadsworth, 2003), 206.

10. Mike Allen and Alan Sipress, "Attacks Refocus White House on How to Fight Terrorism," *Washington Post*, 26 September 2001, p. A3.

11. Remarks by the President in Announcement of the Faith-Based Initiative, 29 January 2001, retrieved from http://www.whitehouse.gov/news/releases/20010129-5.html—[cited 25 November 2002].

12. Dana Milbank and Bradley Graham, "With Crisis, More Fluid Style at White House," *Washington Post*, 10 October 2001, p. A4.

13. Edwin Chen, "A Senator's Decision," *Los Angeles Times*, 24 May 2001, p. A25.

14. A U.S. District Court judge threw out the GAO's lawsuit (*Walker v. Cheney*), ruling that the GAO had no standing in the case. See, for example, Susan Cornwell, "Judge Rejects GAO Suit over Cheney's Papers," 9 December 2002, retrieved from http://news.findlaw.com/politics/s/20021209/energycheneydc.html—[cited 10 December 2002].

15. See Bruce P. Montgomery, "Nixon's Ghost Haunts the Presidential Records Act: The Reagan and George W. Bush Administrations," *Presidential Studies Quarterly* 32 (2002): 789–809. See, too, for example, Dana Milbank, "DiIulio Saga Highlights Primacy Placed on Secrecy," *Washington Post*, 10 December 2002, p. A27.

16. James Gerstenzang and Jonathan Peterson, "Bush's Faith-Based Project Chief Quits after 6 Months," *Los Angeles Times*, 18 August 2001, p. A1.

17. John DiIulio, quoted in Ron Suskind, "Why Are These Men Laughing?" *Esquire*, January 2003, 104. Available at http://ronsuskind.com/writing/esquire/esq_rove_0103.html.

18. This problem was not unique to Bush. It has been argued that this is a common pathology of modern White Houses, at least since Nixon. See Karen M. Hult, "Strengthening Presidential Decision-Making Capacity," *Presidential Studies Quarterly* 30 (2000): 27–46.

19. Jack R. Binns, "Weighing Bush's Foreign Policy," *The Forum* 1, no. 1, article 3 (2002). Available at http://www.bepress.com/forum/vol1/is—[cited 20 November 2002].

20. Fred I. Greenstein, "The Changing Leadership of George W. Bush: A Pre- and Post-9/11 Comparison," *The Forum* 1, no. 2, article 6 (2002): 8. Available at http://www.bepress.com/forum/vol1/is—[cited 5 December 2002].

21. Jane Perlez, "Bush Team's Counsel Is Divided on Foreign Policy," *New York Times*, 27 March 2001.

22. For example, Steven R. Weisman, "Division in Past Bush White House Echoes in Current Struggles," *New York Times*, 24 November 2002.

23. For example, Perlez, "Bush Team's Counsel is Divided on Foreign Policy"; Johanna McGreary, "Odd Man Out," *Time*, 10 September 2001; Binns, "Weighing Bush's Foreign Policy."

24. *Time*, 10 September 2001.

25. Quoted in Milbank and Graham, "With Crisis, a More Fluid Style."

26. Milbank and Graham, "With Crisis, a More Fluid Style."

27. Cohen, Dolan, and Rosati, "A Place at the Table," 131–32; Allen and Sipress, "Attacks Refocus White House"; Bob Woodward, *Bush at War* (New York: Simon & Schuster, 2002).

28. Allen and Sipress, "Attacks Refocus White House."

29. D.T. Max, "The 2,988 Words That Changed a Presidency: An Etymology," *New York Times Magazine*, 7 October 2001. Cf. Woodward, *Bush at War*.

30. Max, "The 2,988 Words That Changed a Presidency."

31. David B. Cohen and Alethia H. Cook, "Institutional Redesign: Terrorism, Punctuated Equilibrium, and the Evolution of Homeland Security in the United States" (paper presented at the annual meeting of the American Political Science Association, 2002), 12.

32. See William W. Newman, "Reorganizing for National Security and Homeland Security," *Public Administration Review* 62 (2002): 129–31. The Homeland Security Council was comprised of the secretaries of treasury, defense, health and human services, and transportation; the attorney general; the directors of the Office of Management and Budget, the CIA, the FBI, and the Federal Emergency Management Administration; and the chiefs of staff to Bush (Card) and Cheney.

33. Cohen and Cook, "Institutional Redesign," 15.

34. Probably the best contemporary source on such policy discussions in the weeks following the September 11 attacks is Woodward, *Bush at War.*

35. See, for example, Dana Milbank, "Who's Pulling the Foreign Policy Strings?" *Washington Post*, 14 May 2002, p. A19. Milbank's answer was Brent Scowcroft, representing the "foreign policy establishment," and Richard Perle, "the intellectual guru of the hard-line neoconservative movement in foreign policy."

36. Morton Abramowitz, "Foreign Policy Infight . . . ," *Washington Post*, 19 August 2002, p. A13.

37. For example, Todd S. Purdum, "Bush Mideast Policy Delayed by Staff Debate," *New York Times*, 22 June 2002.

38. Martin Indyk, "A White House in Search of a Policy," *New York Times*, 11 August 2002. Cf. Binns, "Weighing Bush's Foreign Policy."

39. Christopher Marquis, "Bush Officials Differ on Ways to Force out Iraqi Leader," *New York Times*, 19 June 2002.

40. Ivo H. Daalder and James M. Lindsay, "It's Hawk v. Hawk in the Bush Administration," *Washington Post*, 27 October 2002, p. B3.

41. Abramowitz, "Foreign Policy Infight. . . . "

42. See, for example, Maureen Dowd, "Coup de Crawford," *New York Times*, 21 August 2002; Michael E. O'Hanlon, "How the Hard-Liners Lost," *Washington Post*, 10 November 2002.

43. O'Hanlon, "How the Hard-Liners Lost."

44. See, for example, Ron Suskind, "Mrs. [sic] Hughes Takes Her Leave," *Esquire*, July 2002, 101–7, 110.

45. Carl M. Cannon and Alexis Simendinger, "The Evolution of Karl Rove," *National Journal*, 27 April 2002, 1214.

46. Mike Allen, "Hughes to Sign on with GOP: Contract with Departing Aide Allows Continued Advice to Bush," *Washington Post*, 5 July 200–2, p. A19.

47. Elisabeth Bumiller, "Minus One, Bush Inner Circle Is Open for Angling," *New York Times*, 15 July 2002.

48. Suskind, "Hughes Takes Her Leave," 110.

49. See, for example, Suskind, "Why Are These Men Laughing?"

50. Richard L. Berke and David E. Sanger, "Some in Administration Grumble as Aide's Role Seems to Expand," *New York Times*, 13 May 2002; Terry M. Neal, "Downplaying Politics at the White House," retrieved from washingtonpost.com—[cited 24 July 2002, 3:01 P.M.].

51. Elisabeth Bumiller, "White House Letter: Still Advising, From Afar and Near," *New York Times*, 21 October 2002, p. A12—[accessed through Lexis-Nexus Academic; cited 15 December 2002].

52. For example, Adam Nagoiurney, "Economy Stirs GOP Worry in House Races," *New York Times*, 6 August 2002.

53. See, for example, the range of comments reported in Howard Kurtz, "A Very Public Outing: White House Trashing of Economic Team Was Unexpected," retrieved from washingtonpost.com—[cited 9 December 2002, 8:23 A.M.].

54. Mike Allen and Jonathan Weisman, "Friedman Chosen Top Economic Aide to Bush," *Washington Post*, 13 December 2002, p. A1. On the criticism of Friedman, see, for example, Jonathan Weisman, "Bush's Economic Pick under Fire from Right," *Washington Post*, 11 December 2001, p. E1.

55. Charles M. Cameron, "Studying the Polarized Presidency," *Presidential Studies Quarterly* 32 (2002): 657.

CHAPTER 5

Bush and Public Opinion

MICHAEL A. DIMOCK

In the year following the September 11, 2001, terrorist attacks, George W. Bush enjoyed one of the longest stretches of popularity any president has seen since pollsters have tracked such public attitudes reliably. In addition to rallying behind their president in a time of crisis, the September 11 attacks redefined the criteria by which the public evaluates the presidency, and Bush exhibited the qualities people of all backgrounds were looking for at that time.

But there is a lot of evidence that things are returning to normal with respect to public opinion and the presidency. Democrats and Republicans once again disagree over what the government should be doing, and how good a job the president is doing. While most approve of Bush's leadership in the war on terrorism, there is significant disagreement over his handling of domestic issues, as well as the situation in Iraq.

Presidential images can change quickly and dramatically. The current president's father, George H. W. Bush, entered office perceived by many as a "wimp," yet became one of the most popular presidents in history, if for a short time, due to his decisive and firm response to Iraqi aggression in Kuwait. The tables would turn again on Bush, however, as the 1992 election became a referendum on the domestic economy, largely due to the Clinton campaign's effective campaign rhetoric. Clinton, in turn, faced widespread disapproval after his first two years in office, for presiding over a weak economy and for having achieved little despite the advantage of a Democratically controlled Congress. But budget conflict with the Republicans leading to the 1995 government shutdown gave Clinton's poll numbers a surprising boost, and, though his personal ratings would continue to sink, Clinton's job approval would reach personal peaks in the months following the opening of the Monica Lewinsky investigation.[1]

Already, George W. Bush's public image has been transformed by events. Even before taking office, Bush had to battle his way through an unprecedented electoral deadlock that threatened to exacerbate partisan divisions both in Washington, D.C., and across the nation. The president's early efforts to place tax cuts, Social Security reform, and faith-based programs on the public agenda, while popular, were wiped away by the September

11 terrorist attacks, which redefined the public's image of both Bush individually and the office of the presidency. These changes helped the president to avoid being taken to task for a slumping economy and for links between administration figures and corporate financial scandals. More recently, war with Iraq may once again redefine the president in the eyes of Americans, some of whom support Bush's hard-line stance against Saddam Hussein, and others who do not.

POLITICAL "SCRIPTS"

As these examples suggest, the factors that shape a president's public image are often beyond the power of the president and his staff. Not only are events unpredictable, but public images of the president can be hard to control. As in day-to-day life, it is often the first impressions voters form about presidents that can matter the most. In the process of making judgments about who to vote for in a presidential election, most voters develop images and expectations of a president that will last throughout his or her four or eight years of service. These preconceptions are often based on stereotypes by means of which the public can easily categorize and assess the qualities of a candidate, based on what they learn through the course of a campaign. Put in other terms, people take the limited information about a candidate they pick up and fill in the gaps from stereotypes, media images, cultural references, or their own past experiences to create a more complete picture in their minds. In a sense, they fit the candidate into preexisting "scripts" that they have experience with.[2] The caricatures that result may not capture the candidate's own characteristics perfectly, but they serve a purpose to citizens who need to find ways to simplify the process of evaluating candidates. More importantly from a political perspective, the caricatures that result may be hard for a candidate—or president—to change once they are set in peoples' minds.[3]

Bill Clinton, for example, was perceived as a womanizer long before he came into office, based on allegations and controversies that arose during the 1992 elections. Later events would fit neatly into this preexisting "script" and therefore be taken as more credible than had they occurred to another president. But Bill Clinton also came to office with the accompanying image of a man of ideas and intelligence, who could improve social and economic conditions in the nation.[4] In other words, voters already saw two sides of Clinton's personality long before Election Day, and though most found the scandals attached to the presidency to be distasteful and even abhorrent, they were able to draw a distinction between the personal and the political that allowed Clinton to end his term as one of the more highly regarded presidents of the last forty years.

George W. Bush, too, came to office with an already established image. On the positive side, he was seen as personable, honorable, decisive, and straightforward. On the negative side, there were frequent jabs and jokes about his intelligence. To no small extent, these images can be attributed to the campaigns themselves; in 2000 the Bush campaign emphasized the president's personal character over his political agenda, describing the candidate as a "compassionate conservative" and a "uniter, not a divider." Whether intentionally or not, these caricatures often develop around personality traits or political positions where the candidate is most distinct from his predecessor or opponent. Bush's image of personal honor and conviction was diametrically opposed to the prevailing image of Clinton as a liar and moral failure. The image of Bush as personable, but lacking intelligence was diametrically opposed to the prevailing caricature of Al Gore, as highly intelligent but stiff and robotic.

While presidents come into office with personal images already established, events and issues that arise during their presidency are also very important. Many political events—especially changes in foreign affairs or the economy—would boost or damage the image of any president, regardless of public persona. For example, if history is any guide, there is little doubt Al Gore would have also received a boost in public popularity after September 11, had he been victorious in 2000. However, in other ways, the manner in which events fit into the scripts associated with presidents can play a crucial role in how the president's performance is viewed. After the terrorist attacks, President Bush spent months collecting intelligence, building a coalition, and planning military strategies before taking military action in Afghanistan. Even though many Americans wanted to see the United States respond to the attacks sooner, Bush's reputation for firmness and decisiveness gave him the leeway in this situation to be more cautious and thoughtful. Had Al Gore been in the same position, it might well have been difficult for him to have taken as long to respond without being accused of being indecisive, weak, or insensitive to the emotional toll of the attacks on other Americans.

MANAGING EXPECTATIONS

To a president and his political advisers, maintaining a positive public image can seem like a full time and often fruitless job. All too often there is only so much a president can actually do legislatively or as commander in chief, and all too often good deeds and examples of strong leadership are overlooked by the public, either because they were too complicated to follow, or simply because they did not fit the scripted expectations already in peoples' minds.

Managing public opinion often means framing how people fit political events and presidential actions into their preconceptions of the president. For example, when the special prosecutor's investigation of President Clinton turned to the question of whether he lied to a federal grand jury—and the public—about an affair with Monica Lewinsky, most polling evidence suggests that the public did not question the president's overall capabilities.

Rather, the issue was framed as a failure of personal judgment, and as such, fit into a script the public had already created about the president, and one which most felt did not interfere with the president's ability to govern. By emphasizing the personal nature of the incident, as well as suggesting that he was the target of a conservative smear campaign, the administration was able to deflect much of the potential damage the incident might otherwise have caused.[5]

This example shows the importance of expectations in how the public evaluates presidential performance. By the time Kenneth Starr opened the Lewinsky investigation, the public already had very low expectations regarding the president's personal behavior. While the story was "news," it did not really provide most voters with any "new" information about the president's character or abilities that they had not already surmised. People who already disliked the president, of course, took the events as just one more reason to dislike him. But people who liked, or even were indifferent to the president, had already, at an earlier stage, found a way to compartmentalize the president's personal weaknesses as separate from, and largely irrelevant to, his political strengths. In other words, even the president's strongest supporters already had such low expectations about his personal behavior that new information of this type had virtually no impact.

At many points, President George W. Bush's administration has attempted to manage public opinion about the presidency by emphasizing the president's strengths and attempting to control the expectations people have about the presidency. The president's reputation for honor, determination, and straightforwardness fit well with what the public wanted from their political leader in the weeks and months following the terrorist attacks. Moreover, the administration has continually stressed that the war on terrorism would not be won quickly, diverting public expectations for decisive results. Much like with Clinton, most Americans have come to accept both the positive and negative stereotypes associated with their president. Within weeks of what was one of the most tragic and defining moments in American history, late-night comics were once again joking about the president's limited intelligence. Americans' ability to simultaneously express respect for their commander in chief and laugh at the expense of their president is evidence of the complexity of public opinion about the presidency.

THE 2000 ELECTION OUTCOME

President Bush came into office under extremely unusual circumstances, which shaped public opinion about his presidency in the early days in important and unexpected ways. Ironically, rather than harming the president's popularity by exacerbating partisan antipathy among Democrats, the larger effect of the drawn-out battle over Florida recounts may well have been beneficial to the president, who entered office facing relatively low public expectations about what he could achieve in such a partisan environment.

Soon after the Supreme Court decision ending further recounts in Florida and upholding Bush's victory, less than half of Americans in a nationwide Gallup poll said that Bush won fair and square. Nearly a third (32 percent) said he won on a technicality and 18 percent said he stole the election. But polling also made clear that many were willing to overlook flaws in the electoral system in order to simply have the process over with. In a December NBC/*Wall Street Journal* survey, 42 percent of Americans said that if Bush won Florida's electoral votes it would be because of a flawed system, and not because he actually received the most votes in the state. However, only 32 percent on the same survey said they would not consider a Bush victory to be legitimate. Similarly, while a December ABC/*Washington Post* survey found 62 percent of respondents supporting the elimination of the electoral college system in order to have the president elected by popular vote, the same proportion in the NBC/*Wall Street Journal* poll said they were not bothered by the fact that Bush would win the presidency even though he did not win the popular vote nationwide.

What surprised many political observers was the extent to which "recount fatigue" and the desire to see the nation move on overrode many of the strong feelings about the election and recounting process. Asked to gauge their feelings in a December Gallup poll, the single most prevalent reaction to the Supreme Court's final decision was "relief," an emotion that was widespread among both Democrats and Republicans. While 60 percent of Gore voters said they felt "cheated" by the outcome, far fewer described themselves as "angry" (32 percent) or "bitter" (29 percent). While 85 percent of Gore voters thought Bush did not win the election "fair and square," just one in three said he "stole the election"; the majority (52 percent) said he "won on a technicality." Despite the feeling that Bush did not win fairly, fully 68 percent of Gore voters said they would accept him as the legitimate president.

As a result of these tempered attitudes among many Democrats, the public's initial view of George W. Bush did not differ dramatically from that of other recent presidents. By February 2001, 53 percent of Americans said they approved of the way Bush was handling his job, while only 21 percent disapproved. This is comparable to the 56 percent who gave Bill Clinton an early favorable assessment in February 1993 and the 55 percent who said the same about Ronald Reagan after his first month in office in 1981. (See Table 5.1.) Fully 85 percent of Republicans surveyed approved of Bush's performance in February 2001, compared to 81 percent of Democrats who said the same about Clinton eight years earlier. More importantly, both Clinton and Bush garnered the benefit of the doubt from 52 percent of political Independents, and 29 percent of those on the other side of the fence at the outset of their terms in office.

Though many who felt Bush had not really won the election were willing to give the incoming president a chance, one important effect of the extended election was that the president-elect did not have the opportunity to

TABLE 5.1 Job Approval, One Month into Office

President	Approve (%)	Disapprove (%)
George W. Bush (2/01)	53	21
Bill Clinton (2/93)	56	25
George H. W. Bush (2/89)	63	13
Ronald Reagan (2/81)	55	18
Jimmy Carter (2/77)	71	9

Sources: 1993 and 2001 Pew Research Center; 1977, 1981, and 1989 Gallup.

clearly communicate his agenda to the public prior to taking office. In January, a Pew Research Center survey found just half of Americans saying Bush had done a good job explaining his policies and plans for the future. Nearly two thirds had said the same about Bill Clinton (62 percent) and George H. W. Bush (65 percent) at the outset of their terms. The perception of George W. Bush as a poor communicator was particularly noteworthy among political Independents. In January 1993, 56 percent of those with no partisan leaning said they thought Clinton was clearly communicating his positions—in January 2001 just 37 percent said the same about Bush.

Although these evaluations undoubtedly reflected the fact that the winter's news was dominated by the question of *who* would be president, rather than *what* the incoming president would do, they also reflected the widespread public perception, developed during the election, that Bush lacked certain leadership qualities. A January NBC/*Wall Street Journal* survey found that only 40 percent of respondents were confident Bush had the right set of personal characteristics to be president, down from 47 percent who had said the same about Clinton eight years earlier. When asked to rate the incoming president's qualities, Bush received the best marks for "representing traditional American values," "having high personal standards that set the proper moral tone for the country," and "being easygoing and likeable." His lowest marks came in the areas of "being knowledgeable and experienced enough to handle the presidency" and "being compassionate enough to understand average people."

Many surveys picked up on these early concerns about Bush's knowledge and abilities, as well as another, somewhat negative image that Bush would favor the wealthy. Although 62 percent characterized Bush as "well informed" in a February Pew Research Center survey, this was well below the 79 percent who described Clinton this way at the outset of his term in office. In a *CBS News* survey conducted in early January, just 38 percent thought Bush would really be in charge of what went on in his administration most of the time, while 53 percent thought other people would really be running the government. Fortunately for the president, most people were satisfied with his cabinet appointments and thought it was a good thing that many of his top advisers had previously worked in his father's administration.

While easing peoples' minds about Bush's own capability, the appointment of a new cabinet loaded with Republican insiders and corporate chief executive officers (CEOs) only exacerbated the image of Bush as a corporate insider. Asked, in a January ABC/*Washington Post* survey, whose interests Bush would look out for as president, the military, large corporations, white men, wealthy people, and religious conservatives topped the list, while women's groups, poor people, environmental groups, and labor unions came out on the bottom.

Perhaps more importantly, many Americans were uncertain about Bush's ability to handle international affairs effectively. The January *CBS News* poll found 45 percent of respondents saying they were confident in George W. Bush's ability to deal wisely with an international crisis, while another 45 percent said they were uneasy about his approach, an evaluation that was at best on par with the public's view of Clinton eight years earlier (49 percent confidence, 42 percent uneasy). As we will see, of all evaluations of President Bush, this has changed the most dramatically as his term has unfolded.

THE FIRST ONE HUNDRED DAYS

Unlike the first one hundred days of the Clinton administration, where controversies over cabinet appointments, gays in the military, and rumors of personal scandals drove the president's job approval down seventeen points by early May, Bush's early days in office were viewed as relatively successful. While the president's overall job approval remained steady, Bush was able to enumerate a number of popular positions to the public, including his proposals for tax cuts, education reform, charitable choice, and Social Security reform, all of which were broadly popular. Bush won kudos for his handling of a sticky foreign policy situation with China after the crash landing of an American spy plane with twenty-four crewmembers aboard. Moreover, a number of more contentious administration environmental positions, including the decision to withdraw from the international Kyoto protocol for the reduction of greenhouse gases, largely flew under the radar.

The ability of the Bush administration to promote favorable policies and bury more controversial ones cannot be overstated during this period. In an April Pew Research Center survey, fully, 57 percent of Americans knew about Bush's proposals for increasing education spending, and 90 percent approved of the policy. Similarly, nearly half (46 percent) knew details about the Bush tax-cut plan, and six in ten approved of Bush's position. By contrast, just 20 percent of Americans were aware of America's withdrawal from the Kyoto agreements, a policy that Americans opposed, in the abstract, by roughly two to one. And the same proportion (20 percent) knew about an equally unpopular administration move to decrease regulations on arsenic in drinking water.

Despite the electoral controversies, George W. Bush was never as objectionable to Democrats as Bill Clinton had been to many Republicans during parts of his term in office. Perhaps more importantly, expectations for the Bush administration were set so low that there was little to be disappointed about. By April, Bush's job approval among Democrats had inched upward from 29 to 36 percent, and as many Democrats said Bush had exceeded their expectations as said he was doing worse than expected. Clinton's goodwill among Republicans, by comparison, had slipped quickly—by May 1993 just 15 percent approved of the job he was doing in office.

Equally important, Bush enjoyed remarkably strong backing from his partisan base. In April, fully 87 percent of Republicans approved of Bush's job performance, and 71 percent said they *strongly* approved. While a comparable 82 percent of Democrats approved of Clinton's performance after his first one hundred days in office, less than half (39 percent overall) said they backed him strongly.

But while Bush's overall approval remained solid, many who had refrained from judging the president in the first months of his term were becoming less enchanted with his performance as time passed. From February to May, the proportion saying they could not rate the president's overall job performance dropped from 26 to 15 percent. This eleven-point drop was matched by an eleven-point increase in disapproval (from 21 to 32 percent) while the percentage approving of the president's performance remained steady. Over the same time period the percentage disapproving of Bush's handling of the economy rose from 27 to 41 percent while approval in this area remained steady, again reflecting previously uncertain respondents becoming less satisfied.

These trends would continue through the summer of 2001 as disapproval continued to inch upward—mostly among Democrats and political Independents—even though Bush's job approval never dipped below 50 percent. But the events of September 11 would radically change the way the public viewed the office of the presidency, as well as its current occupant.

SEPTEMBER 11

There are many theories about why presidential popularity soars during times of conflict. Some write the phenomenon off as nothing more than a "rally around the flag" effect—citizens wishing to express their patriotism and love of country by giving the president favorable reviews, even though their underlying perception of his performance has not changed. Others attribute the change directly to the president's actions. For example, the aftermath of the September 11 attacks gave the president the opportunity to win over skeptics by showing his leadership ability at a time of crisis.

More nuanced approaches emphasize the fact that major international crises fundamentally change the context in which the public views the president and the presidency. This context change occurs on two levels. First, an international crisis highlights the president's responsibilities as commander in chief and world leader. Both George W. Bush in 2001 and George H. W. Bush in 1991 benefited from this when crises arose during their terms in office. Rather than being judged on the basis of the economy's performance or other domestic policies, their overall performance was judged primarily on the basis of foreign policy. However, as the elder Bush discovered in 1992, this context shift can change quickly once a crisis is over.

In addition to being judged on different criteria, major crises also change the standards by which presidential performance is evaluated. When the job becomes more difficult, the public is more likely to give the president the benefit of the doubt as to whether he is handling it adequately. In particular, it is hard to criticize a president for failing to perform when a situation is as intractable and overwhelming as it was in the months after September 11.

All of these factors combined to drive Bush's job approval ratings to record levels following the September 11 terrorist attacks. In a Pew Research Center poll conducted in the early part of September, 51 percent approved of Bush's job performance while 34 percent disapproved, the highest disapproval seen in Bush's term. Two weeks later, fully 86 percent approved of the president's performance, and just 7 percent disapproved. (See Figure 5.1.)

To what extent did this surge simply represent the public expressing its patriotism? There is no doubt that this was part of the story. Feelings of patriotism were widespread in the months following the attacks. In fact, in a *Newsweek* survey, 79 percent of Americans said they had displayed an American flag in response to the attacks within ten days of the event, and a Pew Research Center poll a week later found no more than 8 percent saying there was too much flag waving in the country. Most people (73 percent) were happy to see the American flag flown everywhere, and 17 percent said, if

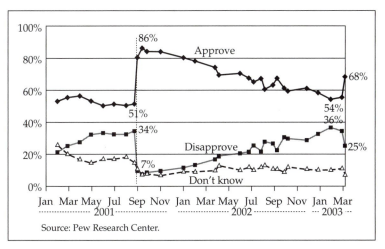

Figure 5.1 Bush Job Approval, 2001–2002.

anything, there were too few flags being flown. These strong feelings about the nation affected survey responses to other, ostensibly unrelated, questions. In Gallup polling from September 7–10, just 43 percent of Americans said they were satisfied with the way things were going in the country overall, while 55 percent said they were dissatisfied. Just days later, satisfaction surged eighteen points to 61 percent, the highest it had been since the 2000 election, while just 36 percent said they were dissatisfied. Given that there is little to suggest that conditions in the nation improved dramatically over that three-week period, there is little doubt that some of this response reflects an increased sense of patriotism and support for the nation.

But there is also little doubt that Bush's actions following the attacks garnered the attention and respect of many Americans. In polling conducted the weekend after the terrorist attacks, fully 85 percent said they approved of Bush's handling of the terrorist attacks, and 83 percent said he had done a good job speaking to the nation. In the Gallup poll, the percentage viewing Bush as a strong and decisive leader, as well as the percentage saying he inspires confidence, jumped from 55 to 75 percent following the attacks. According to a Pew Research center poll, fully 45 percent of Americans said the president had proved to be a stronger leader than they had expected, up from just 21 percent who had held that view five months earlier.

As noted, Republicans avidly supported President Bush from the moment he took office, and the events of September 11 only served to solidify that support. Bush's approval rating jumped thirteen points among Republicans following the attacks, from 83 percent approval in early September to 96 percent two weeks later. (See Figure 5.2.)

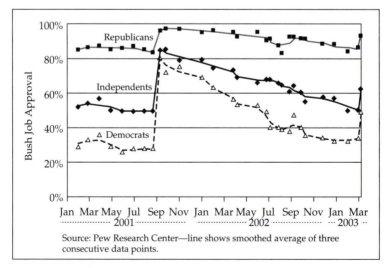

Figure 5.2 Bush Job Approval, by Party, 2001–2002.

But the real turnaround in presidential approval came among Democrats and political Independents, who previously had at best a lukewarm image of the president. In the early September Pew Research Center survey, only 28 percent of Democrats gave the president a positive job evaluation, but just two weeks later fully 81 percent of Democrats said they approved of the president's performance in office. While Bush's leadership and performance undoubtedly swayed many Democrats in the days between these two surveys, and some may have expressed support for the president out of a sense of patriotism, it is also true that the job of being president became a whole lot more difficult on September 11. For many Democrats who still may have disagreed with many of the president's policies in other areas, it was very hard to be critical of the president under the circumstances. When considering more traditional domestic problems earlier in the year, most Democrats felt the president ought to be doing a better job. When considering the overwhelming task of pursuing a war on terrorism, most Democrats were willing to cut the president a bit more slack.

In short, beyond expressions of patriotism and reactions to Bush's leadership and performance in the days following the attacks, it is also clearly the case that the context in which the President was evaluated changed after September 11. Most directly, as terrorism, defense, and foreign relations came to dominate the public's agenda, the role and responsibilities of the presidency took on a new form. Not surprisingly, when asked what they thought the biggest problem facing the nation was, references to terrorism, the threat of war, and national security spiked from 1 percent right before the attacks to 64 percent right after. (See Figure 5.3.) While the president enjoyed better ratings for his handling of a number of issues following the attacks, views on his handling of foreign policy surged the most, and became the primary factor driving the president's overall approval rating.

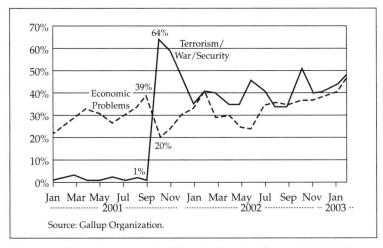

Figure 5.3 Most Important Problem Facing the Nation, 2001–2002.

Comparing public evaluations of the president's performance on two key issues—terrorism and the economy—allows us to analyze which of these responsibilities had the bigger effect on the president's overall job approval rating. For over a year after the attacks, President Bush received significantly higher ratings for his handling of the war on terrorism than for his handling of the economy. Not surprisingly, survey respondents who approved of the president's handling of both the war on terror and the economy during this time uniformly gave the president a positive overall job rating. Similarly, virtually all who disapproved of the president's handling of both issues (almost all Democrats and Independents) gave him low marks overall. But there was another segment of the population, representing anywhere from 11 to 20 percent of Americans, who approved of the president's performance with respect to terrorism, but disapproved of his handling of the economy. When someone with this divided viewpoint rates the president's overall job performance favorably, it suggests that terrorism is a more important issue to that person than is the economy. If he or she disapproves of the president's job performance, it suggests that the economy is weighing more heavily on that individual's mind.

Not surprisingly the issue of terrorism dominated presidential approval ratings in the latter part of 2001. In December, for example, those who approved of his handling of terrorism but disapproved of his handling of the economy approved of his job performance overall by a 73 percent to 19 percent margin, suggesting that the war on terrorism was a much more important factor in most peoples' minds than the economy at that time. This overwhelming focus on the war on terrorism began to fade in January 2002, and economic evaluations began to hold more sway. In October 2002, 20 percent of Americans said they approved of how Bush was handling the war on terrorism but disapproved of his handling of the economy. These people were divided almost 50–50 in their overall evaluation of the president, suggesting that for half of them the economy was at least as important as terrorism in their judgment of the president's performance.

But even a full year after the attacks, it was clear that the war on terrorism was an issue that worked to the president's favor. Nearly every polling firm tracking presidential job approval measured a jump in favorable ratings in the week following the September 11 anniversary, when the president presided over various commemorative events and gave a well-received address to the nation. Historically, presidents facing the sorts of economic conditions President Bush has presided over tend suffer far more in public opinion. In August 2002, the proportion of Americans saying the economy was in good shape fell to 24 percent in the Gallup poll, the lowest in over eight years. Yet fully 65 percent still gave President Bush a favorable rating. The last time the economy was viewed as poorly, during the second year of President Clinton's term in office, his job approval was at 48 percent.

Whether the public will continue to separate their evaluations of the economy from their evaluations of the president remains to be seen, but

Bush has clearly been doing far better than his father in this regard. Within one year of the Gulf war victory, President Bush's job approval rating had fallen forty-eight points, from 89 percent to 41 percent in the Gallup polls. Much of this decline was attributable to public perceptions that the president was failing to deal with economic problems. In March 1992, fully 76 percent said Bush could be doing more to improve economic conditions in the nation; just 21 percent felt he was doing all he could. Interestingly, one year after the terrorist attacks in New York City and Washington, D.C., George W. Bush faces similar criticism on his handling of the economy. In October 2002, the Pew Research Center found that only 31 percent said he was doing as much as he could to improve economic conditions in the nation, while 63 percent said he could be doing more. Yet 61 percent gave the president a favorable rating in the same poll, down just twenty-eight points from the postattack peak approximately one year earlier.

While the president has remained generally popular, the gap between the views of Democrats and Republicans had resurfaced, and the criteria by which Democrats judge the president have changed. Just prior to the terrorist attacks, there was a fifty-six-point gap between the percentage of Republicans who viewed the President favorably (86 percent) and the percentage of Democrats who felt the same (28 percent). While this gap closed to just fifteen points (96 percent of Republicans and 81 percent of Democrats) just after the attacks, by October 2002 the gap between Democrats and Republicans had once again returned to fifty-six points (91 percent among Republicans, 35 percent among Democrats). There is little to suggest that this gap will once again close.

THE BUILDUP TO WAR

While the initiation of military action in Iraq in March 2003 boosted the president's job approval, the boost was significantly smaller than that of September 2001 or the surge in approval George H. W. Bush enjoyed in January 1993. (See Figure 5.1.) Nor did the partisan gap in views of the president, which largely disappeared after September 11, vanish with the arrival of war in Iraq. During the first weeks of military action, Democrats were divided over the president's performance (49 percent approved, 45 percent disapproved). (See Figure 5.2.)

Historically, military engagement has been shown to give the president a significant boost in job approval; thus, the modest increases Bush received in the early days of the war in Iraq surprised some observers. But during the buildup to military action, there were many signs that war might not lead to the kinds of gains seen in previous engagements. While most surveys in the months leading up to military action found clear majorities of Americans supporting the use of force in Iraq to remove Saddam Hussein from power, this support was not nearly as universal as public backing for actions to defend against terrorist attacks at home. When pressed about the specifics, the American public expressed a good deal of caution about U.S. policy in the Middle East.

More importantly, the possibility of war in Iraq divided Americans along partisan lines far more noticeably than the issue of terrorism. Surveys in the months leading up to war clearly showed that the issue of war in Iraq was unlikely to rally Democrats behind the president in the same way the issue of terrorism had. While nearly six in ten Democrats (59 percent said they approved of how the president was handling terrorist threats against the United States, just 36 percent approved of how he was handling the situation in Iraq. In fact, partisan views of Bush's handling of the buildup to war in Iraq were far more similar to views of his handling of the economy— where Republicans and Democrats differed strongly—than to the issue of terrorism. (See Table 5.2.)

While aggregate measures showed majority support for military action in Iraq in the weeks and months before the engagement began, these results masked important partisan divides and significant conditions that the public wanted to see met before war was initiated. For example, in early March 2003— just days before air strikes in Iraq began—a Pew Research Center survey found 59 percent of Americans supporting military action in Iraq in general, but only 38 percent willing to enter into a war without the approval and participation of America's traditional allies; and a majority felt the U.S. should wait for a United Nations resolution to use force first. Only 37 percent said America had enough international support to engage Iraq; 56 percent said the president still needed to convince more of its allies to go along. (See Table 5.3.)

TABLE 5.2 Democrats Critical of Bush's Leadership

Approve of How Bush is Handling . . .	Total (%)	Republicans (%)	Independents (%)	Democrats (%)
Terrorist threats				
Approve	67	87	65	52
Disapprove	25	9	28	37
The economy				
Approve	43	73	36	22
Disapprove	48	19	54	72
Situation in Iraq				
Approve	56	82	52	38
Disapprove	37	15	40	56
Relationships with major allies				
Approve	55	78	51	39
Disapprove	34	14	36	51

Source: Pew Research Center February 2003.

TABLE 5.3 On Eve of War, Partisans Divided on Iraq Policy

Policy	Republicans (%)	Independents (%)	Democrats (%)
Military action in Iraq			
Favor	80	55	45
Oppose	11	35	44
Favor even without support of allies?	59	35	23
Discussion of non-military options?			
Too little	29	48	59
Too much	24	16	16
Right amount	42	29	18
Has Bush explained reasons for war clearly?			
Yes	75	42	31
No	24	54	65

Source: Pew Research Center March 2003—except Discussion of non-military options December 2002.

Democratic concerns about America's policy toward Iraq were particularly stark. Fully 59 percent of Democrats said there was too little talk about ways to deal with Saddam Hussein without using military force, while fewer than half as many Republicans agreed (24 percent). On the eve of war, just three-in-ten Democrats felt George W. Bush had explained clearly why the U.S. might need to use military force in Iraq—nearly two-thirds (65 percent) said he had not. On the eve of war, just 53 percent of Americans—and a third of Democrats—approved of the way the president was handling the nation's foreign policy.

While there is little question that Americans of all political viewpoints supported American troops and the president during the early days of the war in Iraq, these pre-war divisions are indicators that the long-term impact of the Iraqi engagement on the President's job approval may be limited. There is a large and attentive segment of the American population that holds deep concerns about America's position toward Iraq, providing political opportunities for leading Democrats to legitimately criticize the logic and wisdom of the president's foreign policy. The afterglow of even a quick and easy military victory would likely be short-lived, as concerns about the president's domestic and foreign leadership beyond the immediate issue of military engagement have persisted. A month before the war, most Democrats (56 percent) and nearly half of independents (46 percent) said they worried a great deal that it might take a long time to make Iraq a stable and peaceful country after a war.

BUSH UNPOPULAR IN EUROPE, SEEN AS UNILATERALIST

While the war in Iraq has further damaged George W. Bush's image over-seas, even from the President's earliest days in office, foreign publics had a particularly poor impression of the new American president. A Pew Re-search Center study conducted approximately one month before the Sep-tember 11 terrorist attacks found people in Great Britain, France, Ger-many, and Italy all disapproved of the American president's handling of international policy by wide margins. In particular, more than seven in ten people in each country said Bush made foreign policy decisions based entirely on U.S. interests rather than taking into account the views of Eu-ropean allies. Furthermore, this criticism runs beyond Western European nations—the 2002 Pew Global Attitudes survey found majorities in nine-teen of forty-two nations saying the United States pays little or no atten-tion to the interests of countries like theirs when making foreign policy decisions.

While America's image overseas has been criticized for many years, the Bush presidency has only exacerbated the problem. In Western Europe, Bill Clinton was perceived as far more attentive to global issues and concerns. Asked to think back to Bill Clinton's international policies, fully two thirds of British and French, and even higher proportions of Italian and German respondents gave positive appraisals. By comparison, George W. Bush's most favorable assessment came from the Italians, yet even there only 29 percent approved of his handling of foreign policy while 49 percent disap-proved. On a different question, just 20 percent of French respondents, 30 percent of British respondents and 33 percent of Italian respondents said they had even a fair amount of confidence in Bush's handling of world affairs. (See Table 5.4.)

Part of these negative assessments of Bush were clearly linked to his lack of foreign policy experience and the perception that he paid little at-

TABLE 5.4 European Views of How American Presidents Have Handled Foreign Policy

President	Britain (%)	France (%)	Germany (%)	Italy (%)
George W. Bush				
Approve	17	16	23	29
Disapprove	49	59	65	46
*Bill Clinton**				
Approve	66	68	86	71
Disapprove	15	15	9	16

Source: Pew Research Center, August 2001.

*Note: Respondents were asked to consider Clinton retrospectively.

tention to the interests of allies. Roughly three quarters of respondents in Britain, Germany, and France said Bush understands less about Europe than did other American presidents. Bush was also roundly criticized for the same foreign policy decisions that largely flew under the radar domestically. More than 80 percent of respondents in all four European nations surveyed disapproved of Bush's decision to withdraw from the Kyoto protocol, and by three to one or more, foreign publics opposed United States withdrawal from the antiballistic missile (ABM) treaty to develop a missile defense system. Most Americans were unaware of the former, and supported the latter.

Bush's image overseas improved a bit following the September 11 terrorist attacks. In Great Britain, for example, the percentage approving of the president's international policies grew from 17 percent in August 2001 to 40 percent the next spring. But these shifts did little to dispel the prevailing discontent with U.S. leadership among these European publics. In France, approval of Bush's foreign policy doubled from 16 percent to 32 percent, but dislike of Bush did not decline, as roughly six in ten French respondents both before and after the terrorist attacks disapproved of Bush's international policies. In no country did the perception that Bush ignores European interests when deciding on U.S. foreign policy decline over this time period.

More broadly, despite an initial outpouring of public sympathy for America following the September 11, 2001, terrorist attacks, discontent with the United States has grown around the world over the past two years. The Pew Global Attitudes survey, conducted in forty-four nations over the summer and fall of 2002, found that images of the United States, while still generally favorable, have been tarnished in all types of nations, among longtime North Atlantic Treaty Organization (NATO) allies, in developing countries, in Eastern Europe, and, most dramatically, in Muslim societies. Furthermore, war in Iraq was roundly opposed.

On the eve of war with Iraq, a study conducted in Britain, France, Germany, Italy, Spain, Poland, Russia and Turkey found clear majorities in every nation opposed to military action led by the United States. Moreover, there were widespread questions about the Bush administration's motives with respect to Iraq. In France, Germany and Russia, majorities thought the main reason for any U.S. action would be economic (the desire to control oil in the Middle East) and not related to the possible threats posed by the Iraqi regime. Most Turkish respondents saw the looming war in Iraq as part of a larger U.S. war against Muslim countries, and not an effort to achieve stability in the Middle East. By margins of five-to-one or greater, publics in France, Germany, Italy, Spain, Russia and Turkey disapproved of Bush's international policies. This sentiment was prevalent even in Britain, America's strongest ally in the Iraqi conflict where 60 percent disapproved of Bush's handling of foreign policy.

THE 2002 MIDTERMS AND THE OUTLOOK FOR 2004

Republican success in the 2002 midterm election clearly reflected the significant popularity of the president as well as the hard effort he put into campaigning for House and Senate candidates. A postelection survey conducted by *Newsweek* found far more people attributing the Republican victory to President Bush's personal popularity and campaign efforts than to the quality of Republican candidates, ideas, or positions. In fact, a postelection survey conducted by CBS News and the *New York Times* suggests that it was very much Bush's personal leadership, as opposed to his policies, that mattered to voters. When asked if their vote for Congress on November 5 was a vote *for* or *against* George W. Bush, by two to one people said the former (35 percent to 17 percent, with 45 percent saying Bush was not a factor in their vote). But when a separate group of respondents was asked if they considered their midterm vote a vote for or against George W. Bush's *policies*, the results were far more balanced (30 percent for, 24 percent against, 37 percent not a factor).

While events at home and abroad will certainly shape the dynamics of the 2004 presidential election, early indicators suggest that there is room for a strong Democratic opponent to pose a serious challenge to the incumbent President. A Gallup survey conducted in the week before the initiation of military action in Iraq found 45 percent saying they would likely vote for Bush in the 2004 election and 42 percent leaning toward his Democratic challenger. However close this appears, Bush appears stronger than Clinton did at the same point in his first term, when just 40 percent said they would support Clinton for reelection and 54 percent favored a Republican challenger.

Of course, these comparisons to Clinton's first term only serve to reinforce how unreliable such measures are at predicting upcoming elections. Despite these critical evaluations in 1994, President Clinton would go on to a landslide reelection victory over Senator Bob Dole two years later. The test for President Bush will be to hold on to the public's confidence and support. To a large extent, this will mean finding ways to emphasize the generally positive assessments of the president's character and leadership. The public's image of George W. Bush as an honorable, honest, and determined individual has served him well to this point, while more negative impressions about his intelligence and links to big business have been pushed into the background. If the war in Iraq is successful and the public stays focused on terrorism and other foreign threats, the positive aspects of the Bush "script" will likely stay at the forefront. But if economic problems and financial dealings take center stage, these are likely to fit more easily into the negative stereotypes of the president, unless he and his advisors can frame them otherwise.

NOTES

1. Richard F. Fenno, *Learning to Govern: An Institutional View of the 104th Congress* (Washington, D.C.: Brookings, 1996).

2. Samuel L. Popkin, *The Reasoning Voter: Communication and Persuasion in Presidential Campaigns* (Chicago: University of Chicago Press, 1991).

3. See Doris Graber, *Mass Media and American Politics*, 5th ed. (Washington, D.C.: Congressional Quarterly, 2003).

4. Stanley Renshon, *High Hopes: The Clinton Presidency and the Politics of Ambition* (New York: New York University Press, 1996).

5. Molly Andolina and Clyde Wilcox, "Public Opinion: The Paradoxes of Clinton's Popularity," in *The Clinton Scandal and the Future of American Government*. ed. Mark J. Rozell and Clyde Wilcox (Washington, D.C.: Georgetown University Press), 177–94.

CHAPTER 6

Dignified Authenticity

George W. Bush and the
Symbolic Presidency

GARY L. GREGG II

The President stood before Congress and a national television audience holding in his right hand the police badge of George Howard, a man who lost his life trying to save others as the World Trade Center collapsed the morning of September 11, 2001. It was nine days after America watched the towers fall, taking with them our sense of safety from the travails of other lands. Nearly three thousand Americans in total were dead at the Pentagon, in a field in Pennsylvania, and at the bottom of the heap of scrap metal and dust that lay at the heart of New York City. The president came to Capitol Hill as the leader of his people to speak to them and the world about what had happened and to explain what would be America's response.

In the nine days since the terrorist attacks on America, George Bush seemed to have met his place in history, and the public was rallying to his side. Still, having watched the president through the election of 2000 and the first six months in office, one would be hard-pressed to have predicted what would come next. Bush, the man whose syntax and ability at public speaking had been the subject of considerable ridicule, would deliver a historic address in one of the most highly praised presidential performances in decades. The presidential role of commander in chief, shadowed by the awesome military power it implies, met the equally important presidential role of being chief of state in the speech that commanded the attention of nearly every American watching television or listening to the radio that evening. One professional hockey team even adjourned their game as the crowd demanded to hear their president in this time of national crisis.

The president's words were important that evening, but rational arguments seldom are left alone to carry the day in contemporary public politics. The president, with the help of Michael Gerson and his team of speechwriters in the White House, had carefully chosen his words, but the president's delivery and his use of the symbolic tools at his disposal were equally important. Bush, at least for the moment, had become master of the symbolic presidency; he had become quintessentially "presidential."

BEING PRESIDENTIAL AND THE SYMBOLIC PRESIDENCY

"Being presidential" is one of those phrases often invoked, but seldom with any kind of common understanding or definition. No doubt, many of us would argue about what exactly it means to be "presidential," and, at least to a certain degree, it would inevitably involve a discussion of personal preferences. What certainly is clear is that "being presidential" is about more than pure substance and action. It is about style and symbolism, image and imagination. To those concerned with such elements of leadership, *how* one does something is just as important as what is done. The American presidency is about more than just executive orders, staffing decisions, negotiations with Congress, and policy positions. Since George Washington established the precedents that would inspire and constrain his successors, presidential leadership, at least in part, has been about offering symbolic leadership for the nation.[1]

In the United States, we have maintained the ancient fusion of kingship—symbolic leader and decision maker being contained in the same person. This helps explain the unique nature of our relationship to our presidents. We love them and we hate them; we respect some and despise others. This is because we recognize them as more than political decision makers. They are our symbolic representatives; they are part of what we are and we are part of them. As James David Barber has said, this leads to the presidency being "the focus for the most intense and persistent emotions in the American polity."[2]

Everything a president does in some way holds symbolic import. His actions do not always mean the same things to different interpreters, and yet there is little doubt that what a president does and how he does it in public hold important meanings beyond the immediate material and political consequences of his efforts. Advance teams, communications specialists, and speechwriters in the White House script his appearances; the president enacts those scripts; and, mostly through the intermediary of the media, the American people and the world watch, observe, and, sometimes consciously, sometimes not, take in the images and the actions of the man. In an age where the visual image and the related reaction to symbolism has become so all-pervasively important, the public presidency has also become central to governing from the White House and cannot be ignored. Furthermore, the public presidency itself is about more than rational arguments made for specific public policy positions; its also about the photo, the style, the connection made with the public. To one degree or another, the image is also the message.

THE CLINTON CONTEXT

Symbolically, the Bush presidency can best be understood in contrast to the symbolic nature of the Clinton presidency that came immediately before. Bush was clearly inviting us to do this ourselves during the campaign in 2000. He took to ending campaign speeches by raising his right hand and pledging to "uphold the *honor* and *dignity* of the office of president."[3] With this line he was invoking and adding to the constitutional pledge all presidents have taken immediately prior to assuming the presidency, which only requires them to faithfully execute the office and to defend the Constitution itself. He was inviting us to see the *style* of being president existing on the same level as the substance of being president. Style has always been an essential aspect of presidential leadership, and, more to the point, of *being presidential*. In his own amendment of rhetoric, Bush was inviting us to see the incumbent president as the threat to the long tradition of being presidential. Bush was casting himself as the rear guard defense against a postmodern deconstruction of the office represented by Bill Clinton (and by proximity, we were invited to imagine, his Democratic opponent, Vice President Al Gore).

In so many ways, George Washington established the basic elements that are the bundle of precedents and expectations that has become known by the phrase "being presidential." After being inundated with visitors and well-wishers early in his administration, for instance, he developed the practice of setting aside Tuesday afternoons during which the public could be received by their president. These would not be informal gatherings of equals and pals, but neither would they be audiences with royalty based on the European model. They would, however, satisfy the need of the public to see and commune with their president while permitting their president the dignity of separation demanded by the office. In his own words, Washington was trying to create a "just medium between much state and too great familiarity."[4]

Washington had his finger on one of the great symbolic challenges of the presidency—to appear dignified and yet humble, powerful and yet republican. Not all presidents have risen to Washington's challenge. Nearly every gradation between the informality of an Andrew Jackson and the formalism and distance of a Woodrow Wilson can be seen in one presidency or another.

During the late 1960s and into the 1970s, the symbolic power of the American presidency was dealt a series of terrible blows. Lyndon Johnson's Texas informality, the Vietnam war, Nixon's Watergate cover-up and resignation all served to undermine the trust of the American people in the institution of the presidency. The general celebration of presidential power that infused elite opinion during the decades since the presidency of Franklin Delano Roosevelt (FDR) came to an end in the early 1970s following Vietnam and Watergate. It was replaced with a concern that the presidency had grown too powerful and hubristic. It had become, according to Arthur Schlesinger's influential book, "the imperial presidency."[5]

The symbolic reaction of Ford and Carter was clear and understandable but ultimately did not serve themselves or the office. They both sought to create a more humble, informal, and less "imperial" presidency. On certain occasions, Ford ordered the University of Michigan fight song to replace "Hail to the Chief," renamed the living quarters of the White House "the residence" rather than "the mansion," and invited photographers in to see him toast his own English muffins for breakfast. President Carter seemed to be the perfect embodiment of this more informal presidency. A little-known, one-term governor of Georgia, he preferred the informal "Jimmy" and began his presidency by leaving his limousine and walking to the White House following his inauguration. For a time he banned "Hail to the Chief" all together, sometimes carried his own luggage, conducted a televised "fireside chat" in a cardigan sweater, and sold the presidential yacht Sequoia.

Carter himself was to come to the realization that he had taken this humbling of the presidency too far. In his memoirs he would write that in "reducing the imperial presidency, I overreacted at first. We began to receive many complaints that I had gone too far in cutting back the pomp and ceremony. . . . "[6] On the other hand, Ronald Reagan, perhaps because of his time as an actor, seemed to understand the importance of enacting the symbolic presidency and hitting the balance George Washington laid out between "much state and too great familiarity." His inauguration and first actions seemed designed to return the office to its previous formalism and elevated dignity. The grand inaugural balls with white tie and tails, First Lady Nancy Reagan's purchase of new china for the White House, formal East Room press conferences complete with dramatic entrances down the red carpeted hallway, and a return to stirring, elevated rhetoric were hallmarks of Reagan's understanding of the presidency. Out of respect to the institution and the place, he never removed his suit coat while at work in the Oval Office but he would appear in jeans on horseback or "pumping wood," when at his ranch in California. Not too much state, not too much familiarity.

The first President Bush would follow in Reagan's footsteps by maintaining a more formal White House, but the cycle would start again with President Clinton's injection of informality into the public presidency and the structure of the White House itself. Clinton would follow his "pop culture" campaign of 1992 (for instance, his appearance in dark sunglasses playing the saxophone on the *Arsenio Hall* show) with a similarly situated public presidency. He would jog in Washington in short running shorts, would be accused of "selling" the Lincoln Bedroom to high-dollar donors to the Democratic party, and would be so notoriously late for everything that insiders developed the term "Elvis time" for the president's schedule. He would poll almost everything from policy questions to vacation destinations for the first family. He appeared on MTV, a cable music station particularly aimed at American youth interested in pop music, and answered a question about his preferences in underwear. Scandals embroiled the White House for most of Clinton's eight years and culminated in the denials and then revelations of the president having had extramarital relations with an intern in the White House.

His impeachment by the House of Representatives followed, and the Clinton term of office ended two years later in a series of midnight scandals over pardons of criminals with high political connections, expropriating public property from the White House for use in retirement, and reports of vandalism against the White House and executive branch offices.

It is against this backdrop that the symbolic nature of Bush's presidency should be considered. Bush entered office, after all, pledging to change the tone in Washington and change the public character of the presidency. His inaugural address was among the shortest at just twelve minutes and, rather than containing a laundry list of proposed government programs, would be a call to citizenship and the building of community among neighbors. He restored the older dress codes at the White House that had been abandoned by Clinton and banned any man from entering the Oval Office without jacket and tie. Yet at home at his ranch he would appear in boots with jeans held up by a Texas-size belt buckle and sporting a western work shirt. The dignified formalism of his White House would be balanced by the gritty authenticity of his ranch, but the two would not be confused. On Election Day 2002, for instance, he would be seen at the polls in Crawford in his jeans and well-worn brown leather jacket, but a few hours later would emerge from Marine One at the White House dressed in a suit and tie and prepared for work.

Whereas Clinton's overnight guests at the White House were a paparazzo's dream of the brightest stars in Hollywood, Bush would prefer humbler guests, old college friends or the occasional country music singer or professional athlete.[7] Bush would replace "Elvis time" at the White House with a strict demand for punctuality. He would spend less than half the money Clinton spent for public opinion polls and would speak in a plainspoken dialect with misplaced words and syntax that seemed more Crawford diner than Pennsylvania Avenue.[8]

In all, Bush seemed to be conveying what might be called a presidency of "dignified authenticity." His would not have the routine grandeur of formal East Room press conferences, nor would he strive for the elegance of the poet in his speeches, but neither would he display the informality of appearances on pop television programs or distractions of recurring personal scandals. Though there was one president, we seemed to have two Bushes: one displayed understated dignity and formality at the White House, while the other reveled in playing the gritty cowboy at the ranch in Crawford. Though both Bushes would have their critics, for instance on August 28, 2001, the New York Times would editorialize that Bush was endangering America by demonstrating unsafe work habits while cutting wood at his ranch, together they seemed to work to give Bush a balanced presidential image that would be part of what helped him build such trust with the American people after the terrorist attacks in 2001.

Prior to those attacks, some criticized Bush for what seemed like a lack of interest in his use of the symbolic presidency during times of grief and uncertainty. He did not, for instance, visit the site of a school shooting near San Diego (as Clinton regularly did when such things occurred during his presidency), and he did not attend the April 14, 2001, ceremony welcoming home the twenty-four military personnel who had been detained by China after their plane made an emergency landing in that country. The contrast with Clinton could not be clearer. If Clinton's presidency suffered from over-exposure, Bush, critics argued, was suffering from inattention and severe symbolic austerity. Noted presidential scholar Fred I. Greenstein even offered that it was "almost as if he [President Bush] doesn't realize that the president is the symbolic leader of the nation, the head of state" as well as the head of government.[9] Such criticism, however, would not resurface once a real crisis hit the nation with the collapse of the towers that clear autumn day in New York City.

DIGNIFIED AUTHENTICITY AND
THE ATTACKS OF SEPTEMBER 11

Pollsters and political scientists have well documented the historical fact that the American people almost inevitably tend to rally around their president during times of international crisis or following acute acts of violence against America or her interests. These "rally effects" are measured by the rise in the president's job approval ratings when comparing polls done before the event with those done in its aftermath. The terrorist attacks of September 11 would provide just such a pivotal moment in the presidency of George W. Bush.

As soot and ash bellowed through the streets of New York that morning of September 11, 2001, the relationship between the American people and President George W. Bush was ripe for a dramatic change. Few could have predicted the scope and nature of that changed relationship, however. The terrorist attacks and the president's subsequent reactions resulted in a rally effect of unprecedented proportions. In the history of polling, no president had ever gotten a "rally" boost in his job approval ratings of more than eighteen points; Bush's was thirty-five. In the history of polling, most rally effects had dissipated within months of their start and none had ever survived longer than ten months; Bush's lasted through the calendar year and continued through the following winter. Add to this the fact that the rally lasted during a time of great economic uncertainty, falling confidence levels in the economy, corporate scandals, and a collapsing stock market, and the result is a rally effect of historic and wholly unprecedented proportions. The president's extraordinary popularity also continued to last long after all the other measurable indictors of the post September 11 rally had dissipated.[10]

President Bush's rally effect was bigger and lasted longer than FDR's following Pearl Harbor, John F. Kennedy's following the Cuban Missile Crisis, and the first President Bush's during the Gulf war in 1991.[11] The historically high approval ratings for the president were translated also into historic wins for the Republican party in the off-year election of 2002. Parties who hold the White House almost invariably lose seats in Congress during off-year elections. Until 2002, FDR's and Bill Clinton's Democrats in 1934 and 1998, respectively, are the only counterexamples in the last century. Despite a very weak economy, President Bush successfully used his popularity to stump hard for Republican Senate and congressional candidates in 2002 and helped produce a historic victory, with the Republicans picking up seats in the House, and, for the first time in history, taking over the Senate during an off-year election when they held the White House.

Why was Bush's rally effect so large and of such an enduring nature? Why did the American people's higher approval ratings for the president last beyond the time their rally-induced approval ratings for Congress and confidence in the state of the economy had normalized to their pretragedy levels? The answer might well lie in President Bush's masterly use of the symbolic aspects of the presidency to become the nation's military, spiritual, educational, and moral leader. Most commentators write of the attacks of September 11 having transformed the Bush presidency. In reality, Bush transformed his own presidency by reacting to, and ultimately helping shape, the meaning of the terrorist attacks.

The elements of his leadership in the days following the attacks will certainly serve as a model for presidential crisis leadership in the future. Four key elements can be deciphered in the president's postattack leadership, where he set the tone for the nation and bonded with the American people in a way no president has in more than a generation. It all began in an awkward moment with a group of school children doing reading exercises in Mrs. Sandra Kay Daniel's second-grade classroom.

Projecting Reassurance

"The real measure of a person," Bush had written in his pre-election memoirs, "is how he responds to bad news."[12] That sentiment seems to have been on his mind that morning of September 11, when Chief of Staff Andrew Card leaned over and whispered in his ear, "A second plane hit the second tower. America is under attack." The President's eyes darted around the room for a moment and he seemed obviously distant. But he did not panic. He did not excuse himself from the room. He continued to listen to second graders do their reading lessons for him. Only when they were complete, which must have seemed like an eternity later, did he calmly get up and leave the room. His first remarks were quickly scribbled by the President himself and were delivered at the school in front of an audience expecting him to talk about education reform. "I had to convince myself to be as *calm* and *resolute* as possible," he later confided to a journalist, "because I knew people were watching."[13] In those first words to the public, he instructed the nation on the events of the morning, pledged the full resources of the federal government to help the victims, vowed to "hunt down and find" the perpetrators, and asked for a moment of silent prayer. Sketched with his Sharpie pen, these would be the themes that would carry the president and the nation through the crisis.

A little over three hours later, the president had landed at Barksdale Air Force Base in Louisiana, where he would tape another message to the American people.[14] "I think it's important for people to see the government is functioning, because the TV shows our nation has been blasted and bombed," he told aides before deciding to land and give what would become his second statement of the day. "The government is not chaotic. It's functioning smoothly," he would add.[15] In his speech he would again seek to reassure the public of the continuation of government, that the federal government was assisting victims of the tragedy, that the American military was on high alert, and that "we will show the world that we will pass this test."

Some in the media would criticize the president both for his performance delivering the remarks, which they found not to be up to the task at hand, and for not immediately returning to Washington. The president seemed instinctively to predict this latter criticism as he made it repeatedly clear to his security detail that despite what they recommended, he would be returning to Washington before the day was through. He reportedly told one Secret Service agent, "The American people want to know where their dang president is," and against the recommendation of the Secret Service that it would be safer to take a motorcade from Andrews Air Force Base in Maryland to the White House he insisted, "I'm landing on the South Lawn in Marine One. People want to see me land on the South Lawn at the White House and go into the Oval Office, okay?"[16] Bush seemed to understand the need for a traumatized public to see their leader safe, unbowed, and in charge. It is an important image for the symbolic presidency.

The sixteenth century Florentine political thinker Niccolo Machiavelli wanted his prince to gain the skills and knowledge necessary to overcome and tame the powerful forces of fortune that seem to sweep randomly through life. Especially during times of crisis and uncertainty, the American people seem to hold out this same hope for their own prince. Murray Edelman has written, "Because it is apparently intolerable for men to admit the key role of accident, of ignorance, and of unplanned processes in their affairs, the leader serves a vital function by personifying and reifying the processes. As an individual, he can be praised and blamed and given 'responsibility' in a way that processes cannot."[17] In the earliest hours of following the terrorist attacks, President Bush sought to reassure the American people that he was in charge, that random and evil forces would not be allowed to disrupt their lives, and that proper actions were being taken on their behalf. Later, as the crisis wore on, this rhetoric of reassurance would change into repeated attempts to show the American people that they were safe and to urge them to go about their normal lives.

Reflecting the Public Mind

The American people expect the men who hold our highest office to reflect our values and our most profoundly felt emotions. Offering symbolic leadership, to one degree or another, means creating the image that you are one with the entity you are attempting to represent. Taken literally, keep in mind, the very act of representing, is to one degree or another to *"re-present"* the public in government. A central element in Bush's transformed relationship with the American people after September 11 is how genuinely the public perceived him as sharing their pain, but also sharing their more martial emotions demanding justice. Bush would give voice to an anguished public; he would also come to embolden and embody their resolve.

Though it can be seen as a bit of an understatement, his very first public utterance called it "a *difficult* moment for America." Ending that statement by asking for a moment of silence, he symbolized the prayerful questioning of people glued to the terrifying drama on television sets all over the nation. That evening, as he sat in the Oval Office, he would again ask for the nation's prayers and would begin to take on a ministerial role that would culminate three days later in a national prayer service quite unlike anything in recent memory:

> Tonight I ask for your prayers for all those who grieve, for the children whose worlds have been shattered, for all whose sense of safety and security has been threatened. And I pray they will be comforted by a power greater than any of us, spoken through the ages in Psalm 23: "Even though I walk through the valley of the shadow of death, I fear no evil, for you are with me."

The public was shocked and grieving from what they had witnessed and from the uncertainty that came with seemingly random deaths of civilians just like themselves. But the public was also angry and in a mood to seek revenge. From the very beginning, Bush would express his anger at the attacks and, echoing his father dealing with Saddam Hussein's invasion of Iraq a decade before, vowed that the attack against America "will not stand." In his first utterance, he vowed to "hunt down and find those folks who committed this act" and that afternoon defiantly defined the enemy as "faceless cowards." Sitting at his desk in the Oval Office the night of the attacks (a desk fittingly made from the timbers of the HMS *Resolute* and used by other presidents including FDR during World War II and John F. Kennedy and Ronald Reagan during crucial moments in the Cold War), he expressed the "disbelief, terrible sadness, and a *quiet, unyielding anger*" that he sensed taking hold in the public. To the dismay of some of his detractors, he seemed to support and even encourage that righteous indignation of the American people—he was, after all, sharing in it.

This aspect of Bush' post-September 11 leadership would culminate with the president standing among the rubble of the collapsed World Trade Center, arm draped around an aged firefighter, and, speaking to shouting iron workers and firefighters, declaring "I can hear you. The rest of the world hears you. And the people who knocked down these buildings will hear all of us soon." The moment that began completely unscripted and with a malfunctioning bullhorn that a presidential aide happened to find at the site ended with chants of "USA! USA! USA! USA!" *Newsweek*'s Jonathan Alter instantly identified it as a "turning point in history," and Bush himself would later agree that it was "one of those defining moments in American history."[18] Millions across the nation who now knew the president shared their emotions, including anger and an unbending determination that justice would be served, symbolically joined those chanting rescue workers from their living rooms and offices. Criticized by some in the media for being overly bellicose during these first days of the crisis, the president had been expressing a milder form of his own emotions in a way that built trust with the American people and that would allow him to delay a military response until one had been fully planned and was ready to be implemented nearly a month later.

The President himself seemed to understand, at least in retrospect, that he had been playing this role of mirroring the public mood. He would tell journalist and author Bill Sammon that "I guess that's what America appreciated—I was expressing their sentiments. America was hot. And we were sad. We cried."[19] The leader had demonstrated solidarity with his followers in a way that might strengthen both for the challenges ahead.

Instructing the Public Mind

Presidential leadership must be about more than simply reflecting the prevailing mood of the nation, however. FDR said that the presidency was "preeminently a place of moral leadership" and added that "[a]ll our great presidents were leaders of thought at times when certain historic ideas in the life of the nation had to be clarified."[20] During times of crisis, the president uniquely holds the attention of the American people in such a way that he can help define the moment and teach the public. George Bush succeeded in doing just that in the wake of the terrorist attacks.

Beyond the aspects of his rhetoric that will be taken up elsewhere in this chapter, the president seemed to understand he faced three instructional challenges: He would need to carefully define the enemy; he would need to encourage the American people to be very patient; and he would seek to temper the public mood with a balanced rhetoric of war and peace, justice and compassion. Compounding the challenge would be his need to simultaneously rally the world to the American cause.

DEFINING THE ENEMY. In his first public remarks at Emma Booker Elementary School, Bush began to identify the events of that morning as an "apparent terrorist attack" but made no other attempt to fix blame or to use epithets. A few hours later, at Barksdale Air Force Base, the president called them "cowardly acts," and by that evening the terrorists had come to earn the term "evil," which would become the president's favorite epithet for the enemy. The next morning Bush would convene his war cabinet. Flanked on his left by Vice President Dick Cheney, General Henry Shelton, and National Security Assistant Condoleezza Rice, and on his right by Secretary of State Colin Powell, Secretary of Defense Donald Rumsfield, and Attorney General John Ashcroft, Bush would identify the attacks as "acts of war" and identify the challenge as "a monumental struggle of good versus evil."[21] Bush's liberal use of the word "evil" in various formations became rather divisive, as many in the media scoffed at him while others heralded what they called his "moral clarity" and the firmness of his convictions. Overall, the American people responded very favorably to Bush calling it like he saw it.

He would identify Osama bin Laden and the Al Qaeda network by name as the likely suspects and would instruct the American people and the world about their history of terror and their mode of operation. In so doing, he would demonize bin Laden and his terrorist group—thereby rallying the nation to the cause of its extermination.

But the challenge of defining an enemy also carries with it the responsibility of defining those who are not enemies. Bush took this responsibility very seriously and, according to aides, was determined not to allow history to repeat itself with regard to the treatment of Japanese Americans during World War II. At almost every possible moment, Bush would try to define the enemy as terrorists and not Islam itself. He would have an Islamic cleric as part of the National Prayer Service, and he would visit Washington's largest Islamic Center where, shoes off, he would declare "the face of terror is not the true faith of Islam" and that "Islam is peace. These terrorists don't represent peace. They represent evil and war."[22]

He would make special efforts to include Arabs and Muslims whenever he used lists of peoples from around the world lending America moral support and would later host an Iftaar dinner to begin the Muslim holy month of Ramadan. In his nationally televised address to a joint session of Congress on September 20, he would separate the terrorists from Islam by saying the terrorists "practice a fringe form of Islamic extremism that has been rejected by Muslim scholars and the vast majority of Muslim clerics." He would go on to address the Muslim world itself in a way that seemed meant also to provide more instruction to his own people:

> We respect your faith. It's practiced freely by many millions of Americans, and by millions more in countries that America counts as friends. Its teachings are good and peaceful, and those who commit evil in the name of Allah blaspheme the name of Allah. The terrorists are traitors to their own faith, trying, in effect, to hijack Islam itself. The enemy of America is not our many Muslim friends; it is not our many Arab friends. Our enemy is a radical network of terrorists, and every government that supports them.[23]

The president and the administration made some missteps in this obvious effort at using the symbolic powers of the presidency to define the enemy both for the sake of the international coalition and also to protect American Muslims from potential retaliation at home. At one point the president made the regrettable mistake of calling the war on terror a "crusade," and the Defense Department named the military operation in Afghanistan "Infinite Justice," which some Muslims found offensive since they believe only Allah himself could achieve infinite justice. But the White House corrected those possible missteps and continued to make efforts to define the enemy in a way that it would adequately protect innocent Muslims at home and abroad. The president made his point very clear during his national address on September 20: "No one should be singled out for unfair treatment or unkind words, because of their ethnic background or religious faith."[24] The president was teaching the nation about the conflict and about toleration.

COUNSELING PATIENCE. On September 19, the lead editorial in the *New York Times* criticized the president's rhetoric for being overly bellicose and inconsistent in tone. They worried that he was "inflating expectations" for the American people. "The hotter the rhetoric is now," the *Times* editorialized, "the harder President Bush will find it later if his better judgment winds up telling him to delay action, or to concentrate for a while on diplomatic and economic sanctions rather than military force."[25] The editors at the *Times*, however, did not seem to recognize that from the very beginning of the crisis, Bush's rhetoric had been carefully balanced and consistent in pattern. Yes, he would express his own anger at the murder of thousands of innocent Americans and thereby reflect the anger of the public. However, he would also take great pains to instruct the American people on this new kind of war that would be unconventional, oftentimes unpublicized, and above all would require great patience and perseverance.

The attacks of September 11, were not the first attempt by Al Qaeda to kill Americans. They had killed nineteen service men in a bombing of the Khobar Towers in Dhahan, Saudia Arabia, in 1996, simultaneously bombed two U.S. embassies in Africa on August 7, 1998, and two years later sent a small boat full of explosives into the side of the USS *Cole* while it was refueling in Aden, Yemen. The Clinton administration's military response, despite promises of a sustained assault, would amount to two rather sanitary cruise missile strikes that happened to coincide with Monica Lewinsky's return to testify before the grand jury investigating the president. One strike hit a supposed chemical weapons plant in Sudan (later identified as a pharmaceutical factory) and killed a night watchman, while the other hit one of bin Laden's training camps in Afghanistan. Despite the massive nature of Al Qaeda's September 11 attack, Bush set out to counsel the nation to be patient, not to expect their demand for justice to be meted out quickly or even publicly. Over and over again he would use the bully pulpit of the presidency to convince the American people that justice delayed would not be justice denied. He was not willing to settle for a quick strike that would be immediately popular but would not be effective.

The very next morning after the attacks, the President began preparing the nation for a long-term effort and encouraging their patience. Surrounded by his Cabinet and top advisors, he said, "This battle will take time, and resolve."[26] During his radio address on September 15, he vowed "I will not settle for a token act. Our response must be sweeping, sustained and effective. We have much to do, and much to ask of the American people." The first such thing he would ask from the American people, then, would be "patience; for, the conflict will not be short."[27] During his much-celebrated address to the joint session of Congress on September 20, he would meticulously lay out how the current battle was different from wars in the past and warn that "Americans should not expect one battle, but a lengthy campaign, unlike any other we have ever seen." "I ask for your patience, with the delay and inconveniences that may accompany tighter security," he would say later in his remarks, and add, "and for your patience in what will be a long struggle." The end of his address that night seemed designed to help the American people keep their patience while trusting his leadership:

> I will not forget this wound to our country or those who inflicted it. I will not yield; I will not rest; I will not relent in waging this struggle for freedom and security for the American people.

Bush's continuing education plan outlining how this war against terrorism would be unlike any other and his continuing request for patience seemed to pay off as days turned into weeks without a military reaction by the United States. Though America was riled by the deaths of thousands of her innocent countrymen, Bush would wait more than four weeks before beginning to strike back. It was remarkable how America waited with him and continued to do so as months stretched beyond a year with the most visible symbol of the enemy, Osama bin Laden, still unaccounted for and with no end to the war in sight.

Balanced Rhetoric of War and Peace

Bush often spoke of war in the days following September 11, but he also spoke of peace, freedom and compassion. At the end of a question-and-answer session with the press in the Oval Office on September 13, Bush would provide a reaction that would become a symbol of the balance he seemed to hold in his heart and attempted to communicate; a balance between the cold-hearted realism of the warrior and the compassion and care of a humanitarian. He fought a tear brought to his eye by a question that got him thinking about the families and children of the victims, and said, "I am a—I'm a loving guy." Catching himself, however, he abruptly changed course and added, "And I am someone, however, who has got a job to do. And I intend to do it." A rarity for such informal exchanges, all three major networks fed the scene live into homes across America. Though this exchange was certainly unscripted, Bush would try to hit a similar balance in nearly all of his formal remarks as well.

Amongst his vows to achieve justice and to "smoke out" the terrorists, he would strike a gentler chord of humanitarianism and compassion. In his speech to the joint session of Congress where he threatened and outlined strong demands on the government of Afghanistan, he also pointed out that the United States "respects the people of Afghanistan" and that the United States was its largest source of humanitarian aid.[28] He would announce the beginning of the war in Afghanistan not from the Oval Office or some martial setting, but from the Treaty Room of the White House "where American Presidents have worked for peace," Bush would tell the nation.[29] Out the window behind him that Sunday morning could be seen the Jefferson Memorial and children flying kites—not the scene one usually thinks of when contemplating the start of major military operations.

Four days after the war began, Bush would announce the creation of "America's Fund for Afghan Children" and ask America's children to all contribute a dollar for food and medical supplies. "Americans are united in this fight against terrorism," the president would say, and go on to add, "We're also united in our concern for the innocent people of Afghanistan."[30] The balance the president sought to hit would even influence the war itself, as the United States military began using some planes to drop humanitarian supplies to the citizens of Afghanistan while other planes were ferociously bombing targets. After weeks of presidential radio addresses dealing with the war against terror, on November 17, 2001, Laura Bush became the first First Lady to deliver an entire weekly radio address; she focused on the plight of women and children under the Taliban and Al Qaeda in Afghanistan.

Bush would have his moments of emotional release and martial rhetoric but also seemed to be very carefully trying to balance those harsher moments with a softer symbolism of compassion and care. He seemed cognizant of the need not to fall off either end of the spectrum found between soft-headed sentimentalism and hard-nosed militarism.

MINISTERING TO THE NATION'S WOUNDS. George W. Bush may be the most religiously convicted president the nation has seen in some time. His chief speechwriter, Michael Gerson, and other key players in the White House share Bush's faith and a willingness to be open in public about it. Religious phrases and concepts are staples of presidential speeches, but never more so than during times of national crisis or in the wake of tragedy. One thinks particularly of Ronald Reagan's memorable speech following the explosion of the space shuttle Challenger, which ended with the astronauts having "slipped the surly bonds of earth to touch the face of God."[31]

Soon after the attacks, Bush had begun asking the nation for prayer and would appropriate uplifting phrases from the Bible to offer support to the nation. On September 13, quoting from the New Testament book of Matthew that "Blessed are those who mourn for they shall be comforted," Bush declared Friday, September 14, to be a "National Day of Prayer and Remembrance." Since George Washington declared the first Thanksgiving holiday in 1789, presidents have used the symbolic power of declaring special days for the nation. Urging houses of worship to hold noontime memorial services and evening candlelight vigils, Bush's team, headed by Tim Goeglein, special assistant to the president, were busy putting their own service together to be held at the National Cathedral in Washington, D.C.

It rained in Washington on the morning the president called the nation together for prayer. By the time the most powerful collection of people perhaps ever assembled in a house of worship in America emerged from the service, however, the sun had broken through the clouds in a way that few could escape seeing as symbolic of the cathartic effects of the service. The president was aware of the importance of the service, and the White House team charged with putting it together worked nearly around the clock in the days before September 14 in an effort to get the symbolism and tone just right. He seemed to face the challenge of being adequately comforting to the mourners, while setting a tone of resolve and putting his people and the world on notice that a mighty military response would be forthcoming. It would be too easy to fall into mushy sentimentalism or, on the other side, into jingoistic militarism. Bush's answer would be as close to a sermon as one could expect from a president in the modern era. He would later tell the *Washington Post*'s Bob Woodward, "I saw it as a moment to make sure that I helped comfort and helped get through the mourning process. I also really looked at it from a spiritual perspective, that it was important for the nation to pray."[32]

In his relatively short remarks of just sixty-five sentences, the president invoked the name of God twelve times and mentioned prayer eleven times. Discussing the new unity felt across the nation, he remarked, "Our unity is a kinship of grief, and a steadfast resolve to prevail against our enemies." The cadence of his speech oscillated between these two emotional posts of the nation—grief and resolve. He called the nation to pray for the dead and the suffering and reminded us, "the Lord of life holds all who die, and all who mourn." But he also sought to set out a new responsibility for the nation to "answer these attacks and rid the world of evil" while using anecdotes of courage and grace to uplift our spirits. Before stepping down from the pulpit and walking silently to his pew, where the cameras would catch the father [former President Bush] reaching over to approvingly touch and comfort his son, the president ended with what can only be described as a prayer more likely to be heard from a local minister on that Sunday than the President of the United States.

> On this national day of prayer and remembrance, we ask almighty God to watch over our nation, and grant us patience and resolve in all that is to come. We pray that He will comfort and console those who now walk in sorrow. We thank Him for each life we now must mourn, and the promise

of life to come. As we have been assured, neither death nor life, nor angels nor principalities nor powers, nor things present nor things to come, nor height nor depth, can separate us from God's love. May He bless the souls of the departed. May He comfort our own. And may He always guide our country. God bless America.[33]

On this day and the days ahead, the president would come to function as the national minister. He would embrace firefighters who were working seemingly endless hours and who had lost dear friends in the attacks; he would hug and weep with victim's families; and he would express the nation's sorrow and offer comforting words to his mourning and apprehensive people. Almost thirty years ago, Michael Novak observed that the presidency was "the nation's most central religious symbol."[34] So it certainly would be in the hands of George W. Bush that tumultuous September.

CREATING AND MANIPULATING
THE SYMBOLS OF THE PRESIDENCY

Presidents themselves can be powerful symbols in American public life. People seem to find some magic in the mere touch of the man who represents the power and majesty of the nation. Anyone who has ever been to a presidential rally can attest to the phenomena of watching citizens grasping wildly across the rope line in hopes of shaking the hand that wields the power of the presidency. Photo opportunities also provide presidents with an arsenal of symbolically powerful tools they can use and manipulate. Photo opportunities are often aimed at enhancing the president's image by appropriating the image of the office. Presidents have not been shy about using the White House, Oval Office, Air Force One, and the Presidential Seal to political advantage. During times of war, the symbolic arsenal of the presidency can be enhanced even further.

George W. Bush has made ample use of the symbolic trappings of the office. During the 2002 elections, the President used Air Force One to help add status and prestige to congressional candidates all over the nation. Some would even fly to other locations simply to arrive back in their hometown on the famous plane where Bush managed the earliest hours of the war against terror.[35] Bush would also make use of human symbols, in much the same way Ronald Reagan did so effectively two decades before, by inviting people with symbolic importance to sit in a prominent position and be recognized at his speech to the joint session of Congress. Sitting with Laura Bush and attracting the eye of the television audience were Mayor Rudolph Guiliani (who had become one of the heroes of the tragedy), Prime Minister Tony Blair of Great Britain, injured rescue workers from New York, and a pregnant Lisa Beamer, widow of Todd Beamer, one of the heroes who rushed the hijackers and lost their lives on Flight 93. The president was appropriating the developing symbols of the attacks as he sought to define the moment for the nation.

Over the next year, Bush would continue to appropriate the symbols of September 11 as he would remind the nation of the continuing effort to rout out terrorism and secure the homeland. He would throw out the first pitch of the World Series at Yankee Stadium, as a way to symbolize "America's desire to continue life undeterred after the attacks."[36] He would appear with American military personnel, firefighters, and police officers. He would sign the Afghan Relief Act, not surrounded by the traditional lawmakers in blue suits, but surrounded by women and young children, some in traditional Muslim dress.

Though the language relating to the antiterror campaign and remembrance of September 11 would become routine in most presidential appearances, the White House would also come to sponsor special memorials, such as the White House ceremony marking the six-month anniversary of the attacks on March 11, 2002. On the one-year anniversary of the terrorist attacks, Bush would begin his day with a ceremony outside the White House, and then would travel to each of the three sites of the attacks for televised memorials (the Pentagon, Pennsylvania, and Ground Zero in New York). He would then end his day with a prime-time address to the nation from New York City. His speech was short, but the visual of the president standing at Ellis Island was dramatic. Only the Statue of Liberty, with its torch majestically burning bright, punctuated the dark night sky behind the president standing alone. Spread throughout the months following the attacks, events like these allowed the president to remind the nation of that terrible day, of America's response, and of his role in that response. The White House would also put a continuous reminder on their Web site. Calling it "The Spirit of Freedom," it contains a montage of dramatic images related to the events of September 11 paired with selections from presidential remarks. It is difficult to imagine the events of September 11 and their aftermath without thinking about President Bush, and that is no doubt one of the key aspects of his record-breaking popularity. The White House would miss no opportunity to keep that memory alive.

CONCLUSION

The terrorist attacks of September 11 left many Americans shaken, confused, and desiring revenge. During such times, we rely on our president to function as our chief of state, to combine symbolic actions with words that comfort, rally, and help define the moment. In times of crisis, America relies on our president to help set the proper tone and teach us about the moment at hand. From the earliest hours of the crisis, George W. Bush seemed to understand that the nation would call him to play this role, and his communications team worked with him to perform it masterfully. The transformation that seemed to take place was less about the carnage itself than about the president's reaction. He struck a chord within the hearts and minds of the American people that would continue to resonate for more than a year and despite great economic challenges, would allow him to help his party do what history says is almost impossible—build on their majority in the House of Representatives and take control over the U.S. Senate during a midterm election.

Although there are those who dismiss symbolism in politics as nonempirical nonsense, or even brand it the tool of oppression by the powerful through the quiescence of the powerless, symbolism is critically important to the office. To recognize this is to recognize the subtle but pervasive impact that the office has had upon each citizen and each generation since George Washington took the oath in 1789. As Robert Denton has said, "To describe the President as Priest, Prophet, and King is to acknowledge the respect, expectations, hopes, and values of the American people."[37]

George W. Bush came to office promising to change the tone that predominated the Clinton presidency. The image he developed, which I have called "dignified authenticity," put him in a very good position to deal with the attacks of September 11. Because he had not been known for his eloquence, expectations were low for his public performances, but his image seemed honest and solid. In the wake of our loss of innocence in the carnage of September 11, Bush was able to capture many hearts and minds in America and to define the moment for the nation. Americans respected his dignity and trusted his authenticity. The result was a transformed presidency and a transformed political landscape.

NOTES

1. Gary L. Gregg II, "The Symbolic Dimensions of the First Presidency," in *Patriot Sage: George Washington and the American Political Tradition* ed. Gary L. Gregg and Matthew Spalding. (Wilmington, Del.: ISI Books, 1999), 165–98.

2. James David Barber. *Presidential Character* (Englewood Cliffs, N.J.: Prentice-Hall, 1972), 4.

3. Also see Bush's use of these words in George W. Bush, *A Charge to Keep: My Journey to the White House* (New York: Perennial, 1999), 134.

4. William B. Allen, ed. *George Washington: A Collection* (Indianapolis: Liberty Fund, 1988), 545.

5. Arthur M. Schlesinger. *The Imperial Presidency* (New York: Popular Library, 1974).

6. James E. Carter, *Keeping Faith: Memoirs of a President* (New York: Bantam Books, 1982), 27.

7. Adam Nagourney, "A List of Guests Throws Light on the Bush Style," *New York Times*, 19 August 2002.

8. Ralph Z. Hallow, "As Polling Goes, Bush Is No Clinton," *Washington Times*, 10 April 2002, p. A4.

9. Quoted in John F. Harris, "On the World Stage, Bush Shuns the Spotlight," *Washington Post National Weekly Edition*, 23–29 April 2001, p. 11.

10. Retrieved from http://www.gallup.com/poll/releases/pro020912.asp?Version=p.

11. Retrieved from http://www.gallup.com/poll/releases/pr010918.asp.

12. Quoted in Bill Sammon, Fighting Back: *The War on Terrorism—from inside the Bush White House* (Washington, D.C.: Regnery Publishing, 2002), 85.

13. Bill Sammon, *Fighting Back: The War on Terrorism—from inside the Bush White House* (Washington, D.C.: Regnery Publishing, 2002), 94.

14. Because of logistical difficulties, the tape would not be broadcast until after 1:00 P.M.

15. Sammon, *Fighting Back*, 113.

16. Ibid., 120, 127.

17. Murray Edelman, *The Symbolic Uses of Politics* (Urbana, Ill.: University of Illinois Press, 1964), 78.

18. Sammon, *Fighting Back*, 190–91.

19. Ibid., 157.

20. Quoted in Wilfred E. Brinkley, *The Power of the Presidency: Problems of American Democracy* (Garden City, N.Y.: Doubleday, Doran, 1937), 267.

21. "Bush's Remarks to Cabinet and Advisors," *New York Times*, 13 September 2001, p. A16.

22. David E. Sanger, "A Nation Challenged: The President; Bin Laden is Wanted in Attacks, 'Dead or Alive,' President Says," *New York Times*, 18 September 2001.

23. Retrieved from http://www.whitehouse.gov/news/releases/2001/09/20010920-8.html.

24. Retrieved from http://www.whitehouse.gov/news/releases/2001/09/20010920-8.html.

25. "Wartime Rhetoric," *New York Times*, 19 September 2001, p. A26.

26. "Bush's Remarks to Cabinet and Advisers," *New York Times*, 13 September 2001, p. A16.

27. Retrieved from http:www.whitehouse.gov/news/releases/2001/09/20010915.html.

28. Retrieved from http:www.whitehouse.gov/news/releases/2001/09/20010920-8.html.

29. Retrieved from http:www.whitehouse.gov/news/releases/2001/10/20011007-8.html.

30. Retrieved from http:www.whitehouse.gov/news/releases/2001/10/20011011-8.html.

31. Ronald Reagan, *Speaking My Mind: Selected Speeches* (New York: Simon & Schuster, 1989), 292.

32. Bob Woodward, *Bush at War* (New York: Simon & Schuster, 2002), 67.

33. Retrieved from http://www.whitehouse.gov/news/releases/2001/09/print/20010914-2.html.

34. Michael Novak, *Choosing Our King: Powerful Symbols in Presidential Politics* (New York: MacMillan, 1974), xiv.

35. Elisabeth Bumilller, "Peace and Political Status at 39,000 Feet," *New York Times*, 29 October 2002, p. A24.

36. Retrieved from www.whitehouse.gov.kids/baseball/.

37. Robert E. Denton Jr., *The Symbolic Dimensions of the American Presidency: Description and Analysis* (Prospect Heights, Ill: Waveland Press, 1982), 121.

The Way We Go to War

The Iraq Resolution

LOUIS FISHER

On October 10, 2002, Congress passed legislation authorizing President George W. Bush to use military force against Iraq. Did Congress actually decide to go to war? Not really. Members of Congress transferred that choice to Bush. They decided only that he should decide. Ultimately it was his determination, not the decision of lawmakers.

Why is that important? Doesn't the president, as commander in chief, have the constitutional authority to decide on war? He does not. The framers recognized that the president needed certain *defensive* powers to respond to sudden attacks. Taking the country from a state of peace to a state of war, however, is vested in Congress. The framers placed the war power there and the power of the purse. Presidents have no constitutional authority to make military and financial commitments of tens of billions of dollars.

Placing the war power in elected representatives was a vital part of forming "a republic." It is the difference between believing in representative government—democracy—and believing in monarchy. A nation dedicated to "We the People" places ultimate authority in elected lawmakers. Members of Congress take an oath to defend the Constitution, not the president. Nevertheless, in this area of the war power, the United States has been drifting toward monarchy and away from a republic.

PRESERVING A REPUBLIC

To judge how well President Bush asked for authority, and how well Congress granted it, requires some discussion of what it means to have "a republic." We know the word but probably not its meaning. Yet it appears in our Pledge of Allegiance, which we recited as schoolchildren: "I pledge allegiance to the Flag of the United States of America, and to the Republic for which it stands, . . . " The flag, by itself, is not important. It is a symbol of the real thing: the republic. If we lose the democratic qualities associated with a republic, the flag is emptied of meaning. It would "stand" for nothing.

The framers knew the meaning of a republic. They fought and died for it. In breaking with England, they repudiated the monarchical principles promoted by such writers as William Blackstone in his *Commentaries on the Laws of England*. He gave all of foreign affairs and the war power to the Executive, who had the sole power to make war, send and receive ambassadors, make treaties, issue letters of marque and reprisal (authorizing private citizens to undertake military actions), and raise and regulate fleets and armies.

The break with Blackstone was decisive and complete. Not a single one of his prerogatives over external affairs was assigned solely to the president. Those powers were either given exclusively to Congress (the power to declare war, issue letters of marque and reprisal, and raise and support armies and navies) or were shared between the Senate and the president (the power to appoint ambassadors and to make treaties).

In Federalist No. 39, James Madison identified the fundamental qualities of a republic: "a government which derives all its powers directly or indirectly from the great body of the people." This system of government necessarily places the primary power and authority in Congress. Self-government means rule by the people—not direct rule, but indirect rule through the representatives they elect. Also in Federalist No. 39, Madison explained the connection between a republic and the spirit of the American Revolution:

> . . . [N]o other form would be reconcilable with the genius of the people of America; with the fundamental principles of the Revolution; or with that honorable determination which animates every votary of freedom, to rest all our political experiments on the capacity of mankind for self-government. If the plan of the convention, therefore, be found to depart from the republican character, its advocates must abandon it as no longer defensible.

Blackstone was not to be planted on American soil. In other essays, Madison went to great lengths to describe the many checks and balances needed to keep each of the three branches within their proper spheres. Still, in Federalist No. 51 he said that "[i]n republican government, the legislative authority necessarily predominates."

From 1789 to the present time, the decision to take the country from a state of peace to a state of war has remained largely where the framers placed it: in Congress. Major wars were either declared or authorized by Congress. There were only two exceptions to this pattern: Harry Truman going to war against North Korea in 1950, and Bill Clinton mounting an offensive war against Yugoslavia in 1999. Presidents on many occasions used military force without seeking authority from Congress, but these actions were modest in scope and duration.[1]

DID PRESIDENT BUSH MAKE HIS CASE?

When the administration first began talking about war against Iraq, White House spokesman Ari Fleischer cautioned on a number of occasions that

President Bush was not rushing into war. Instead, he was described as a deliberate man who carefully studied all options. On August 21, 2002, President Bush called himself "a patient man. And when I say I'm a patient man, I mean I'm a patient man, and that we will look at all options, and we will consider all technologies available to us and diplomacy and intelligence."[2]

Administration officials assured reporters that Bush "has no war plans on his desk."[3] At that same press conference on August 21, Bush noted that "there is this kind of intense speculation that seems to be going on, a kind of a—I don't know how you would describe it. It's kind of a churning—." Secretary of Defense Donald Rumsfeld supplied the missing word: "frenzy." Bush agreed with that choice. The country was too preoccupied, he said, with military action against Iraq.

Yet five days later, the administration switched to a frenzied mode. Vice President Dick Cheney delivered a forceful speech that implied there was only one option: going to war. He warned that Saddam Hussein would "fairly soon" have nuclear weapons, and that it would be useless to seek a Security Council resolution requiring Iraq to submit to weapons inspectors. The threat by Hussein made preemptive attack against Iraq imperative.[4] Cheney predicted that Iraq would have a nuclear weapon "perhaps within a year," and stated that there was "no doubt" that Iraq "now has weapons of mass destruction."[5]

The press read Cheney's speech "to be ruling out anything short of an attack."[6] Editorials concluded that Cheney's speech "left little room for measures short of the destruction of Saddam Hussein's regime through preemptive military action."[7] Two reporters for the *Washington Post* noted the abrupt transition: "this week's frenzy of attention to Iraq was entirely generated by a White House whose occupants returned from the August recess anxious and ready to push the debate to a new level."[8] What happened to the options carefully being weighed by Bush? Tension within the administration was evident when Secretary of State Colin Powell, in a September 1 interview with the BBC, recommended that weapons inspectors should return to Iraq as a "first step" in resolving the dispute with Iraq. Ari Fleischer, asked whether Powell's statement revealed a conflict within the administration on Iraq policy, labored to convince reporters that Cheney and Powell were in agreement "that arms inspectors in Iraq are a means to an end, and the end is knowledge that Iraq has lived up to its promises that it made to end the Gulf War, that it has in fact disarmed, that it does not possess weapons of mass destruction."[9] Of course, Cheney had already announced that Iraq *did* possess weapons of mass destruction.

Senate Minority Leader Trent Lott (R-Miss.) seemed to acknowledge the disarray within the administration. He said on September 3: "I do think that we're going to have to get a more coherent message together."[10] When asked whether he was comfortable with the White House's presentation of the case for war against Iraq, he responded: "I'd like to have a couple more days before I respond to that."[11]

The meaning of "regime change" shifted with time. On April 4, 2002, in an interview with a British television network, President Bush said: "I made up my mind that Saddam needs to go. . . . The policy of my Government is that he goes. . . . The policy of my Government is that Saddam Hussein not be in power."[12] On August 1, he stated that the "policy of my Government . . . is regime change—for a reason. Saddam Hussein is a man who poisons his own people, who threatens his neighbors, who develops weapons of mass destruction."[13] Clearly, Hussein had to go.

The commitment to regime change and offensive war changed significantly when President Bush addressed the United Nations on September 12. After cataloguing Saddam Hussein's noncompliance with Security Council resolutions, apparently building a case for regime change and military operations, Bush laid down five conditions that could lead to a peaceful resolution. If Iraq wanted to avoid war, it needed to immediately and unconditionally pledge to remove or destroy all weapons of mass destruction, end all support for terrorism, cease persecution of its civilian population, release or account for all Gulf war personnel, and immediately end all illicit trade outside the oil-for-food program. The underlying message: If Iraq complied with those demands, Saddam Hussein could stay in power. What happened to the policy of regime change?

On October 21, after Congress had passed the Iraq Resolution, Bush again said that Hussein could stay. He announced that if Hussein complied with every UN mandate, "that in itself will signal the regime has changed."[14] An exquisite sentence, but one that calls to mind a typical response to a magician's trick, where one asks: "Could you do that again, only this time more slowly?" Now Saddam Hussein could stay in office if he changes.

After the September 12 UN speech offering peace to Iraq if it complied with the five demands, Iraq agreed four days later to unconditional inspections. Given Iraq's record since 1991, there were abundant reasons to be skeptical of its promise. But the response should have been to test Iraq's sincerity by sending inspection teams there to learn—on the ground—whether it would give full access to buildings and presidential palaces. Instead, the administration began to belittle the importance of inspections. Pentagon spokeswoman Victoria Clarke warned that inspections would be difficult if not impossible to carry out.[15] If so, why have Bush go to the United Nations and place that demand on Iraq and the Security Council?

On September 26, during a campaign speech in Houston, Texas, Bush delivered the standard litany of offenses committed by Saddam Hussein, but added, perhaps with careless language: "this is a guy that tried to kill my dad at one time."[16] The remark made some wonder whether the commitment to war was motivated by reasons of national security or partly by a "family grudge match."[17] The administration continued to rely on a broad assortment of charges against Iraq, many of them going beyond the issue of weapons of mass destruction. Senator Paul Sarbanes (D-Md.) questioned the claim by Secretary of State Colin Powell that Iraq, to avoid military action, would have to comply with a number of UN resolutions, including one that prohibits illicit trade beyond the program that allows Iraq to trade oil for food. Sarbanes asked: "Are we prepared to go to war to make sure they comply with UN resolutions on illicit trade outside the oil for food program? Will we take military action or go to war in order to make them release or account for all Gulf war personnel whose fate is still unknown? Would we do that?"[18]

Senator Richard Lugar (R-Ind.) also challenged the administration's rationale of finding Iraq at fault for a long list of infractions, including brutality by Saddam Hussein against his own people. In conversations with top officials of the executive branch he knew they did not believe that those actions would justify a U.S. war.[19] Nevertheless, the administration continued to provide a laundry list of charges beyond what was supposedly the essential issue: weapons of mass destruction.

Why the zigs and zags? Going to war is a serious enterprise and calls for consistency, clarity, and coherence. It is supposed to be *reasoned* deliberation. In an op-ed piece, Michael Kinsley acknowledged that ambiguity can be useful in dealing with other nations. Sending mixed signals can keep an enemy off balance. Yet Kinsley concluded: "the cloud of confusion that surrounds Bush's Iraq policy is not tactical. It's the real thing. And the dissembling is aimed at the American citizenry, not at Saddam Hussein." Kinsley said that arguments that "stumble into each other like drunks are not serious. Washington is abuzz with the 'real reason' this or that subgroup of the administration wants this war."[20]

WHAT ROLE FOR CONGRESS?

As the administration prepared for war with Iraq, initially it concluded that President Bush did not need authority from Congress. The White House Counsel's office gave a broad reading to the President's power as commander in chief, and argued that the 1991 Iraq Resolution provided continuing military authority to the President, passing neatly from father to son.[21] These legal positions were strained and unconvincing. The framers made the President commander in chief, not a monarch. They designated him commander in chief to avoid fragmented direction of military operations and to assure civilian supremacy over the military.[22]

The President's unilateral prerogatives over the military were confined to defensive powers "to repel sudden attacks," especially when Congress was not in session. That point was easily understood by the judiciary. In *Talbot* v. *Seeman* (1801), Chief Justice John Marshall noted: "The whole powers of war being, by the constitution of the United States, vested in congress, the acts of that body can alone be resorted to as our guides in this inquiry."

In *The Prize Cases* (1863), the Supreme court carefully restricted the President's power to defensive actions, remarking that he "has no power to initiate or declare a war either against a foreign nation or a domestic State."

The executive branch took exactly the same position. During oral argument, the attorney representing President Abraham Lincoln duly noted that the President's actions in question has nothing to do with "the right *to initiate a war, as a voluntary act of sovereignty.* That is vested only in Congress."

Citing the Iraq Resolution of 1991 was perhaps beguiling but misplaced. That statute authorized military action to implement UN Security Council resolutions calling for Iraq's removal from Kuwait. When Congress passed the statute, did it somehow sanction military operations authorized by *future* Security Council resolutions? That position is not credible. It would mean that Congress had somehow shifted part of its war power to the Security Council. It would allow the UN Charter—adopted only by the President and the Senate pursuant to the treaty process—to strip the House of Representatives of its constitutional authority over war. There is no evidence that Congress intended, or could intend, such a result.[23]

The White House also claimed that Congress, by passing the Iraq Liberation Act of 1998, had already approved U.S. military action against Iraq for violations of Security Council resolutions.[24] There was nothing to this argument. The statute begins by itemizing a number of congressional findings about Iraq: invasion of Iran and Kuwait, the killing of Kurds, using chemical weapons against civilian opponents, and other offenses. It supported, as a nonbinding "sense of Congress," efforts to remove Saddam Hussein from power and replace him with a democratic government. However, the statute explicitly states that nothing in the law "shall be construed to authorize or otherwise speak to the use of United States Armed Forces (except as provided in section 4(a)(2)) in carrying out this Act."[25] This particular section provided up to $97 million in military supplies to Iraqi opposition groups, as part of the transition to democracy in Iraq. It did not authorize war.

Ari Fleischer announced that Bush "intends to consult with Congress because Congress has an important role to play."[26] However, for Bush and his aides to simply "consult" with Congress would not meet the needs of the Constitution. No doubt policy making works better when the president consults with lawmakers, but consultation is not a substitute for receiving statutory authority. Congress is a legislative body that discharges its constitutional duties by passing statutes to authorize and define national policy. It exists to legislate and legitimate, particularly for military and financial commitments. Only congressional authorization of a war against Iraq would satisfy the Constitution.

For one reason or another, Bush decided in early September to seek authorization from Congress. On several talk shows on Sunday, September 8, administration officials moved away from a unilateralist tone and built the case for a broad coalition. Cheney, having advocated preemptive strikes against Iraq in his earlier speech, took this position in an NBC *Meet the Press* interview: "We're working together to build support with the American people, with the Congress, as many have suggested we should. And we're also, as many have suggested we should, going to the United Nations."[27]

Although the administration had taken most of the year to decide on what to do about Iraq, Congress was expected to act quickly. According to one newspaper story, White House officials "have said that their patience with Congress would not extend much past the current session."[28] In fact, the administration wanted Congress to complete action on an authorizing resolution before the lawmakers adjourned for the election. National security assistant Condoleezza Rice said that President Bush wanted lawmakers to approve the resolution before they left town. She said that Bush "thinks it's better to do this sooner rather than later."[29]

Why the rush? Senator Robert C. Byrd (D-W.Va.) deplored "the war fervor, the drums of war, the bugles of war, the clouds of war—this war hysteria has blown in like a hurricane."[30] What could explain the shift from a laidback policy in August to a pent-up demand a month later? White House Chief of Staff Andrew Card gave one reason for waiting until September to advocate military action against Iraq: "from a marketing point of view, you don't introduce new products in August."[31]

In 1990, after Iraq had invaded Kuwait, President George Bush did not ask Congress for authority before the November elections. Instead, he first went to the Security Council and asked for a resolution authorizing action, which he received on November 29. Only in January 1991, when Congress returned for the new session, did lawmakers debate and pass legislation that authorized military operations by the president.

For reasons that were never explained, Congress in 2002 had to act with alacrity. In an op-ed piece that supported the administration's strategy, former Secretary of State George Shultz argued that the "danger is immediate." Iraq's making of weapons of mass destruction "grows increasingly difficult to counter with each passing day."[32] Senate Majority Leader Tom Daschle (D-S.D.) suggested that Bush would have an easier time getting congressional support if he first gained Security Council approval,[33] but the administration insisted that Congress had to act first.

There was no constitutional obligation for Congress to await action by the Security Council, but acting in the months before the November elections invited partisan exploitation of the war issue. Several Republican nominees in congressional contests made a political weapon out of Iraq. They compared their "strong stand" on Iraq to "weak" positions by Democratic opponents. Some of the key races in the nation appeared to turn on what candidates were saying about the war issue.[34] Because of the steady focus on the war, Democrats were unable to redirect the political agenda to such issues as corporate crime, the state of the stock market, and the struggling economy.[35]

Democrats never developed a credible strategy, appearing to favor a prompt vote on the Iraq Resolution to get that issue "off" the table. It was reported that Senator Daschle hoped to expedite action on the Iraq Resolution "to focus on his party's core message highlighting economic distress before the November midterm elections."[36] Senator John Edwards (D-N.C.)

urged quick action: "In a short period of time, Congress will have dealt with Iraq and we'll be on to other issues."[37]

This approach had multiple drawbacks, both moral and practical. Could Democrats openly authorize war merely to refocus the campaign on their domestic program? As noted by Senator Mark Dayton (D-Minn.), trying to gain "political advantage in a midterm election is a shameful reason to hurry decisions of this magnitude."[38] Second, voting on the Iraq Resolution could never erase the White House's capacity to dominate the headlines, if not through the Iraq Resolution then through ongoing negotiations with the UN Security Council. Third, although these Democrats wanted to put the issue of war against Iraq "behind" them, in terms of a vote, the war would always be in front.

The partisan flavor intensified when President Bush, in a speech in Trenton, N.J., on September 23, said that the Senate "is more interested in special interests in Washington and not interested in the security of the American people."[39] The administration quickly explained that his remark was in the context of the legislative delay on the Department of Homeland Security, but Democrats faulted Bush for using the war as leverage in the House and Senate races.[40]

After the Trenton speech, Democrats could have announced that President Bush had so politicized the Iraq Resolution that it could not be debated with the care and seriousness the legislation required. Daschle, in particular, could have used his position as Senate Majority Leader to delay a vote until after the elections. Perhaps he did not have the votes with the Senate Democratic Caucus to prevail. If he failed to rally his troops, he would have highlighted his weaknesses as leader and advertised the divisions within his own ranks. In the end, as evidenced by the vote on the Iraq Resolution, Senate Democrats were divided anyway. Several Senate Democrats criticized Daschle for working too closely with Bush on the Iraq Resolution and getting nothing in return. Bush's comments in Trenton, they said, made it look like Daschle was being "played for a fool."[41]

UNSUBSTANTIATED EXECUTIVE CLAIMS

Bush and other top officials invited members of Congress to sessions where they would receive confidential information about the threat from Iraq, but the lawmakers said they heard little that was new. After one of these briefings, Senator Bob Graham (D-Fla.) said: "I did not receive any new information."[42] House Minority Whip Nancy Pelosi (D-Cal.), also the ranking Democrat on the House Intelligence Committee, remarked that she knew of "no information that the threat is so imminent from Iraq" that Congress could not wait until January to vote on an authorizing resolution."[43] None of the charges against Iraq in Bush's address to the United Nations were new. After a "top secret" briefing by Defense Secretary Rumsfeld in a secure room in the Capitol, Senator John McCain (R-Ariz.) soon rose and left, saying "It was a joke."[44]

The administration kept a steady drumbeat for war, releasing various accounts to demonstrate why Iraq was an imminent threat. On September 7, President Bush cited a report by the International Atomic Energy Agency (IAEA) that the Iraqis were "6 months away from developing a weapon. I don't know what more evidence we need."[45] However, the report did not exist.[46] The administration promoted a story about Mohamed Atta, the leader of the September 11 attacks, meeting with an Iraqi intelligence officer in Prague in April 2001. Yet on information available from Czech intelligence, President Vaclav Havel concluded that there was no evidence the meeting ever took place. Central Intelligence Agency (CIA) Director George Tenet told Congress that his agency had no information that could confirm the meeting.[47]

The administration tried to make a link between Iraq and Al Qaeda, but the reports could never be substantiated.[48] On September 25, Bush claimed that Saddam Hussein and Al Qaeda "work in concert."[49] On the following day, he claimed that the Iraqi regime "has longstanding and continuing ties to terrorist organizations, and there are Al Qaida terrorists inside Iraq."[50] Ari Fleischer tried to play down Bush's remark, saying he was talking about what he feared *could* occur.[51] Senator Joseph Biden (D-Del.), who attended a classified briefing that talked about the relationship between Iraq and Al Qaeda, said that credible evidence had not been presented.[52] There was some evidence of Al Qaeda activity in the northern part of Iraq, but that is Kurdish territory made semi-autonomous because of American and British fighter planes that police the no-fly zones. Besides, members of Al Qaeda are present in some sixty countries. Presence alone is not a basis for using military force.

Allies in Europe, active in investigating Al Qaeda or radical Islamic cells, could find no evidence of links between Iraq and Al Qaeda. Interviews with top investigative magistrates, prosecutors, police, and intelligence officials could uncover no information to support the claims by the Bush administration. Investigative officials in Spain, France, and Germany, after dismissing a connection between Iraq and Al Qaeda, worried that a war against Iraq would increase the terrorist threat rather than diminish it.[53]

On September 27, Secretary Rumsfeld announced that the administration had "bulletproof" evidence of Iraq's links to Al Qaeda. He said that declassified intelligence reports, showing the presence of senior members of Al Qaeda in Baghdad in "recent periods," were "factual" and "exactly accurate." However, when reporters sought to substantiate the claim, officials offered no details to back up the assertions. Having claimed bulletproof support, Rumsfeld admitted that the information was "not beyond a reasonable doubt." Senator Chuck Hagel (R-Neb.) told Secretary of State Powell: "To say, 'Yes, I know there is evidence there, but I don't want to tell you any more about it,' that does not encourage any of us. Nor does it give the American public a heck of a lot of faith that, in fact, what anyone is saying is true."[54]

In his speech to the nation on October 7, on the eve of the congressional vote, President Bush said that Iraq "has trained Al Qaida members in bomb-making and poisons and deadly gases."[55] Intelligence officials played down the reliability of those reports.[56] Bush claimed that satellite photographs "reveal that Iraq is rebuilding facilities at sites that have been part of his nuclear program in the past."[57] The administration decided to declassify two before-and-after photos of the Al Furat manufacturing facility.[58] Five busloads of two hundred reporters descended on the site and were given a ninety-minute tour by Iraqi generals. The reporters found few clues to indicate a weapons program.[59]

True, a quick visit by reporters means little. They had neither the time nor the expertise to explore all the buildings and examine them carefully. But it is also true that satellite photos are unable to penetrate buildings and analyze their interiors. Only a ground search by experienced inspectors can do that.

Bush's October 7 speech addressed the concern that a change in leadership in Iraq might create instability and make matters worse in the Middle East. His response: "The situation could hardly get worse for world security and for the people of Iraq." Yet in an analysis released a day later, the U.S. intelligence agencies explained how the situation could get worse. The report predicted that Saddam Hussein was unlikely to initiate a chemical or biological attack against the United States. However, should he conclude that a U.S. attack could no longer be deterred, he might launch such a counterattack, both against the United States and Israel. Under attack, he might decide that "the extreme step of assisting Islamist terrorists in conducting a WMD [weapons of mass destruction] attack against the United States would be his last chance to exact vengeance by taking a large number of victims with him."[60] Thus, the analysis seemed to suggest that military action against Iraq could provoke precisely what Bush said he wanted to prevent.

Released at the same time as the intelligence analysis was an exchange from a closed congressional hearing on October 2. Senator Carl Levin (D-Mich.) asked a senior intelligence witness: "If [Saddam] didn't feel threatened, did not feel threatened, is it likely that he would initiate an attack using a weapon of mass destruction?" The response: "My judgment would be that the probability of him initiating an attack—let me put a time frame on it—in the foreseeable future, given the conditions we understand now, the likelihood I think would be low." Levin took it to the next step: "If we initiate an attack and he thought he was in extremis or otherwise, what's the likelihood in response to our attack that he would use chemical or biological weapons?" The answer this time: "Pretty high, in my view."[61]

ACTING ON THE RESOLUTION

There was little doubt that President Bush would find support in the House. The question was whether the vote would divide along party lines. The partisan issue blurred when House Minority Leader Dick Gephardt (D-Mo.) broke ranks with many in his party and announced support for a slightly redrafted resolution. He said: "We had to go through this, putting politics aside, so we have a chance to get a consensus that will lead the country in the right direction."[62] Of course, politics could not be put aside. Even when leaders of the two parties and the two branches appealed for nonpartisan or bipartisan conduct, their comments were generally viewed as calculated to have some partisan benefit. Gephardt's interest in running for the presidency was well known, as was Daschle's and several other members of Congress. Democratic Senators John Edwards (N.C.) and Joseph Lieberman (Conn.), interested in a 2004 bid for the presidency, came out in support of the Iraq Resolution. Another potential Democratic candidate for president, Senator John Kerry of Massachusetts, initially expressed doubts about the Iraq Resolution but later voted for it.[63] Lawmakers who opposed the Iraq Resolution also thought through their own political agendas and interests.

One Democratic lawmaker concluded that Gephardt, by supporting Bush, had "inoculated Democrats against the charge that they are antiwar and obstructionist."[64] Why were Democrats so concerned about the antiwar charge? There was no evidence that the public, in any broad sense, supported war against Iraq. Available polls revealed no public appetite for immediate military action. A *New York Times* poll published on October 7 indicated that 69 percent of Americans believed that Bush should be paying more attention to the economy. Although support was high for military action (with 67 percent approving U.S. military action against Iraq with the goal of removing Hussein from power), when it was asked, "Should the U.S. take military action against Iraq fairly soon or wait and give the U.N. more time to get weapons inspectors into Iraq?" 63 percent preferred to wait. To the question "Is Congress asking enough questions about President Bush's policy toward Iraq?" only 20 percent said too many, while 51 percent said not enough. When asked whether Bush was more interested in removing Hussein than weapons of mass destruction, 53 percent said Hussein and only 29 percent said weapons.[65]

A *Washington Post* story on October 8 described the public's enthusiasm for war against Iraq as "tepid and declining."[66] Americans gave Bush the benefit of the doubt but were not convinced by his arguments. Because of those doubts, "support could fade if the conflict in Iraq becomes bloody and extended."[67] These public attitudes led the *New York Times* to wonder: "Given the cautionary mood of the country, it is puzzling that most members of Congress seem fearful of challenging the hawkish approach to Iraq."[68]

More fundamentally, the vote on the resolution was inescapably and legitimately a political decision. Lawmakers would be voting on whether to commit as much as $100 billion or $200 billion to the war, stretching over a period of years. Their actions would stabilize or destabilize the Middle East, strengthen or weaken the war against terrorism, enhance or debase the nation's prestige. Politics would always be present, as would partisan calculations and strategy.

When the House International Relations Committee reported the resolution, it divided thirty-one to eleven. Democrats on the committee split ten to nine in favoring it. Two Republicans, Jim Leach of Iowa and Ron Paul of Texas, opposed it. The forty-seven-page committee report consists of only five pages of text analyzing the resolution.[69] President Bush's speech to the United Nations occupies another five pages. Twenty-one pages are devoted to an administration document called "A Decade of Deception and Defiance: Saddam Hussein's Defiance of the United Nations" (September 12, 2002). It was prepared as a background paper for Bush's speech to the United Nations. Some of it describes what is supposedly the administration's main concern: the development of weapons of mass destruction. Other sections focus on conditions in Iraq that, while deplorable, could hardly justify war: Iraq's refusal to allow visits by human rights monitors, the expulsion of UN humanitarian relief workers, violence against women, child labor and forced labor, the lack of freedom of speech or of the press, and refusal to return to Kuwait state archives and museum pieces.

A key section of the report reads: "The Committee hopes that the use of military force can be avoided. It believes, however, that providing the President with the authority he needs to use force is the best way to avoid its use. A signal of our Nation's seriousness of purpose and its willingness to use force may yet persuade Iraq to meet its international obligations, and is the best way to persuade members of the Security Council and others in the international community to join us in bringing pressure on Iraq or, if required, in using armed force against it."[70]

ECHOES OF TONKIN GULF

In this way, the committee both authorized military force and hoped that it would not be necessary. It would not make the decision to go to war. That judgment would be left to the president. The Iraq Resolution bears a melancholy resemblance to the Tonkin Gulf Resolution of 1964, which Congress passed almost unanimously (with only two dissenting votes in the Senate). Passage of this resolution was not an endorsement of war either. Instead, members of Congress thought that by offering broad, bipartisan support to President Lyndon B. Johnson, war with North Vietnam could be avoided.

During Senate debate on the Tonkin Gulf Resolution, Gaylord Nelson reviewed the statements by his colleagues and noticed that "every Senator who spoke had his own personal interpretation of what the joint resolution means." He found that "there is no agreement in the Senate on what the joint resolution means."[71] To clarify the resolution, he offered an amendment to state that President Johnson would seek "no extension of the present military conflict" and that "we should continue to attempt to avoid a direct military involvement in the southeast Asian conflict." Senator J. William Fulbright, floor manager of the resolution, refused to accept the amendment because it would force the two Houses to go to conference to resolve the differences between the versions passed by each chamber. However, Fulbright remarked that Nelson's amendment expressed "fairly accurately what the President has said would be our policy, and what I stated my understanding was as to our policy." Fulbright believed that the resolution "is calculated to prevent the spread of the war, rather than to spread it."[72] The military expansion that began in February 1965 led to the deaths of 58,000 Americans and several million in Southeast Asia.

Congressional debate in 2002 contains some similarities to and differences from the Tonkin Gulf Resolution. On October 10, 2002, the House passed the Iraq resolution, 296–133. The vote contrasts markedly with the unanimous House vote in 1964. Yet the resolutions are virtually identical in transferring to the president the sole decision to go to war. In each case, lawmakers were willing to trust in the president, not in themselves.

After the House vote in 2002, Senator Daschle announced his support for the resolution. Although he suggested that Senators might "go back and tie down the language a little bit more if we can," he insisted that "we have got to support this effort. We have got to do it in an enthusiastic and bipartisan way."[73] Why the need for enthusiasm and bipartisanship? Why wasn't the argument on the merits? Trust in the President or a call for bipartisanship are not substitutes for analyzing the use of military force against another country. Senator Kerry, who had earlier raised substantive arguments against going to war against Iraq, now accepted presidential superiority over Congress: "We are affirming a president's right and responsibility to keep the American people safe, and the president must take that grant of responsibility seriously."[74] With that kind of reading, Congress had little reason to participate in the debate other than to offer words of encouragement and support to a president who already seemed to possess all the constitutional authority he needed to act single-handedly. Congress was no longer an authorizing body. It merely endorsed what the president had already decided.

A similar position appears in Daschle's statement that "it is important for America to speak with one voice at this critical moment."[75] That attitude flavored Senate debate in 1964 on the Tonkin Gulf Resolution, but why should legislators consider agreement with the president more important than a conscientious and individual allegiance to their constitutional duties? A member of Congress takes an oath to support and defend the Constitution, not the president. As the 1964 experience demonstrated, unity does not assure wise policy. That comes from honest and free deliberation. During debate on the Department of Homeland Security, Daschle said he intended "to give the President the benefit of the doubt." Byrd took sharp exception: "I will not give the benefit of the doubt to the President. I will give the benefit of the doubt to the Constitution."[76]

Senator Byrd watched the congressional debate drift slowly from a willingness of lawmakers to analyze issues and weigh the merits to wholesale legislative abdication to the president. To Byrd, the fundamental question of why the United States should go to war was replaced by "the mechanics of how best to wordsmith the president's use-of-force resolution in order to give him virtually unchecked authority to commit the nation's military to an unprovoked attack on a sovereign nation." Having followed the arguments presented by President Bush and after questioning the top executive branch officials responsible for crafting the resolution, Byrd did not find the threat from Iraq "so great that we must be stampeded to provide such authority to this president just weeks before an election."[77]

Republican Senators Lugar, Hagel, and Arlen Specter (Pa.), after raising serious questions about the resolution, decided by October 7 to support it.[78] On October 10, the Senate voted seventy-seven to twenty-three for the resolution. The only Republican voting against the resolution was Lincoln Chafee of Rhode Island. An Independent, James Jeffords of Vermont, also voted no. Lee Hamilton, who served as a Representative from Indiana for 34 years (1965–99), filling key positions in the Intelligence and International Relations committees, noted that Congress "is really handing over to the president not just the question of how you conduct the war, but the authority to decide whether or not to go to war."[79]

CONCLUSIONS

Congress failed to discharge its constitutional duties when it passed the Iraq Resolution. Instead of making a decision about whether to go to war and spend billions for a multiyear commitment, it transferred those legislative judgments to the president. Legislators washed their hands of the key decisions to go to war and for how long. Of course they can reenter the debate and seek to cut off funds if the war goes badly, but legislation to terminate funding would have to survive a presidential veto, forcing Congress to find a two thirds majority in each chamber for the override. Lawmakers would also have to be willing to cut off funds for soldiers engaged in combat.

Constitutionally, Congress should not have voted on the Iraq Resolution before the election, which colored the votes and the political calculations. It would have been better for Congress as an institution, and for the country as a whole, to have President Bush request the Security Council to authorize inspections in Iraq. Depending on what the Security Council did or did not do, and on what Iraq agreed or did not agree to do, Congress could then have debated whether to authorize war. Having learned what the Security Council and Iraq actually did, rather than on what they might do, Congress would have been in the position to make an informed choice. It chose, instead, to vote under partisan pressures, with inadequate information, and thereby abdicated its constitutional duties to the president.

In the end, Congress had two models to choose from. It could have acted after the election, as it did in 1990–91. It could have acted in the middle of an election, as in 1964. The first maintained the integrity of the legislative institution by minimizing partisan tactics and scheduling legislative debate after the Security Council voted. The second placed Congress in a position of voting hurriedly without the information it needed, and with information it did receive (the two "attacks" in Tonkin Gulf) of dubious quality. In 2002, Congress picked the Tonkin Gulf model. There may be times when Congress might have to authorize war in the middle of an election. The year 2002 was not one.

After passage of the Iraq Resolution, President Bush went to the Security Council and persuaded them to adopt a resolution unanimously, fifteen to zero, for strengthened inspections in Iraq. Over the space of three months the inspectors did their work, ordering the destruction of some missiles, but finding no weapons of mass destruction. Rather than allow the inspections to continue, the Bush administration returned to the Security Council to seek a second resolution, this one to authorize military action against Iraq. The administration hoped to receive at least nine votes, but was unable to do so. Though he lacked the solid backing of the international community achieved with the first resolution, President Bush decided to go to war against Iraq with only England supplying significant armed forces. Having spurned the Security Council and the other nations that refused to endorse military action, the United States launched war against Iraq and planned to occupy the country for many years to come.

If the consequences in the years to come will not be as disastrous as they were for Southeast Asia, it will be because of good fortune, not because President Bush articulated persuasive reasons for war, and not because Congress fulfilled its constitutional duties. The political process followed in 2002 did great harm to "a republic." The experience left us with a question: Do we still have an interest in living in—and fighting for—representative democracy? If not, how can we pretend to advise other countries how to establish democratic regimes?

NOTES

1. Louis Fisher, *Presidential War Power* (Lawrence: University Press of Kansas, 1995), 1–38, 46–54.

2. *Weekly Compilation of Presidential Documents* 38 (2002): 1393–94.

3. Elizabeth Bumiller, "U.S. Must Act First to Battle Terror, Bush Tells Cadets," *New York Times*, 2 June 2002, p. A1.

4. Elizabeth Bumiller and James Dao, "Cheney Says Peril of a Nuclear Iraq Justifies Attack," *New York Times*, 27 August 2002, p. A1.

5. *New York Times*, 27 August 2002, p. A8.

6. Dana Milbank, "Cheney Says Iraqi Strike Is Justified," *Washington Post*, 27 August 2002, p. A1.

7. "Mr. Cheney on Iraq" (editorial), *Washington Post*, 27 August 2002, p. A14.

8. Dan Balz and Dana Milbank, "Iraq Policy Shift Follows Pattern," *Washington Post*, 6 September 2002, p. A19.

9. Dana Milbank, "No Conflict on Iraq Policy, Fleischer Says," *Washington Post*, 3 September 2002, p. A14.

10. Alison Mitchell and David E. Sanger, "Bush to Put Case for Action in Iraq to Key Lawmakers," *New York Times*, 4 September 2002, p. A1.

11. Helen Dewar and Mike Allen, "Senators Wary about Action against Iraq," *Washington Post*, 4 September 2002, p. A16.

12. *Weekly Compilation of Presidential Documents*, 38 (2002): 573.

13. Ibid., 38 (2002): 1295.

14. David E. Sanger, "Bush Declares U.S. Is Using Diplomacy to Disarm Hussein," *New York Times*, 22 October 2002, p. A15.

15. Todd A. Purdum and David Firestone, "Chief U.N. Inspector Backs U.S., Demanding Full Iraq Disclosure," *New York Times*, 5 October 2002, p. A1.

16. *Weekly Compilation of Presidential Documents* 38 (2002): 1633.

17. Mike Allen, "Bush's Words Can Go to the Blunt Edge of Trouble," *Washington Post*, 29 September 2002, p. A22.

18. Todd S. Purdum, "The U.S. Case against Iraq: Counting up the Reasons," *New York Times*, 1 October 2002, p. A14.

19. David E. Sanger and Carl Hulse, "Bush Appears to Soften Tone on Iraq Action," *New York Times*, 2 October 2002, p. A13.

20. Michael Kinsley, "War for Dummies," *Washington Post*, 11 October 2002, p. A37.

21. Mike Allen and Juliet Eilperin, "Bush Aides Say Iraq War Needs No Hill Vote," *Washington Post*, 26 August 2002, p. A1.

22. See Fisher, *Presidential War Power*, 1–12.

23. For a full exploration of the arguments presented by the White House Counsel's office, see Louis Fisher, "The Road to Iraq," *Legal Times*, 2 September 2002, pp. 34–35.

24. "Bush Rejects Hill Limits on Resolution Allowing War," *Washington Post*, 2 October 2002, p. A12.

25. 112 Stat. 3181, § 8 (1998).

26. Ron Fournier, "White House Lawyers Give Bush OK on Iraq," *Washington Times*, 26 August 2002, p. A3.

27. Mike Allen, "War Cabinet Argues for Iraq Attack," *Washington Post*, 9 September 2002, p. A1.

28. David Firestone and David E. Sanger, "Congress Now Promises to Hold Weeks of Hearings about Iraq," *New York Times*, 6 September 2002, p. A1.

29. Mike Allen, "War Cabinet Argues for Iraq Attack," *Washington Post*, 9 September 2002, p. A1.

30. *Congressional Record*, 148:S8966 (daily edition, 20 September 2002).

31. Dana Milbank, "Democrats Question Iraq Timing," *Washington Post*, 16 September 2002, p. A6.

32. George P. Schulz, "Act Now: The Danger Is Immediate. Saddam Hussein Must Be Removed," *Washington Post*, 6 September 2002, p. A25.

33. Bradley Graham, "Cheney, Tenet Brief Leaders of Hill on Iraq," *Washington Post*, 6 September 2002, p. A1.

34. Jim VandeHei, "GOP Nominees Make Iraq a Political Weapon," *Washington Post*, 18 September 2002, p. A1.

35. Dana Milbank, "Democrats Question Iraq Timing," p. A1.

36. David Firestone, "Liberals Object to Bush Policy on Iraq Attack," *New York Times*, 28 September 2002, p. A1.

37. Dana Milbank, "In President's Speeches, Iraq Dominates, Economy Fades," *Washington Post*, 25 September 2002, p. A6.

38. Mark Dayton, "Go Slow on Iraq," *Washington Post*, 28 September 2002, p. A23.

39. *Weekly Compilation of Presidential Documents* 38 (2002): 1598.

40. Carl Hulse and Todd S. Purdum, "Daschle Defends Democrats' Stand on Security of U.S.," *New York Times*, 26 September 2002, p. A1.

41. Jim VandeHei, "Daschle Angered by Bush Statement," *Washington Post*, 26 September 2002, p. A6.

42. Mike Allen and Karen DeYoung, "Bush to Seek Hill Approval on Iraq War," *Washington Post*, 5 September 2002, p. A1.

43. Jim VandeHei and Juliet Eilperin, "Democrats Unconvinced On Iraq War," *Washington Post*, 11 September 2002, p. A1.

44. Jim VandeHei, "Iraq Briefings: Don't Ask, Don't Tell," *Washington Post*, 15 September 2002, p. A4.

45. *Weekly Compilation of Presidential Documents*, 38 (2002): 1518.

46. Dana Milbank, "For Bush, Facts Are Malleable," *Washington Post*, 22 October 2002, pp. A1, A22.

47. James Risen, "Prague Discounts An Iraqi Meeting," *New York Times*, 21 October 2002, p. A1; James Risen, "How Politics and Rivalries Fed Suspicions of a Meeting," *New York Times*, 21 October 2002, p. A9; Peter S. Green, "Havel Denies Telephoning U.S. on Iraq Meeting," *New York Times*, 23 October 2002, p. A11.

48. Dana Priest, "U.S. Not Claiming Iraqi Link to Terror," *Washington Post*, 10 September 2002, p. A1.

49. *Weekly Compilation of Presidential Documents* 38 (2002): 1619.

50. Ibid., p. 1625.

51. Mike Allen, "Bush Asserts That Al Qaeda Has Links to Iraq's Hussein," *Washington Post*, 26 September 2002, p. A29.

52. Karen De Young, "Unwanted Debate on Iraq-Al Qaeda Links Revived," *Washington Post*, 27 September 2002, p. A19.

53. Sebastian Rotella, "Allies Find No Links between Iraq, Al Qaeda," *Los Angeles Times*, 4 November 2002, p. A1.

54. Eric Schmitt, "Rumsfeld Says U.S. Has 'Bulletproof' Evidence of Iraq's Links to Al Qaeda," *New York Times*, 28 September 2002, p. A8.

55. *Weekly Compilation of Presidential Documents*, 38 (2002): 1717.

56. Karen De Young, "Bush Cites Urgent Iraqi Threat," *Washington Post*, 8 October 2002, p. A21.

57. *Weekly Compilation of Presidential Documents*, 38: 1718.

58. "AlFurat Manufacturing Facility, Iraq" *Washington Post*, 8 October 2002, p. A21.

59. John F. Burns, "Iraq Tour of Suspected Sites Gives Few Clues on Weapons," *New York Times*, 13 October 2002, p. A1.

60. "Analysts Discount Attack by Iraq," *Washington Post*, 9 October 2002, p. A1.

61. "C.I.A. Letter to Senate on Baghdad's Intentions," *New York Times*, 9 October 2002, p. A12.

62. "For Gephardt, Risks and a Crucial Role," *Washington Post*, 3 October 2002, p. A15.

63. Dan Balz and Jim VandeHei, "Democratic Hopefuls Back Bush on Iraq," *Washington Post*, 14 September 2002, p. A4.

64. David E. Rosenbaum, "United Voice on Iraq Eludes Majority Leader," *New York Times*, 4 October 2002, p. A12.

65. Adam Nagourney and Janet Elder, "Public Says Bush Needs to Pay Heed to Weak Economy," *New York Times*, 7 October 2002, pp. A1, A14.

66. Dana Milbank, "With Congress Aboard, Bush Targets a Doubtful Public," *Washington Post*, 8 October 2002, p. A21.

67. Ibid.

68. Editorial, "A Nation Wary of War," *New York Times*, 8 October 2002, p. A30.

69. H. Rep. No. 107–721 (2002).

70. Ibid., pp. 4–5.

71. *Congressional Record*, 110:18458 (1964).

72. Ibid., p. 18462.

73. John H. Cushman Jr., "Daschle Predicts Broad Support for Military Action against Iraq," *New York Times*, 7 October 2002, p. 10.

74. Helen Dewar and Juliet Eilperin, "Iraq Resolution Passes Test, Gains Support," *Washington Post*, 10 October 2002, p. A16.

75. Jim VandeHei and Juliet Eilperin, "House Passes Iraq War Resolution," *Washington Post*, 11 October 2002, p. A6.

76. *Congressional Record*, 148: S9187, S9188 (daily ed. September 25, 2002).

77. Robert C. Byrd, "Congress Must Resist the Rush to War," *New York Times*, 10 October 2002, p. A35.

78. Helen Dewar, "Armey, Lugar Reverse Stand on Resolution," *Washington Post*, 8 October 2002, p. A21.

79. Jonathan Riehl, "Broad Resolution Allows Bush to Set Terms of War without Review," *CQ Weekly Report*, 12 October 2002, p. 2679.

CHAPTER 8

Executive Privilege in the Bush Administration

The Conflict between Secrecy and Accountability

MARK J. ROZELL

Although well established now as a legitimate presidential power, executive privilege remains controversial. Executive privilege is controversial in part because some presidents have overreached in exercising this authority. Presidential attempts to conceal evidence of wrongdoing during the Watergate scandal that led to President Richard Nixon's resignation and during the scandal that led to President Bill Clinton's impeachment gave executive privilege a bad name.

The phrase "executive privilege" does not appear in the Constitution. To be precise, that phrase was not a part of the common language until the Eisenhower's administration, leading some to suggest that executive privilege therefore cannot be constitutional.[1] These semantic, textualist challenges to executive privilege's constitutionality fail when viewed through a broader, historical lens of past interbranch disputes. In fact, every president since George Washington has exercised some form of what is today called executive privilege, whatever the words chosen to describe their actions.[2] As Louis Fisher has pointed out, "one could play similar word games with 'impoundment,' also of recent vintage, but only by ignoring the fact that, under different names, Presidents have from an early date declined to spend funds appropriated by Congress."[3]

Executive privilege is an implied power derived from Article II.[4] It is most easily defined as the right of the president and high-level executive branch officers to withhold information from those who have compulsory power—Congress and the courts (and therefore, ultimately, the public). This right is not absolute, as executive privilege is often subject to the compulsory powers of the other branches. The modern understanding of executive privilege has evolved over a long period as the result of presidential actions, official administration policies, and court decisions. Today, executive privilege is considered most legitimate when used to protect, first, certain national security needs, and second, the confidentiality of White House deliberations when it is in the public interest to do so. Related to the second, executive privilege may be appropriate in circumstances where confidentiality is necessary to protect ongoing investigations in the executive branch.

After the Watergate scandal, several presidents exercised executive privilege either very cautiously or ineffectively. Not until the Clinton administration did a post-Watergate president make a concerted effort to exercise this presidential power.[5] Yet most of President Clinton's uses of executive privilege were indefensible because he asserted this power in circumstances that were far beyond widely accepted norms. In the early stages of his administration, President George W. Bush has also made substantial use of executive privilege in circumstances where the exercise of that power is highly debatable.

This chapter focuses on the various uses of executive privilege during the early stage of President George W. Bush's administration. President Bush has exercised the privilege in an attempt to reestablish what he perceives as a more correct balance of powers between the legislative and executive branches. Still, because President Bush has departed from recognized executive privilege norms, he has ultimately weakened executive privilege.

I. BACKGROUND

The most important modern articulation of executive privilege standards was the Reagan administration's executive privilege memorandum.[6] On November 4, 1982, President Ronald Reagan issued an executive privilege memorandum to heads of executive departments and agencies. The Reagan procedures were generally similar to a 1969 Nixon memorandum. For example, President Reagan's guidelines affirmed the administration policy "to comply with Congressional requests for information to the fullest extent consistent with the constitutional and statutory obligations of the Executive Branch."[7] The memorandum reaffirmed the need for "confidentiality of some communications,"[8] and added that executive privilege would be used "only in the most compelling circumstances, and only after careful review demonstrate[d] that assertion of the privilege [was] necessary."[9] Finally, the memorandum stated that "executive privilege [would] not be invoked without specific Presidential authorization."[10]

Despite similarities with previous memoranda the Reagan memorandum developed clearer procedures than had existed before. All congressional requests for information would be accommodated unless "compliance raise[d] a substantial question of executive privilege."[11] Such a question would arise if the information "might significantly impair the national security (including the conduct of foreign relations), the deliberative processes of the Executive Branch or other aspects of the performance of the Executive Branch's constitutional duties."[12] Under these procedures, if a department head believed that a congressional request for information might concern privileged information, he or she would notify and consult with both the attorney general and the counsel to the president. Those three individuals would then decide to release the information to Congress, or have the matter submitted to the president for a decision if any one of them believed that it was necessary to invoke executive privilege. At that point, the department head would ask Congress to await a presidential decision. If the president chose executive privilege, he would instruct the department head to inform Congress "that the claim of executive privilege [was] being made with the specific approval of the President."[13] The Reagan memorandum allowed for the use of executive privilege even if the information originated from staff levels far removed from the Oval Office.

The administration of the first President Bush did not adopt any new formal executive privilege procedures. In 1994 the Clinton administration issued a memorandum that defined new procedures for handling executive privilege disputes. The Clinton administration adopted the very broad view that all White House communications are presumptively privileged. Furthermore, the administration's position was that Congress has a less valid claim to executive branch information when conducting oversight than when conducting legislation.

II. GEORGE W. BUSH'S EXERCISE OF EXECUTIVE PRIVILEGE

In the early stages of the Bush presidency, the administration was involved in three policy disputes that either had implications for the development of executive privilege or had a direct claim of privilege by the president. It became clear early in President Bush's term that the president was committed to regaining lost ground on executive privilege. President Bush not only wanted to revitalize executive privilege, but to expand the scope of that power substantially. President Bush's actions appear motivated by his belief in the sovereignty of the executive branch.

Nonetheless, President Bush chose some very nontraditional cases for reestablishing executive privilege. In one case, he tried to expand the scope of executive privilege for former presidents, and even to allow them to transfer this constitutional authority under Article II to designated representatives. In another case, the Bush administration tried to expand executive privilege to protect Department of Justice (DOJ) documents from investigations long ago closed. The Bush administration has been pushing the use of executive privilege in circumstances where there is little precedent for such action. In so doing, President Bush has contributed to the further downgrading of executive privilege rather than to achieving his purpose of reaffirming this constitutional principle.

A. The Presidential Records Act of 1978 and Executive Order 13223.

In 1978, Congress passed the Presidential Records Act[14] to establish procedures for the public release of the papers of presidential administrations.

The Act allowed for the public release of presidential papers twelve years after a president had left office. The principle behind the law was that these presidential records ultimately belong to the public and should be made available for inspection within a reasonable period of time. The Act (Section 2206) gave responsibility for implementing this principle to the National Archives and Records Administration (NARA).[15] The 1978 Act retained the public disclosure exemptions of the Freedom of Information Act so that certain materials involving national security or state secrets could be withheld from public view for longer than the twelve-year period.[16]

On January 18, 1989, President Reagan issued Executive Order 12267,[17] which expanded certain implementation regulations of NARA. President Reagan's executive order identified three situations in which records could be withheld: national security, law enforcement, and the deliberative process privilege of the executive branch.[18] The executive order gave a sitting president primary authority to assert privilege over the records of a former president.[19] Furthermore, although Executive Order 12267 recognized that a former president has the right to claim executive privilege over his administration's papers, the archivist of the United States did not have to abide by his claim. The incumbent president could override the archivist with a claim of executive privilege, but only during a thirty-day review period.[20] After that period, absent a formal claim of executive privilege, the documents were to be automatically released.

On November 1, 2001, President George W. Bush issued Executive Order 13233[21] to supersede President Reagan's executive order and to vastly expand the scope of privileges available to current and former presidents. President Bush's executive order dropped the law enforcement category and added two others: the presidential communications privilege and the attorney-client or attorney work-product privileges. Under the new executive order, former presidents may assert executive privilege over their own papers, even if the incumbent president disagrees.[22] Indeed, President Bush's executive order also gives a sitting president the power to assert executive privilege over a past administration's papers, even if the former president disagrees.[23] President Bush's standard therefore allows any claim of privilege over old documents by an incumbent or past president to stand.[24] Furthermore, the Bush executive order requires anyone seeking to overcome constitutionally based privileges to have a "demonstrated, specific need" for presidential records.[25] The Presidential Records Act of 1978 did not contain such a high obstacle for those seeking access to presidential documents to overcome. Thus, under the Bush executive order, the presumption is always in favor of secrecy, whereas previously, the general presumption was in favor of openness.

The Bush executive order set off challenges by public advocacy groups, academic professional organizations, press groups, and some members of Congress. All were concerned that the executive order vastly expanded the scope of governmental secrecy in a way that was damaging to democratic institutions. Several groups, including the American Historical Association, the Organization of American Historians, and Public Citizen, initiated a lawsuit to have the executive order overturned. Congress held hearings that were highly critical of the executive order.[26] Although the controversy remains unresolved as of this writing, it is clear that President Bush's executive order improperly supersedes an Act of Congress and attempts to expand executive privilege far beyond the traditional standards for the exercise of that power.

Thus, the groups opposed to the president's action were correct for the following reasons. First, the handling of presidential papers is a matter that should be handled by statute and not by executive order. Presidential papers are ultimately public documents—a part of our national records—and are paid for with public funds. They should not be treated merely as private papers.

Second, although there is legal precedent for allowing an ex-president to assert executive privilege,[27] the standard for allowing such a claim is very high, and executive privilege cannot stand merely because an ex-president has some personal or political interest in preserving secrecy.[28] An ex-president's interest in maintaining confidentiality erodes substantially once he leaves office, and it continues to erode even further over time.[29] The Bush executive order does not acknowledge any such limitation on a former president's interest in confidentiality.

Third, the executive order makes it easy for such claims by former presidents to stand, and almost impossible for those challenging the claims to get information in a timely way. The legal constraints will effectively delay requests for information for years as these matters are fought out in the courts. These obstacles alone will settle the issue in favor of former presidents, because many citizens with an interest in access to information will conclude that they do not have the ability or the resources to stake a viable challenge. The burden will shift from those who must justify withholding information to fall instead on those who have made a claim for access to information.

Fourth, executive privilege may actually be frivolous in this case because there are already other secrecy protections in place for national security purposes. In a nutshell, the Bush administration is trying to expand executive privilege substantially to cover what existing statutes and regulations already cover. Furthermore, a general interest in confidentiality is not enough to sustain a claim of executive privilege over old documents that may go back as far as twenty years.[30]

B. Cheney Energy Task Force

President Bush appointed Vice President Richard Cheney to direct an energy policy task force for the purpose of developing the administration's energy policy. In April 2001, two Democratic members of Congress, Henry

Waxman and John Dingell, requested information from Vice President Cheney about the composition and activities of the task force. Their request was in response to press reports that the task force had been meeting in secrecy with representatives of various groups that had a direct interest in the development of a national energy policy. The lawmakers asked the General Accounting Office (GAO) to investigate the activities of the task force. The GAO initially responded with a broad-based request for information about the task-force meetings. The GAO also requested information regarding the identities of individuals present at task-force meetings, the identities of persons consulted by the task force about the development of energy policy, and the costs of the meetings. The vice president's counsel mostly refused this request and provided only a limited number of documents that the GAO considered unhelpful. After several months of wrangling over access to the information, on August 2, 2001, the vice president wrote to Congress that the GAO lacked authority to seek access to the task-force information. According to Vice President Cheney, the GAO only has the authority to review the results of programs, and not to seek information from a task force involved in program development.

Comptroller General of the United States David Walker strongly objected to the assertion that the GAO's scope of authority is limited to reviewing program results. Nonetheless, the GAO narrowed the scope of its information request and decided to seek only the names of advisers to the task force, as well as the dates, locations, and the subjects of meetings. The GAO and the members of Congress had thus dropped their insistence that Vice President Cheney disclose substantive details about discussions that took place in those meetings.

The conflict between the GAO and the vice president's office appeared headed to a court showdown until the terrorist attacks on the United States on September 11, 2001. Walker issued a statement in late September that the dispute remained unresolved, but that "given our current national focus on combating terrorism and enhancing homeland security, this matter is not a current priority."[31] On January 27, 2002, Vice President Cheney declared that the administration was steadfast in its refusal to provide even the most basic information about the meetings because of an important principle involved: that to do so would contribute to a further withering away of traditional presidential prerogatives. The conservative group Judicial Watch filed a lawsuit against the Cheney task force to try to compel public disclosure of information about the names of persons who had met with the task force.[32] The liberal National Resources Defense Council also initiated a lawsuit to get access to administration information on the development of energy policy.[33] On January 30, 2002, the GAO announced its intention to initiate a lawsuit to force Vice President Cheney to reveal the names of the participants in the task force meetings, and to give other details about the meetings.[34]

This controversy did not result in a direct presidential claim of privilege. Nonetheless, in his August 2 letter to the Congress, Vice President Cheney asserted that to provide the information requested by GAO would interfere with the constitutional duties of the executive branch by undermining the confidentiality of internal deliberations. Walker correctly pointed out that Vice President Cheney had thereby introduced "the same language and reasoning as assertions of Executive Privilege."[35] Walker also noted that the GAO had merely requested factual information, such as the names of persons who attended meetings and the costs of meetings, and not deliberative information.[36]

Because of this narrow scope of inquiry, any claim of executive privilege in this controversy, whether made explicitly by the president or implicitly by the vice president, lacked credibility. The vice president was on stronger ground in his refusal to cooperate with the initial request for information about the task force in the summer of 2001 because that inquiry was overly broad. The definition of "records" sought initially by GAO went on for half a page, reaching to e-mails, voicemails, drawings, plans, checks and canceled checks, bank statements, ledgers, books, diaries, logs, video recordings, telexes, notes, invoices, and drafts. Because of that initially broad information request, it is plausible that Vice President Cheney perceived the later narrowed request as merely a first effort by the GAO to ultimately drag him into a multistep process of getting more and more detailed information over time. Vice President Cheney may also have been concerned that releasing the names of those who met with the administration task force would result in those individuals being called in the future to testify to Congress. Nonetheless, these concerns are not sufficient to sustain a claim of executive privilege, because the narrow scope of the GAO request for information did not involve either direct presidential decision making or even deliberative matters. Thus, the administration pursued a two-pronged strategy of (1) making the traditional arguments for executive privilege without making a formal claim of that principle, and (2) claiming that the GAO lacked statutory authority to access executive branch information about task-force matters.

On December 9, 2002, the U.S. District Court for the District of Columbia dismissed the GAO suit. The court ruled that Walker lacked standing and thus delivered a potentially serious setback to the scope of the GAO's investigative authority. Walker chose not to file an appeal.

C. Department of Justice Documents and Congressional Oversight

President Bush made his first formal claim of executive privilege on December 12, 2001. This claim was in response to a congressional subpoena for prosecutorial records from the DOJ. The House Government Reform Committee, chaired by Representative Dan Burton, was investigating two separate matters that concerned DOJ decision making. First, the committee was examining the decision by former Attorney General Janet Reno to refuse to appoint an independent counsel to investigate allegations of campaign finance abuses in the 1996 Clinton-Gore campaign. Second, the committee was examining allegations of Federal Bureau of Investigation (FBI) corruption in its Boston office's handling of organized crime in the 1960s and 1970s. The committee made it clear that it was not requesting DOJ documents or other materials pertaining to any ongoing criminal investigations.

President Bush instructed Attorney General John Ashcroft not to comply with the congressional request for any deliberative documents from the DOJ. Ashcroft clashed with Burton over the administration's refusal to cooperate with the legislative investigations. At the core of this battle was a dispute over whether an administration can withhold any and all documents that involve prosecutorial matters, even if those matters are officially closed. Burton and members of the committee were upset that the Bush administration was trying to expand the scope of its authority to withhold information from Congress by refusing documents from terminated DOJ investigations. They were also upset that the Bush DOJ had declared that the unfinished investigation of the 1996 campaign finance controversy was closed. Burton and his colleagues clearly believed that Reno had hampered legitimate investigations, and that President Bush's desire to have certain Clinton-era controversies ended had the effect of denying full public disclosure of governmental misconduct. Burton penned a strongly worded letter to Ashcroft protesting the administration's "inflexible adherence to the position" that all deliberative materials from the DOJ be routinely withheld from Congress.[37] Burton pointed out that the administration had not made a valid claim of executive privilege and therefore had no right to withhold the documents requested by his committee.[38]

White House Counsel Alberto Gonzales recommended that the president assert executive privilege in response to any congressional subpoena for the documents or if Ashcroft appeared before the committee. The committee subpoenaed the documents and called Ashcroft to appear at a hearing on September 13, 2001. Because of the terrorist attacks two days before the scheduled hearing, Ashcroft's appearance was delayed. A new hearing was then scheduled for December 13, 2001. President Bush wrote a memorandum to Ashcroft asserting executive privilege.[39] At the hearing (Ashcroft was not present) Burton fumed, "This is not a monarchy. . . . the legislative branch has oversight responsibility to make sure there is no corruption in the executive branch."[40] In place of Ashcroft, the chief of staff of the DOJ Criminal Division issued the administration's statement before the committee. The statement claimed that revealing information about DOJ investigations would have a "chilling effect" on future DOJ deliberations. Nonetheless, during the hearing, the witness, Michael Horowitz, admitted that although the administration had adopted the policy that Congress should never receive access to deliberative documents, in the future, the DOJ could conduct a case-by-case analysis of the validity of congressional requests for such documents.[41] This statement indicated for the first time that there was some flexibility on the administration's part with regard to the principle of withholding deliberative materials.

President Bush's executive privilege memorandum to Ashcroft emphasized the deliberative nature of some of the prosecutorial materials requested by the committee. The president also expressed concern that releasing materials regarding confidential recommendations to an attorney general "would inhibit the candor necessary to the effectiveness of the deliberative processes by which the Department [of Justice] makes prosecutorial decisions." [42] More vaguely, the president asserted the separation of powers doctrine and the need "to protect individual liberty," and he stated that "congressional access to these documents would be contrary to the national interest."[43]

The DOJ followed with a letter to Burton emphasizing the president's assertion of executive privilege over the subpoenaed documents and expressing a desire to reach some accommodation. Assistant Attorney General Daniel Bryant expressed the unwillingness of the DOJ to release certain memoranda pertaining to Reno's decision not to appoint a special counsel to investigate allegations of campaign improprieties in the 1996 Clinton-Gore campaign.[44] Regarding the investigation of allegations of FBI corruption, he expressed at some length the DOJ's willingness to "work together" with the committee to provide "additional information without compromising the principles maintained by the executive branch."[45] Burton responded that the offer of accommodation was meaningless because, ultimately, the administration remained unwilling to allow the committee to review the most crucial documents for the purposes of an investigation.[46] Gonzales followed with the assurance that the administration did not have a "bright-line policy" of withholding all deliberative documents from Congress.[47] Yet Gonzales continued that, with regard to such memoranda, "the Executive Branch has traditionally protected those highly sensitive deliberative documents against public or congressional disclosure,"[48] a characterization that Burton strongly rejected.[49]

It is truly puzzling that President Bush took his first official executive privilege stand over materials concerning closed DOJ investigations. The Bush administration had made it clear that it was necessary to regain the lost ground of executive privilege after the years of Clinton scandals and misuses of that power. Yet it chose to regain some of that lost ground in a circumstances in which there appeared little justification for the exercise of that power. There were no national security implications to the legislative investigation. There was no clear public interest at stake in protecting old investigative documents and other materials. This claim of privilege did not even fall into the category of protecting the integrity of ongoing criminal investigations.

The dispute over certain DOJ documents became especially heated when news stories reported that the FBI had abused its authority when it investigated organized crime in the 1960s and 1970s. There was credible evidence that the FBI had caused the wrongful imprisonment of at least one person while it protected a government witness who committed multiple murders even while he was in protection. Burton demanded access to ten key DOJ documents in order to investigate the allegations of wrongful conduct by the FBI.[50] The documents that Burton requested were, on average, twenty-two years old.[51] The administration refused to turn over DOJ documents, and Burton threatened to take this controversy to the courts.

Burton had the complete support of the committee, as evidenced by a February 6, 2002, hearing at which all the members, Republican and Democrat alike, joined in lambasting the administration's actions, and declared their intention to carry the fight for the documents as far as necessary.[52] The complete unanimity of the committee was remarkable, especially given that the administration—during a period of war and with extraordinarily high levels of public approval—had made direct appeals for support to GOP members of the committee on the eve of the hearing. At the opening of the hearing, several GOP members openly declared their disdain for this tactic and said that, regardless of party affiliation or of a president's popularity, they were ready to defend Congress's prerogatives.

The administration witness at the hearing, Daniel Bryant, an assistant attorney general in the DOJ Office of Legislative Affairs, asserted the position that all prosecutorial documents are "presumptively privileged" and never available for congressional inspection.[53] This claim ran counter to a long history of congressional access to DOJ prosecutorial documents, especially in cases of closed investigations where the need for secrecy has disappeared.[54] It also appeared to run counter to earlier administration policy clarifications that there was no blanket policy of withholding such materials from Congress. Bryant stated that the administration was willing to give an oral presentation about the general contents of the disputed documents to members of the committee, but not to allow the members to actually see the documents.[55] This offer only brought more comments of disdain from committee members.

On March 1, 2002, the two sides reached an accommodation in which the committee would be permitted to openly view six of the ten disputed documents. The agreement allowed both sides to declare victory. The committee claimed that it had won the right to access to the most important documents that were necessary for its investigation of the Boston FBI office scandal. The administration took the view that it had allowed access only to a narrow category of documents—in this case, those that concerned an indicted FBI agent were considered necessary to Congress's oversight function. The administration continued to insist that it did not have to give Congress access to deliberative documents. Ultimately, the committee accepted this agreement because of a lack of a consensus that members should instead continue to push for all ten documents. The administration prevailed in withholding three key documents pertaining to Reno's decision not to appoint a special counsel to investigate campaign finance abuses by the 1996

Clinton-Gore campaign. The inability of the committee to achieve a total victory indeed reflected the unwillingness of certain Democratic members to push for these three documents.

The resolution of this controversy was somewhat reminiscent of many former executive privilege battles, especially the ones during the Reagan years. In each of those battles the administration staked out a strong stand on executive privilege and signaled a refusal to compromise; Congress persisted and used its authority to pressure the administration to turn over the disputed materials; the administration ultimately relented on either all the documents, or at least the key ones; both sides walked away and declared victory. In this case though, the committee achieved only a partial victory. Furthermore, that the administration held the line on certain categories of documents signaled the likelihood of additional such information disputes between the branches during the Bush presidency.

III. EXECUTIVE PRIVILEGE IN THE EARLY GEORGE W. BUSH PRESIDENCY SUMMARIZED

Although President Bush wanted to quickly reestablish executive privilege, he attempted to do so by means of some very nontraditional cases. One concerned executive privilege for former presidents and with regard to the papers of past administrations. The common standard is that a former president's interest in maintaining secrecy over his administration's documents wanes substantially over time. President Bush's executive order attempts to override an act of Congress and to vastly expand presidential privileges for ex-presidents. A second controversy concerned the exercise of a form of executive privilege by a sitting vice president. The common standard for years has been that presidents alone have the authority to either assert executive privilege or to direct an administration official to do so. Even though Vice President Cheney did not use the words "executive privilege" in refusing access to information, he used legal language and justifications identical to an actual claim of executive privilege. Furthermore, Vice President Cheney did not assert the right to withhold deliberative materials or presidential advice but rather very benign-seeming factual information, such as names of people present at certain meetings of the task force and the costs and the subjects of those meetings. The third controversy again involved protecting materials from closed, not ongoing, criminal investigations.

None of these cases concerned national security. The administration never made a convincing case that there was strong public interest involved in protecting the release of these materials to Congress. With the nation at war abroad and fighting terrorism domestically, it is not hard to imagine a stronger circumstance in which the administration might stake a claim to executive privilege to protect national security and the public interest. In its first months in office, the Bush administration had instead made some flimsy attempts at restoring executive privilege.

President Bush's efforts on executive privilege nonetheless were consistent with an overall administration strategy of attempting to tip the balance of federal governmental powers increasingly in favor of the executive branch. If the administration sustains strong public support for the war on terror, then it stands to reason that the president will continue to try to enhance his ability to exercise greater powers with fewer congressional restraints. Such a scenario creates the likelihood of future battles with Congress over executive privilege.

CONCLUSION

What is the current standing of executive privilege? The debate on executive privilege over the past generation has shifted significantly. Few call it a myth any longer. The principle of executive privilege is widely accepted today, although there is considerable debate about the parameters of this presidential power. It certainly has not helped that the George W. Bush administration has overreached in its exercise of this power.

To clarify the parameters of this power, some advocate the adoption of a statutory definition of executive privilege, and others express the hope that future court decisions will provide more guidance and specificity over executive privilege. Yet neither proposed solution is necessary or desirable. The resolution to conflicts over executive privilege resides in the theory of separation of powers as envisioned by the framers of the Constitution. Congress and the courts possess the institutional powers needed to challenge presidential exercises of executive privilege. So long as the other branches vigorously protect their prerogatives, presidential misuses of executive privilege will be curtailed. There is no need for a legislatively or judicially imposed solution to prevent such possible future misuses of executive privilege when these branches already possess the constitutional powers needed to successfully challenge presidents.

The early stage of the Bush administration demonstrates that even during periods of high popularity, presidents are often constrained in their efforts to expand or overreach their constitutional authority. President Bush has revived the national debate over executive privilege. He shows little interest in backing away from battles with Congress over this presidential power. It is thus likely that the debate over executive privilege will continue, as long as Congress still vigorously challenges presidential assertions of that power.

NOTES

1. See Raoul Berger, *Executive Privilege: A Constitutional Myth.* (Cambridge: Havard University Press, 1974), 1–2 (arguing that executive privilege is unconstitutional and a "myth" because the "very words 'executive privilege' were conjoined

only yesterday, in 1958"); Saikrishna Bangalore Prakash, "A Critical Comment on the Constitutionality of Executive Privilege," *Minnesota Law Review* 83 (1999): 1143, 1146 (asserting that the existence of executive privilege is not supported by the Constitution, because it is neither explicitly nor implicitly mentioned in the text).

2. Mark J. Rozell, "Executive Privilege and the Modern Presidents: In Nixon's Shadow," *Minnesota Law Review* 83 (1999): 1069, 1070.

3. Louis Fisher, "Raoul Berger on Public Law," *Political Science Reviewer* 8 (1978): 173, 181.

4. See United States v. Nixon, 418 U.S. 683, 705 (1974) ("Whatever the nature of the privilege of confidentiality of Presidential communications in the exercise of Art. II powers, the privilege can be said to derive from the supremacy of each branch within its own assigned area of constitutional duties"). The key members of the Committee of Style at the Constitutional Convention—Alexander Hamilton, Rufus King, and Governeur Morris—shaped the language of article II to allow the executive to exercise vast powers. The Vesting Clause, U.S. Constitution, art. II, sec. 1, the lack of any enumeration of duties in the Commander in Chief Clause, U.S. Constitution art. II, sec. 2, and the many silences about such powers as war, diplomacy, and control over executive departments all left the president with a vast reserve of unspecified authority. Several selections from the Federalist Papers support the exercise of executive branch secrecy. See *Federalist* No. 64, 392–93 (John Jay) (Clinton Rossiter, ed., New York: Penguin Books, 1961) (noting that "[i]t seldom happens in the negotiation of treaties . . . but that perfect *secrecy* and immediate *dispatch* are sometimes requisite," and asserting that "[t]he convention [*sic*] have done well, therefore, in so disposing of the power of making treaties that although the President must, in forming them, act by the advice and consent of the Senate, yet he will be able to manage the business of intelligence in such manner as prudence may suggest"); *Federalist* No. 70, at 424 (Alexander Hamilton) (Clinton Rossiter, ed., 1961) (stating that "decision, activity, secrecy, and dispatch" are valuable characteristics for an executive to have).

5. Rozell, "Executive Privilege and the Modern Presidents," 1071–72.

6. Memorandum from Ronald Reagan, President of the United States, to the Heads of Executive Departments and Agencies (4 November 1982).

7. Reagan, memorandum, at 1.

8. Ibid.

9. Ibid.

10. Ibid.

11. Ibid.

12. Ibid at 1–2.

13. Ibid at 2.

14. Presidential Records Act of 1978, Pub. L. No. 95–591, § 2(a), 92 Stat. 2523, 2523–27, codified as amended at 42 U.S.C. §§ 2201–2207 (2000).

15. 44 U.S.C. § 2206 (2000).

16. Ibid., § 2204(c)(1).

17. Exec. Order No. 12,667, 3 C.F.R. 208 (1989), *reprinted in* 44 U.S.C. § 2204.

18. Ibid., § 1(g), 3 C.F.R. at 208.

19. Ibid., § 3, 3 C.F.R. at 209.

20. Ibid., § 4(b), 3 C.F.R. at 210.

21. Exec. Order No. 13,233, 3 C.F.R. 815 (2001), *reprinted in* 44 U.S.C.A. § 2204 (Supp. 2002).

22. Ibid., § 3(d)(1)(ii), 3 C.F.R. at 817.

23. Ibid., § 3(d)(2)(ii), 3 C.F.R. at 817.

24. See letter from Alberto R. Gonzales, Counsel to the President, to Steve Horn, United States House of Representatives (2 November 2001) (explaining that former presidents "are to have the primary responsibility for asserting privileges over the records of a former President" but that the sitting president may assert such privileges in "compelling circumstances" even against the wishes of a former president); Exec. Order No. 13,233 § 3(d), 3 C.F.R. at 817.

25. Exec. Order No. 13,233 § 2(c), 3 C.F.R. at 816; quoting United States v. Nixon, 418 U.S. 683, 713 (1977).

26. See, for example, *Hearings Regarding Executive Order 13,233 and the Presidential Records Act before the House Subcomm. on Gov't Efficiency, Fin. Mgmt. & Intergovernmental Relations and the House Comm. on Gov't Reform*, 107th Cong. 30 (2001) [hereinafter *Hearings Regarding Executive Order 13,233*] (statement of Anna K. Nelson) ("The Bush Administration, unwittingly perhaps, has thwarted the intention of Congress to open these government records to the public.")

27. See Nixon v. Adm'r of Gen. Serv., 433 U.S. 425, 449 (1976) (adopting the solicitor general's view that some constitutionally based privileges "survive the individual President's tenure").

28. See ibid. at 439 ("We reject the argument that only an incumbent President may assert [the presidential privilege of confidentiality] and hold that appellant, as a former President, may also be heard to assert [it]").

29. Ibid., at 451.

30. See, for example, Hearings Regarding Executive Order 13,233 (*supra* n. 26) at 52 (statement of Mark J. Rozell); *Hearings on "H.R. 4187, the Presidential Records Act Amendments of 2002" Before the House Subcomm. on Gov't Efficiency, Fin. Mgmt. & Intergovernmental Relations*, 107th Cong. 1 (2002).

31. Press Release, David M. Walker, Comptroller General of the United States, U.S. General Accounting Office, Statement on the National Energy Policy Development Group (28 September 2001).

32. Judicial Watch, Inc. v. Nat'l Energy Policy Dev. Group, 219 F. Supp. 2d 20 (D.D.C. 2002).

33. Nat'l Res. Def. Council v. Dep't of Energy, 191 F. Supp. 2d 41 (D.D.C. 2002).

34. See Walker v. Cheney, No. 02-0340 (D.D.C. filed 22 February 2002).

35. Letter from David M. Walker, Comptroller General of the United States, U.S. General Accounting Office, to J. Dennis Hastert, Speaker of the House of Representatives (17 August 2001).

36. Ibid., at 2.

37. Letter from Dan Burton, Chairman, House of Representatives Committee on Government Reform, to John Ashcroft, Attorney General, U.S. Department of Justice (29 August 2001).

38. Ibid., at 2.

39. Memorandum from George W. Bush, President of the United States, to the Attorney General (12 December 2001).

40. See Ellen Nakashima, "Bush Invokes Privilege on Hill," *Washington Post*, 14 December 2001, p. A43 (quoting Burton).

41. See *Investigation into Allegations of Justice Department Misconduct in New England: Hearings Before the Comm. on Gov't Reform*, 107th Cong. 382 (2001) [hereinafter

Investigation into Allegations] (statement of Michael E. Horowitz, Chief of Staff, Criminal Division, U.S. Department of Justice) ("[W]e remain willing to work informally with the committee to provide the information to the committee about the decisions related to these subpoenaed documents that you had not previously requested . . . "). This prepared statement is a truly unimpressive brief on behalf of the administration's claim of privilege. It contains a string of unconnected quotations taken out of context to try to prove the obvious point that administrations have secrecy needs. The statement never gets beyond broad generalities to make a case why secrecy was needed in this particular dispute. Some of the evidence presented is simply wrong (e.g., the claim that George Washington withheld all information from Congress in the St. Clair incident), leaves out important facts (e.g., that four days after a former Bush administration stand on executive privilege, the president relented and gave everything to Congress), and claims as authoritative a widely discredited assertion by former attorney general Benjamin Civiletti that allowing members of Congress to investigate the process of federal prosecutions would destroy the civil liberties of persons under investigation. Benjamin R. Civiletti, *Justice Unbalanced: Congress and Prosecutorial Discretion*, vols. 5–6 (The Heritage Foundation, Lecture No. 472, 1993).

42. Bush (*supra* n. 39) at 1.

43. Ibid.

44. See letter from Daniel J. Bryant, Assistant Attorney General, Office of Legislative Affairs, U.S. Department of Justice, to Dan Burton, Chairman, House of Representatives Committee on Government Reform (19 December 2001) ("The Department has a strong confidentiality interest in the extremely sensitive prosecutorial decisionmaking documents called for by the subpoenas").

45. Ibid., at 2.

46. See letter from Dan Burton, Chairman, House of Representatives Committee on Government Reform, to John Ashcroft, Attorney General, U.S. Department of Justice (3 January 2002). ("[I]f you were prepared to advise the President to invoke executive privilege over the . . . documents, there is little likelihood that you would ever permit Congress to receive deliberative memoranda").

47. Letter from Alberto R. Gonzales, Counsel to the President, to Dan Burton, Chairman, House of Representatives Committee on Government Reform (10 January 2002).

48. Ibid.

49. Letter from Dan Burton, Chairman, House of Representatives Committee on Government Reform, to Alberto R. Gonzales, Counsel to the President (11 January 2002).

50. Letter from Dan Burton, Chairman, House of Representatives Committee on Government Reform, to John Ashcroft, Attorney General, U.S. Department of Justice 2 (4 February 2002).

51. Ibid.

52. See *Investigation into Allegations* (*supra* n. 41), at 471 (statement of Henry A. Waxman) ("This administration's effort to operate in secret goes far beyond national security or any other important national interest"); ibid. at 481–82 (statement of Charles E. Grassley) ("I fear that there is a widespread, deliberate policy by agencies to deny or delay giving information to Congress. . . . Getting to the bottom of the . . . scandal and fixing the cause of this injustice far outweighs any need to preserve the deliberate process").

53. Ibid. at 505 (statement of Daniel J. Bryant, Assistant Attorney General, Office of Legislative Affairs, U.S. Department of Justice).

54. See ibid. at 516 (statement of Mark J. Rozell) (providing three examples in which Congress received access to Department of Justice deliberative documents).

55. Ibid. at 504 (statement of Daniel J. Bryant, Assistant Attorney General, Office of Legislative Affairs, U.S. Department of Justice).

CHAPTER 9

George W. Bush and Congress

The Electoral Connection

MICHAEL NELSON

As with any other president, George W. Bush's relationship with Congress has been shaped by a number of political factors. Some of these are as old and enduring as the Constitution. Others are as contemporary and variable as the personal background and temperament of the president. Still others have to do with the character of the party system and the nature of the times in which the president serves.

Bush's relationship with Congress went through three phases during his first two years in office, and entered a fourth phase as a result of the 2002 midterm election. In this chapter, I first consider the factors that influence the relationship between presidents and Congress, then turn to the particular circumstances of President Bush and the 107th Congress. Finally, I assess the results of the midterm election and what they augur for the remainder of Bush's term.

Much has been made, and rightly so, of the consequences for the Bush presidency of the September 11, 2001, terrorist attacks on the World Trade Center in New York City and the Pentagon near Washington as well as of Operation Iraqi Freedom—the war against Iraq that Bush launched on March 19, 2003. Important as these events were, nothing has shaped Bush's relationship with Congress more than the elections of 2000, 2002, and, in prospect, 2004. The connection between the president and Congress has been, first and foremost, an electoral connection.[1]

PRESIDENT AND CONGRESS, 1789–2000

The Constitutional Convention created a government marked less by separation of powers than, in the political scientist Richard Neustadt's apt phrase, by "separated institutions sharing powers."[2] Institutional separation means that in stark contrast to parliamentary governments, which typically draw the leaders of the executive branch from the legislature, the president is forbidden by Article I, section 6, of the Constitution to appoint any sitting member of Congress to the cabinet or White House staff. These severely separated branches, however, are constitutionally enjoined to share in the exercise of virtually all the powers of the national government. Although Congress is empowered to "make all laws," the president reports to it on "the state of the Union," recommends to it "such measures as he shall judge necessary and expedient," and may veto any laws it passes, subject to override by a two thirds vote of both the House of Representatives and the Senate. The Senate may (or may choose not to) give "Advice and Consent" concerning presidential appointments to the executive branch and the judiciary. In matters of war, the president is "Commander in Chief of the Army and Navy" but Congress has the power to "declare war," to "raise and support Armies," and to "provide and maintain a Navy." In matters of peace, no treaty proposed by the president can take effect unless two thirds of the Senate ratifies it.

What would encourage the institutionally separated president and Congress to cooperate in the exercise of these shared powers? Historically, political parties have been the bridge that spanned the executive and legislative branches and helped bind them together, uniting what the Constitution divided. Politically speaking, no president is an island. Each takes office with hundreds of fellow partisans in Congress who share a stake in his political success and thus have a powerful incentive to help rather than hinder him in the pursuit of a legislative agenda.

Parties are most likely to foster cooperation, of course, under circumstances of united government, when the party that controls the presidency also constitutes a majority of the House and Senate. If divided government prevails—that is, if the opposition party controls one or both houses of Congress—then the institutional separation that the Constitution created is buttressed by the party system rather than bridged. Under divided government, the relationship between the branches is not just one of president versus Congress, but of Democratic president versus Republican Congress or Republican president versus Democratic Congress. In recent years, ideology has further reinforced this divide, making the relationship between the branches one of conservative Republican president versus liberal Democratic Congress, or liberal Democratic president versus conservative Republican Congress.[3]

Throughout most of American history, united government has been the norm. When the voters elected a new president, they almost always gave him a Congress controlled by the same party. For example, during the first two thirds of the twentieth century, from 1901 to 1969, united government prevailed for fifty-four years, or 79 percent of the time. For twenty two of those years, Republicans controlled the presidency and Congress; the Democrats controlled both branches for thirty two years. Each of the twelve presidents who took office during this period began his term with a Congress of his own party. The only time voters changed from united to divided government was at midterm when, for example, they sent Democratic president Harry S. Truman a Republican Congress in 1946, or saddled Republican president Dwight D. Eisenhower with a Democratic Congress in 1954.

The elections of 1968 marked a great historical divide, ending the era of united government and ushering in an era of divided government. For the first time since 1848, the voters elected a new president, Republican Richard Nixon, and saddled him with a Congress controlled by the opposition party. From 1969 to 2001, during the third of a century that preceded George W. Bush's election as president, united government prevailed only 19 percent of the time. Most recently, Bill Clinton enjoyed a Democratic Congress during his first two years as president, but in 1994 the voters elected a Republican House and Senate, and in 1996 they reelected both the Democratic president and the Republican Congress.

What accounts for the recent era of divided government? What difference does the presence of united or divided government make in the relationship between the president and Congress?

CAUSES OF DIVIDED GOVERNMENT

Perhaps the obvious explanation for the recent prevalence of divided government is also the accurate one: the voters divide the government because they do not wish to entrust complete control to either major party.[4] Except in 1992, when they elected a president and Congress of the same party, a majority of voters in recent Election Day exit polls have said they hoped divided government would be the outcome. Three reasons seem to account for voters' unwillingness to do what previous generations of voters did as a matter of course.

First, the era of divided government coincides with the era of declining trust in government. In 1964, most Americans gave trusting responses to National Elections Studies (NES) questions such as "How much of the time do you think you can trust the government in Washington to do what is right?" and "Do you think that quite a few of the people running the government are crooked, not very many are, or do you think hardly any of them are crooked?" Since the 1970s, most respondents have answered distrustfully. For example, in response to the question "Would you say that the government is pretty much run by a few big interests looking out for themselves or that it is run for the benefit of all the people?" two thirds answered trustfully in 1964 and two thirds answered distrustfully in 2000.[5]

Second, the political parties have become much more ideologically polarized than the electorate. Around 60 percent of voters locate themselves in one of the middle three positions on the NES's seven-point liberalism-conservatism scale, down only slightly from the 68 percent who did so as recently as the 1970s.[6] The parties, however, especially in Congress, have moved toward the extremes. In the 1960s and 1970s, when the Democratic Party in Congress still included many southern conservatives and the Republican Party had a substantial northeastern liberal wing, neither congressional party strayed too far from the center of the political spectrum or, consequently, from the voters. In recent decades, however, the Democrats have lost most of their southern seats to the Republicans while winning many previously Republican seats in the Northeast. Congressional Republicans have become so conservative and congressional Democrats so liberal that, as Marc Hetherington and Suzanne Globetti point out, by the time of the 105th Congress "only one Democratic [House] member, Ralph Hall of Texas, would have had to switch [parties] for all the Republicans to be more conservative than all the Democrats."[7]

The third reason that voters choose divided government is that they want what the Republican Party has to offer without having to sacrifice what the Democratic Party has to offer. As Gary Jacobson has written, "Most voters continue to desire a balanced budget, low tax rates, low inflation, a less intrusive government, greater economic efficiency, and a strong national defense. At the same time, they dislike paying the necessary price: cuts in middle-class entitlements and other popular domestic spending programs, greater exposure to market forces, and greater environmental risk."[8] Many voters think they can get all of what they want by entrusting the Republicans with control of one branch of government and the Democrats with control of the other.

CONSEQUENCES OF DIVIDED GOVERNMENT

At one time, the consequences of divided government were matters of scholarly dispute. In an influential 1991 study of federal lawmaking from 1946 to 1990, David Mayhew concluded that divided governments are no less likely to enact major legislation than united governments.[9] Since then, however, other political scientists have challenged that finding even for the period Mayhew studied. For example, after taking into account the number of important issues on the legislative agenda in each two-year Congress, Sarah Binder discovered that divided governments were markedly less productive than united governments.[10] Still other scholars have identified other effects of divided government that were important even if legislative output was not.[11]

One of these effects was divided government's dilution of democratic accountability. In the absence of united government, both political parties are able to evade responsibility when things go wrong, each blaming the other and the branch that it controls for whatever makes the voters unhappy about the performance of the federal government. During the 1980s and early 1990s, for example, Republican presidents and Democratic Congresses did little more than point accusatory fingers at each other as the annual federal budget deficit quintupled from less than $60 billion to nearly $300 billion. The voters, not knowing which party to believe, believed neither. Serious deficit reduction came only in 1993, the first year in more than a decade that the same party controlled both the presidency and Congress.

Another important effect of divided government was on the federal judiciary, which became a political football in the partisan battle between presidents and Senates of different parties. From 1900 to 1968, during the era of united government, only three of forty-five (7 percent) Supreme Court nominations were rejected by the Senate. Two of these rejections came in 1968, a year of de facto divided government because the Republicans firmly expected to win control of the presidency but not the Senate in that year's elections. Since 1969 four of seventeen (24 percent) Supreme Court nominations have been rejected, including four of the twelve (33 percent) that were made when the president and Senate were controlled by different parties. In addition, as John Anthony Maltese has shown, the "selling of Supreme Court nominees" has become indistinguishable from overtly (and appropriately) partisan battles about public policy.[12] During the 1990s, an equally partisan approach—rejection by inaction—characterized the Republican Senate's response to many of Clinton's nominations to fill vacancies on the federal district and circuit courts.

In any event, the growing ideological polarization between the parties in Congress removes all doubt that whether the government is divided or united matters a great deal in the current political era. What made Mayhew's finding plausible when he published it was that neither party was homogeneous during the period he studied. The congressional Republican Party included a significant number of liberal northeasterners whom Democratic presidents could draw on to build legislative coalitions. Republican presidents benefited in turn from the many southern conservatives in the congressional Democratic Party. But in recent years, as southern Democratic voters have moved into the Republican Party, the Republican congressional caucus naturally has become more conservative. This in turn has led many northeastern Republican voters to move into the Democratic Party, making that party's congressional caucus more liberal. The willingness of either congressional party to work cooperatively with the president when the government is divided has gone down correspondingly.

GEORGE W. BUSH AND THE 107th CONGRESS

George W. Bush is in many ways a typical president of the era of divided government. Like Richard Nixon, Gerald Ford, Ronald Reagan, and George Bush, he is a Republican. (Of the seven presidents of this era, only Jimmy Carter and Bill Clinton have been Democrats.) Like three of his four most recent predecessors, Bush is a former state governor with no previous experience in Washington. And like all but Reagan in 1980, Bush was elected president without a mandate to make dramatic changes in domestic policy. His margin of victory in 2000 was the least decisive of any successful presidential candidate since 1824. Bush lost the national popular vote to Democratic nominee Al Gore by more than 500,000 votes. His majority in the electoral college was not only controversial, resting on a postelection Supreme Court decision that effectively awarded him Florida's twenty-five votes, but also narrow: 271–267. Far from having coattails in the accompanying congressional elections, Bush saw his party lose one seat in the House and four seats in the Senate, leaving the upper chamber evenly divided between fifty Republicans and fifty Democrats. Exit polls on Election Day 2000 revealed little support for Bush's policies. His main advantage over Gore was the "voters' preference for him as a candidate and leader."[13]

Bush did assume office with two advantages that most of his predecessors in the era of divided government lacked. First, as governor of Texas, he had a history of working cooperatively with a strong legislature controlled by the opposition party. Neither Carter nor Clinton had faced that challenge in their own states: the legislatures they dealt with as governor were weak and Democrat-controlled. The strength of Bush's relationship with the Texas legislature was demonstrated when he was introduced to a prime-time national television audience by Democratic Speaker Pete Laney on the night Gore conceded the election. Bush's second advantage was that at the time he became president, his party enjoyed a nine-seat majority in the House and, because Vice President Richard Cheney was constitutionally empowered to break tie votes in the Senate, a one-seat working majority in that body. These majorities were tiny, but the growing ideological polarization of the parties in Congress meant that Bush could count on almost every Republican member to support his position on almost every important matter.

Offsetting the advantages that Bush enjoyed at the outset of his administration were some particular difficulties that he suffered as he prepared to deal with the 107th Congress, especially the Senate. Senators in the era of divided government increasingly use the filibuster as a matter of course— by one measure, the share of major legislation that encountered an actual or threatened filibuster rose from 12 percent in 1969–70 to 50 percent in 1997–98.[14] What this meant was that on almost any issue that came before the Senate, as few as forty-one senators—enough to keep the body from imposing cloture by the three-fifths majority required to end a debate—could thwart the majority from working its will by preventing a vote from taking place. Not fifty-one votes but sixty would be needed to pass controversial legislation that Bush supported but the Democrats opposed. The same was true of the nominees for judicial and executive positions whose confirmation Bush sought. As noted earlier, senators in the opposition party had become increasingly unwilling to defer to the president's nominations, especially for federal judgeships.

Throughout his first two years as president, Bush's approach to Congress resembled the one he had taken to the Texas legislature: outline his goals in broad terms rather than detailed language, allow Congress to work its will, then claim whatever compromise emerged from the legislative process as a victory.[15] Although Bush pursued this strategy consistently (he seldom issued veto threats and cast no vetoes), circumstances beyond his control caused Congress to respond differently at different times. Indeed, Bush's relationship with the 107th Congress went through four distinct phases: general success, frustration, limited success, and postelection triumph.

PHASE ONE: GENERAL SUCCESS

During the early weeks of his presidency, Bush strove to set the legislative agenda by focusing on several priorities, including reducing taxes, reforming education, fostering energy production, revamping Social Security, and creating an Office of Faith-Based and Community Initiatives that would deepen the involvement of religious organizations in the administration of federal social programs.[16] Although Bush had campaigned in 2000 as "a uniter, not a divider," most of these initiatives were strongly conservative. In pursuing them, he benefited enormously from a Congressional Budget Office (CBO) forecast, issued ten days after he took office, that the federal budget surplus for the next ten years would be $5.6 trillion, including $3.1 trillion that was not dedicated to the Social Security trust fund and thus was available for other purposes.

Bush moved quickly to claim $1.6 trillion of the projected surplus for income tax reductions and the elimination of the estate tax. As a way of preventing Senate Democrats from defeating his proposal with a filibuster, he worked with House Speaker Dennis Hastert of Illinois and Senate Majority Leader Trent Lott of Mississippi to include the tax cuts in the annual congressional budget resolution, which by Senate rules is not subject to filibuster. Bush also campaigned for his tax bill in states he had carried in 2000 where Democratic senators faced reelection in 2002, such as Georgia, South Dakota, and Louisiana. "If you like what you hear today, maybe e-mail some of the good folks of the United States Senate from your state," he told one cheering crowd.[17] On March 8, 2001, the House passed the president's tax bill on a near party-line vote. The Senate reduced the amount of the cuts to $1.35 trillion before passing it on May 23. Bush accepted the Senate version— "I'm a practical man," he said. "I want to get it done"—and signed the bill with great fanfare on June 7.[18]

Bush also made considerable progress on his plan to overhaul public education by requiring annual testing, rewarding successful schools financially and punishing unsuccessful ones, and creating a limited tuition voucher program that would enable students from low-income households to transfer from poorly performing public schools to private schools. From the beginning, the president formed an alliance on education policy with important Democrats, especially Massachusetts Senator Edward M. Kennedy and Representative George Miller of California. As with the tax cut, Bush accepted whatever amendments were needed to secure passage of his bill, abandoning the voucher program and approving substantial new funds for special education.

In the area of appointments, Bush selected a demographically diverse and, with the exception of his conservative nominee for attorney general, former Missouri Senator John Ashcroft, generally uncontroversial cabinet.[19] He seasoned his nominations with familiar and widely admired Washington figures, including Colin Powell as secretary of state, Donald Rumsfeld as secretary of defense, and Democrat Norman Mineta as secretary of transportation. Bush thus avoided the sort of bruising confirmation battles that had caused his father and Clinton such troubles at the start of their administrations.[20] He also waited until May 11, 2001, before sending his first round of federal appeals court nominees to the Senate, a decision that he soon had reason to regret.

PHASE TWO: FRUSTRATION

From the beginning, Republicans had worried that their one-seat majority in the Senate was endangered by the precarious health of two of their most senior members, Strom Thurmond of South Carolina, who was ninety-eight years old, and North Carolina senator Jesse Helms, age seventy-nine. These fears were realized on May 24, 2001, but in an entirely unexpected way. Sen. James Jeffords, a liberal Republican from Vermont, announced that he had become an Independent and would caucus with the Senate Democrats. Jeffords had voted against the president's tax cut, and White House staff members had clumsily sought revenge. They leaked threats that Bush might veto a dairy program that was vital to Vermont farmers and neglected to invite Jeffords to a White House ceremony honoring a teacher from his state. But this was only the proximate cause of Jeffords's decision to defect. He had felt uncomfortable and isolated for some time in his party's increasingly conservative caucus. Jeffords's decision gave the Democrats a fifty-one–forty-nine working majority in the Senate. Sen. Tom Daschle of South Dakota became the new Senate majority leader, thus gaining control of the scheduling of Senate business. Democrats assumed the chairmanships of every Senate committee and subcommittee.

Daschle refocused the Senate's agenda on Democratic issues, such as a "bill of rights" for patients in their dealings with health maintenance organizations (HMOs), energy conservation, and raising the minimum wage. In the face of threatened Republican filibusters, few of these measures passed, and the ones that did had little chance of being enacted by the House. Meanwhile, the disciplined conservative Republican majority in the House remained focused on Bush's agenda. Voting along party lines, the House passed measures such as the president's energy bill, which would have opened parts of Alaska's Arctic National Wildlife Refuge (ANWR) to increased oil and gas production; his fetal protection bill, which proposed to make it a federal crime to harm or kill an unborn child while committing a violent offense against a pregnant woman; and his version of patients' rights legislation. Like the bills that the Democratic Senate was passing, these measures were stymied in the other chamber.

The change in the chairmanship of the Senate Judiciary Committee, from Utah Republican Orrin G. Hatch to Vermont Democrat Patrick Leahy, was an especially important consequence of Jeffords's defection. During Hatch's tenure, President Clinton's nominations for judgeships on the nation's federal appeals courts had often been left to languish. In 1996, for example, the Judiciary Committee set a record of sorts by not confirming a single one of Clinton's appeals court nominees. Hatch and his fellow Senate Republicans looked forward to working closely with Bush on judicial nominations. As noted earlier, however, Bush did not announce his first round of nominees until May 11, just two weeks before Jeffords defected and Leahy became chair of the committee. Leahy kept all but three of Bush's first eleven nominees bottled up in committee for the rest of the year.

In August 2001, Bush received more bad news: a revised CBO forecast reduced the projected budget surpluses almost to nothing. By September 10, the president's job approval rating was 51 percent, the lowest of any elected president in modern history at the eight-month mark of his administration.

PHASE THREE: LIMITED SUCCESS

The September 11, 2001, terrorist attacks on New York and Washington ushered in the third stage of Bush's relationship with the 107th Congress. Virtually overnight, his approval rating shot up 35 percentage points, cresting soon afterward at 90 percent. Presidents typically receive short-terms boosts in public approval as a result of the "rally-round-the-flag" effect, which John E. Mueller has defined as "being associated with an event which (1) is international and (2) involves the United States and particularly the president directly; and it must be (3) specific, dramatic, and sharply focused."[21] When such an event occurs, the public rallies to the president as, in a sense, the anthropomorphic symbol of national unity, a kind of living flag. The rally effect sparked by the September 11 attacks was steeper (Bush's thirty-five-point jump in approval nearly doubled the previous record), higher (his peak of 90 percent was the highest any president has ever achieved), and longer lasting (Bush remained above his pre-September 11 peak for more than a year) than any in recorded history.[22]

Because Bush's surge in popular support was tied to the September 11 attacks, he was able to get his way on nearly all matters relating to national security during the remaining sixteen months of the 107th Congress. Democrats united with Republicans to support the president's September 20, 2001, declaration, which he delivered to a cheering Congress and a prime-time national television audience, of a "war on terror." Bush vowed to target not just the Al Qaeda terrorist network that had launched the attacks and "every [other] terrorist group of global reach," but also "any nation that continues to harbor or support terrorism," especially Iraq.

Administration-sponsored antiterrorism legislation flowed through Congress like water. In September, Congress enacted a resolution authorizing the president to "use all necessary and appropriate force" against those involved in the World Trade Center and Pentagon attacks, as well as against nations "that harbored such organizations or persons"; a $40 billion supplemental appropriations bill to help New York City and the nation recover from and respond to the attacks; and a $15 billion package of loans and guarantees for the airline industry, which was suffering from a September 11-induced loss of business. In October Congress passed the U.S.A. Patriot Act, a sweeping antiterrorism bill that granted broad authority to law enforcement agencies to tap telephones, conduct searches, and monitor Internet communications in their pursuit of suspected terrorists. In November it passed a bill creating a new Transportation Security Administration within the Department of Transportation to administer airport security. A year later, in October 2002, Congress approved the president's request to endorse the use of force in Iraq "as he determines to be necessary and appropriate." The leaders of both congressional parties supported all of these laws and, with the exception of the Iraq resolution, all were passed with strong bipartisan majorities.[23]

The president's high public approval ratings were not fungible, however. Rooted in national security concerns, they did not extend to bipartisan congressional support for his domestic agenda. Indeed, much of the domestic legislation that Bush signed in 2002 involved popular, mostly Democratic initiatives that he and the great majority of Republicans in Congress accepted only grudgingly. These included the McCain-Feingold campaign finance reform act; a bill aimed at curbing corporate fraud; and a six-year, $248 billion increase in federal farm subsidies. Bush's own agenda of welfare reform, energy production, support for faith-based social programs, and a ban on human cloning was endorsed by the Republican House but languished in the Democratic Senate. Two of his nominees for judgeships on the Fifth Circuit Court of Appeals, Charles W. Pickering of Mississippi and Priscilla Owen of Texas, were rejected by the Senate Judiciary Committee on party-line votes.

Bush's June 2002 proposal for a Department of Homeland Security lay at the intersection of national security policy and domestic policy and thus received a mixed response from Congress. The department would absorb twenty-two existing federal agencies, including the Coast Guard, Customs Service, Immigration and Naturalization Service, Federal Emergency Management Agency, and Secret Service. The result would be an organization with 170,000 employees and a $37.5 billion annual budget, making it one of the four largest departments in the executive branch. Loath as Congress usually is to reorganize the bureaucracy on anything approaching this scale, both the House and the Senate quickly demonstrated their willingness to approve the new department as an important part of the president's war on terror. But Senate Democrats balked at a provision to grant managers within the department extensive latitude to hire, transfer, and fire employees. For them, this was a matter not of national security, but of Republican indifference to the concerns of federal employee unions, an important Democratic constituency. The controversy remained unresolved on the eve of the 2002 midterm election.

THE MIDTERM ELECTION

Unlike any of his predecessors, President Bush experienced both united and divided government during his first two years in office. The experience convinced him long before the fall 2002 election campaign began that his best strategy for leading Congress was to increase the number of Republican representatives and senators and decrease the number of congressional Democrats. He threw himself into the midterm election earlier and more energetically than any president in history.

The political challenge that Bush faced as he sought to increase Republican representation in Congress was on the face of it insurmountable, but on closer inspection merely formidable. In the post–World War II era, the president's party had lost an average of twenty-six seats in the House of Representatives in midterm elections. In 2002 the loss of even six seats would give control of the House to the Democrats. Since the Civil War, only two presidents, neither of them Republicans, had seen their party gain seats in the House at midterm.[24] Senate midterm elections have been more variable, but the average loss for the president's party in midterms from 1946 to 1998 was still four seats. Even worse from the Republicans' standpoint, their party was more "exposed" in 2002 than the Democrats: twenty Republican seats were at stake in the election, compared with only fourteen Democratic seats.[25] Because Senators Thurmond, Helms, Phil Gramm of Texas, and Fred Thompson of Tennessee were retiring in 2002, four of the Republican seats—but none occupied by Democrats—were open, and thus more vulnerable to capture by the opposition party than seats defended by incumbents usually are. As for the president's party taking control of the Senate away from the other party in a midterm election, that had not happened since 1882.

Republican optimism revived when they looked more closely at the historical evidence, however. For example, in midterm elections that had taken place when the president's approval rating was above 60 percent, the average loss for his party in the House was not twenty-six seats, but five.[26] Bush's approval rating remained well above 60 percent throughout the entire midterm election year. What's more, the Republicans seemed likely to benefit in 2002 from the reallocation of House seats that occurred after the 2000 census. Bush had carried seven of the eight states that gained additional seats in the House, most of them in the South and West, in the 2000 election. Of the ten mostly northeastern and midwestern states that lost seats, six had been carried by Gore. On the Senate side, seven of the fourteen Democrats running for reelection in 2002 represented states Bush had carried, but only three of the twenty seats the Republicans were defending were in states carried by Gore.

Bush, advised by his chief political aide, Karl Rove, decided well in advance of the election to become actively involved in the campaign for a Republican majority in Congress. The president helped his party in five major ways:

1. *Candidate recruitment.* Bush actively recruited strong Republican challengers to incumbent Democratic senators, even to the point of intervening in state party politics to do so. In Minnesota, Rove and Vice President Cheney heavily pressured Tim Pawlenty to run for governor instead of senator to clear the way for former St. Paul mayor Norm Coleman, whom the president regarded as more electable. (Both Coleman and Pawlenty won.) Bush personally recruited Representative Saxby Chambliss of Georgia to challenge Max Cleland, the state's incumbent Democratic senator, and Representative John Thune of South Dakota to run against incumbent Democrat Tim Johnson. The president also made clear to state Republican activists that he supported Representative John E. Sununu over incumbent Republican Senator Robert Smith in the New Hampshire Senate primary and former Tennessee governor Lamar Alexander over Representative Ed Bryant in that state's Republican primary for senator. He cleared the field for state attorney general John Cornyn in Texas. In every instance, Bush's main concern was to recruit the candidate who had the best chance of winning. In every instance, too, the candidate whom Bush recruited became the Republican nominee. And in every instance but one (Thune lost very narrowly), the Republican nominee was elected.

2. *Fundraising.* During the course of the 2001–2002 election cycle, Bush was the featured attraction at sixty-seven fundraising events that raised a record $141 million in campaign contributions for the Republican Party and its candidates. As vice president, Cheney raised an additional $40 million, also a record. Added together, these $181 million equaled almost exactly the $184 million margin by which the Republican Party outspent the Democratic Party in the 2002 midterm.[27] As part of their effort, Bush and Cheney appeared at early fundraising events designed to help ward off prospective challengers to Republican incumbents. For example, a year before the election, Bush helped Senator Jeff Sessions of Alabama raise so much money that a likely Democratic challenger, Representative Bud Cramer, decided not to run.

3. *Willingness to invest his political capital.* As noted earlier, much of the explanation for Bush's remarkably high approval ratings in the aftermath of September 11 lies in the president's role as chief of state, the living symbol of national unity. To the extent that presidents act in highly visible ways to fulfill their other role as chief of government—that is, as the leader of their party—they forfeit some of their chief of state–based public approval. In particular, political campaigning typically reduces the president's approval rating because it brings his partisanship into sharp relief. Bush's approval rating went down roughly 5 percentage points as a result of his involvement in the 2002 campaign, but he regarded that as a price worth paying in order to help his party. Political capital, in Bush's view, is for spending and investing, not for hoarding. To the extent that he could increase Republican representation in Congress, he calculated, the return on his investment of time and reputation would be a good one. In any event, Bush's pre-election approval rating was still 63 percent, remarkably high for a president at midterm.[28]

4. *Campaigning.* Throughout the fall, Bush campaigned ardently for Republican candidates. For example, in the five days leading up to the election, he traveled ten thousand miles to speak at Republican rallies in seventeen cities in fifteen states. Several of these appearances were in states where the Republican nominee was trailing and where, if the Democrat had won, Bush risked being blamed for the defeat.

5. *Dominating the national agenda.* At Bush's request, Congress spent much of September and early October 2002 debating the resolution authorizing the use of force against Iraq. Media coverage of this debate crowded out the issues that the Democrats were hoping to emphasize during the months leading up to the election, especially the soft economy and corporate malfeasance. Instead, the political focus was on national security, the issue on which voters are consistently most trusting of the Republican Party.

The results of the election vindicated Bush's decision to become actively involved in the campaign. The Republicans gained six seats in the House, doubling their majority in that body, and two seats in the Senate, transforming them from minority to majority status. Political analysts were quick to describe the historic nature of the Republican victory. It marked the first time in more than a century that the president's party had regained control of the Senate in a midterm election. It was the first election since 1934—and the first ever for a Republican president—in which the president's party gained seats in both houses of Congress in a first-term midterm election. At the state level, where Republicans maintained their majority of the nation's governorships, it was the first election in which the president's party made gains in the state legislatures at midterm. Republicans picked up around 200 state legislative seats instead of losing 350, the average loss in midterm elections. For the first time since 1952, Republicans outnumber Democrats in the nation's state legislatures.

Analysts also were quick to credit Bush with his party's success. Twelve of the sixteen Senate candidates for whom he campaigned were victorious, as were all but two of the twenty-three House candidates he supported. An election-eve *CBS News* poll indicated that 50 percent of the voters were basing their decision on their opinion of the president, many more than the 34 percent who had done so in 1990 or the 37 percent who had done so in 1998. Of these 50 percent, 31 percent were pro-Bush and only 19 percent opposed him.[29]

Not surprisingly, Republicans claimed a mandate for the president. Scott Reed, for example, who had been Robert Dole's campaign manager in the 1996 presidential election, said, "I attribute about 85 percent of it to Bush and his polling numbers." Remarkably, some Democrats reached the same conclusion. Democratic consultant Raymond Strother described Bush as "an incredible force. It reminds you of Franklin Roosevelt."[30] Tony Coelho, who was Gore's campaign chairman in 2000, said, "He got his mandate, he got his victory, and now he can govern for two years."[31] Democratic National Committee chair Terry McAuliffe, said, "I pin a lot of it on that this is a president who has had very high approval ratings."[32] The news media generally agreed. *Time* magazine, for example, described "an election that seemed to give George W. Bush a strong mandate to lead the American people."[33]

PHASE FOUR: POSTELECTION TRIUMPH

Some immediate consequences flowed from Bush's victory. The president not only asked for a postelection, "lame duck" session of Congress but, rejecting the advice of Senate Republican Leader Lott not to press for major legislation until the new year, he also insisted that legislators act on some important matters. Senate Democrats quickly capitulated to the president's position on the Department of Homeland Security and passed his version of the bill. Democrats on the Judiciary Committee cleared two of Bush's eleven original appeals court nominees, Dennis W. Shedd and Michael W. McConnell, so that their nominations could be approved on the Senate floor. Congress also enacted the administration-sponsored terrorism insurance bill, which passed on most of the costs of a major terrorist attack from private insurance companies to the federal government.

The Democrats took these actions in response to two of the president's most persistent themes on the campaign trail. One of the standard lines in Bush's stump speech had been, "The way to make sure our judges get approved on a timely basis is to change the leadership in the United States Senate."[34] The president also had regularly assailed Democratic senators for, in his view, placing the interests of federal employee unions above those of homeland security. Many Senate Democrats blamed the defeat of two of their party's incumbents, Jean Carnahan of Missouri and Max Cleland of Georgia, on these issues. The president's supporters "are in a better negotiating position following the elections of last week," said Senator John B. Breaux of Louisiana, explaining why he was changing his vote on homeland security.[35] Breaux was especially fearful that his fellow Louisiana Democrat, Mary Landrieu, might lose a December runoff election if Senate Democrats did not yield on the issue.

BUSH AND THE 108TH CONGRESS:
THE ELECTORAL CONNECTION IN 2004

Bush's postelection political momentum was slowed dramatically by two events. First, Landrieu was reelected despite heavy campaigning by the president for her Republican opponent. The Bush political juggernaut, it seemed, was not as irresistible as it had appeared to be in November. Second, on December 5, Republican Senate Leader Trent Lott told the audience at a one hundredth birthday party for Strom Thurmond that when the South Carolinian had run for president as the nominee of the segregationist States' Rights Party in 1948, Lott's own state of Mississippi had voted for him. "We're proud of it. And if the rest of the country had followed our lead, we wouldn't have had all these problems over all these years, either."[36] Controversy over Lott's remark dominated the nation's political agenda for the next two weeks, culminating on December 20 in his resignation from the Republican leadership. Lott's departure brought about the selection of a Republican Senate leader with whom Bush had a more comfortable relationship, Senator Bill Frist of Tennessee. But it placed the Republicans on the defensive on an issue of particular sensitivity, racial relations.

Although Bush had declined to claim a mandate after the 2002 elections, he made clear that he planned to pursue an ambitious domestic policy agenda, resubmitting nearly all the legislative proposals that the Democratic Senate had stymied during the 107th Congress. The president's agenda included a market-oriented prescription drug plan for seniors, renewal of the 1996 Welfare Reform Act, tort reform to limit damages in medical malpractice lawsuits, an energy plan that would open parts of ANWR to drilling, and a ban on partial-birth abortions. Bush also proposed a new $726 billion tax cut, much of it devoted to eliminating the tax on investment dividends. He revived the judicial nominations of Pickering and Owen, both of whom the Democrat-controlled Senate Judiciary Committee had rejected in 2002. In a bid for Latino support, as well as for a more conservative judiciary, Bush pressed the Senate hard to confirm the appeals court nomination of Miguel Estrada.

Bush also made clear that he would pursue the toppling of Saddam Hussein's government in Iraq during the spring of 2003—through military means if necessary. As far as the administration was concerned, the resolution of support that Congress had passed the previous October was all the authorization he needed to launch an invasion. Politically, he was correct. Responding to public opinion, members of Congress voiced overwhelming and bipartisan support when the president launched Operation Iraqi Freedom on March 19, 2003. In early April, Congress approved his request for approximately $75 billion to fund the war.

Bush was much less successful in pressing his domestic agenda. The House continued to be supportive, but the Senate resisted most of his proposals. Oil drilling in ANWR was voted down by Democrats and a handful of moderate Republicans. A similar coalition voted to reduce Bush's tax cut proposal to $350 billion, although concentrated in a shorter time. Estrada's nomination was filibustered by Senate Democrats, who also threatened to filibuster the Owen and Pickering nominations if they reached the floor. Bush's proposals concerning medical malpractice, welfare reform, and most other matters were pushed to the congressional "back burner."

No single explanation accounts for the 108th Congress's strong support of Bush's war policies and strong resistance to his domestic agenda during the early months of 2003. But the looming 2004 presidential election surely played an important role. Although state governorships, not the U.S. Senate, have been the main spawning ground of successful presidential candidates since the mid-1970s, no fewer than four Democratic senators entered the race for their party's presidential nomination: John Edwards of North Carolina, Bob Graham of Florida, John Kerry of Massachusetts, and Joseph Lieberman of Connecticut. The reason for these candidates' early start was that the Democratic National Committee had approved a rule allowing states to hold their 2004 presidential primaries a month earlier than in the past, making January and February, rather than March, the period in which the nominating contest may well be settled.

The main effect of this change was that the work of the Senate was colored by presidential politics from the very beginning of the 108th Congress. With an eye on the November 2004 match-up with Bush, Senators Edwards, Graham, Kerry, and Lieberman (along with their congressional allies) had every incentive to support the president on matters that the majority of voters supported, such as the war with Iraq. But this stance threatened their standing with Democratic activists and voters, many of whom opposed the war. Since Democratic activists and voters would be choosing the party's nominee, the senators and their supporters were especially concerned to demonstrate their liberal Democratic credentials by ardently opposing Bush's domestic proposals.

What about the third branch of government—especially the Supreme Court? The nine justices serving during the 2002–03 term constituted the oldest Court in history. Although vacancies on the Supreme Court have historically occurred an average of once every two years, at the start of 2003 it had been almost nine years since the last vacancy, the longest period of its kind since 1823. Seven of the nine justices were appointed by a Republican president, and some of them may have been postponing their retirement with hopes that a Republican president and Senate would choose their successors. In all, the chances that Bush will have the opportunity to nominate one or two justices to the Supreme Court during the 108th Congress are unusually high.

Republican control of the Senate also substantially increases the prospect that Bush's nominees will be approved. Historically, 88 percent of Supreme Court nominations have been confirmed when the president's party controlled the Senate, compared with 54 percent in situations of divided government.[37] But Senate Democrats have the power to filibuster, and they may use it if Bush does what he once said he would do—namely, appoint justices in the mold of Antonin Scalia and Clarence Thomas, the two youngest and most conservative members of the current Court.[38] The likelihood of a filibuster would increase if Bush made such a nomination during the election campaign in 2004.

Finally, although the united party government that resulted from the 2002 midterm election conferred considerable advantages on President Bush, it also increased his political risks. With full control of the government comes full responsibility for the government's performance. As one White House official said, "Republicans have the keys to the car."[39] If the voters are satisfied with the federal government's performance on Election Day 2004, Bush will receive full credit. But if they are dissatisfied, it will be impossible for him to deflect responsibility for a weak economy, a dangerously unstable Iraq, or other perceived policy failures onto a Democratic Congress. It is perhaps instructive that the two recent presidents who suffered the worst midterm elections during their first terms, Ronald Reagan and Bill Clinton, went on to resounding victories in their campaigns for reelection.

NOTES

1. I borrow the phrase from David Mayhew, *Congress: The Electoral Connection* (New Haven, Conn.: Yale University Press, 1974).

2. Richard E. Neustadt, *Presidential Power: The Politics of Leadership* (New York: Wiley, 1960), 33.

3. Keith T. Poole and Howard Rosenthal, *Congress: A Political History of Roll Call Voting* (New York: Oxford University Press, 1997).

4. For evidence to support this argument, see Morris P. Fiorina, *Divided Government* (Boston: Allyn & Bacon, 1996), chap. 5. For an argument that the voters do not create divided government intentionally, see John R. Petrocik and Joseph Doherty, "The Road to Divided Government: Paved without Intention," in *Divided Government: Change, Uncertainty, and the Constitutional Order*, ed. Peter F. Galderisi (Lanham, Md.: Rowman & Littlefield, 1996).

5. Marc J. Hetherington and Suzanne Globetti, "The Presidency and Political Trust," in *The Presidency and the Political System*, 7th ed., ed. Michael Nelson (Washington, D.C.: CQ Press, 2002), 261–62.

6. Gary C. Jacobson, *The Politics of Congressional Elections*, 5th ed. (New York: Longman, 2002), 254.

7. Hetherington and Globetti, "The Presidency and Political Trust," 272.

8. Ibid., 259.

9. David R. Mayhew, *Divided We Govern: Party Control, Lawmaking, and Investigations, 1946–1990* (New Haven, Conn.: Yale University Press, 1991).

10. Sarah A. Binder, "The Dynamics of Legislative Gridlock, 1947–1996," *American Political Science Review* 93 (1999), 519–33; and Sarah A. Binder, "Congress, the Executive, and the Production of Public Policy: Divided We Govern?" in *Congress Reconsidered*, 7th ed., ed. Lawrence C. Dodd and Bruce I. Oppenheimer (Washington, D.C.: CQ Press, 2002), 293–314. Other scholars also have cast doubt on Mayhew's conclusion that divided government made little difference for legislative productivity. See, for example, John J. Coleman, "United Government, Divided Government, and Party Responsiveness," *American Political Science Review* 93 (1999), 821–35; and George C. Edwards III, Andrew Barrett, and Jeffrey Peake, "The Legislative Impact of Divided Government," *American Journal of Political Science* 41 (1997), 545–63.

11. See, for example, Michael Nelson, "The Election: Ordinary Politics, Extra-ordinary Outcome," in *The Elections of 2000*, ed. Michael Nelson (Washington, D.C.: CQ Press, 2001), 55–92.

12. John Anthony Maltese, *The Selling of Supreme Court Nominees* (Baltimore, Md.: Johns Hopkins University Press, 1995).

13. Paul J. Quirk and Sean C. Matheson, "The Presidency: The Election and the Prospects for Leadership," in Nelson, *The Elections of 2000*, 178.

14. Barbara Sinclair, "Hostile Partners: The President, Congress, and Lawmak-ing in the Partisan 1990s," in *Polarized Politics: Congress and the President in a Partisan Era* (Washington, D.C.: CQ Press 2000), 145–47.

15. Bush's legislative style as governor is described in Bill Minutaglio, *First Son: George W. Bush and the Bush Family Dynasty* (New York: Times Books, 1999), chap. 15.

16. Roger H. Davidson and Walter J. Oleszek, *Congress and Its Members*, 8th ed. (Washington, D.C.: CQ Press, 2002), 299.

17. "Bush Tax Cuts Clear First Hurdle," *World News Tonight*, American Broad-casting Company (ABC), 8 March 2001.

18. Richard Stevenson and David Rosenbaum, "Bush Fails to Win Over Mod-erate Democrats on Tax Plan," *New York Times*, 26 April 2001.

19. Bush named eight women or minorities to his fourteen-member cabinet, the same number as in Bill Clinton's first cabinet.

20. Davidson and Oleszek, *Congress and Its Members*, 298.

21. John E. Mueller, *War, Presidents, and Public Opinion* (New York: Wiley, 1973), 208.

22. Marc J. Hetherington and Michael Nelson, "Anatomy of a Rally Effect: George W. Bush and the War on Terrorism," *PS: Political Science and Politics*. Vol. 36, No. 1 (2003): 37–42.

23. Senate Democrats supported the Iraq resolution by 29–21. House Democrats opposed it by 81–126. (House and Senate Republicans supported the resolution by 215–6 and 48–1, respectively.)

24. The two presidents were Franklin D. Roosevelt (1934) and Bill Clinton (1998).

25. The concept that a party is at greater risk in an election if more of its seats are exposed to capture by the other party owes to Bruce I. Oppenheimer, James A. Stimson, and Richard W. Waterman, "Interpreting U.S. Congressional Elections: The Exposure Thesis," *Legislative Studies Quarterly* 11 (1986): 227–47.

26. Rhodes Cook, "A Popular President, His Party Benefits," *The Rhodes Cook Letter*, November 2002, 5.

27. Paul R. Abramson, John H. Aldrich, and David W. Rohde, *Change and Con-tinuity in the 2000 and 2002 Elections* (Washington D.C.: CQ Press, 2003).

28. Bush's approval rating returned to 68 percent in the afterglow of the Republican victory. David W. Moore, "Bush's Approval at 68%," retrieved from http://www.gallup.com/poll/releases/pr021115.asp?Version=p.

29. Adam Nagourney and Janet Elder, "In Poll, Americans Say Both Parties Lack Vision," *New York Times*, 3 November 2002. An election-eve Gallup poll reported that 53 percent would be using their vote "in order to send a message that you support [or oppose] George W. Bush." Of these, 35 percent said they would vote to support him and 18 percent said they would vote to express their opposition. In 1998, the last election in which the president's party gained seats, the split was 23 percent to 23 percent among the 46 percent who said they were using their vote to express their

attitude toward President Clinton. David W. Moore and Jeffrey M. Jones, "Late Shift toward Republicans in Congressional Vote," retrieved from www.gallup.com/poll/ releases/pro21104.asp?Version=p—[cited 4 November 2002].

30. Manuel Roig-Franzia and David S. Broder, "Georgia Effort Shows GOP Strengths," *Washington Post*, 7 November 2002.

31. Dana Milbank and Mike Allen, "White House Claims Election Is Broad Mandate," *Washington Post*, 7 November 2002.

32. Dan Balz, "GOP Controls Both Houses," *Washington Post*, 6 November 2002.

33. Karen Tumulty, "The Making of a Comeback," *Time*, 17 November 2002.

34. Dana Milbank, "The Virtual Candidate," *Washington Post*, 2 November 2002.

35. Neil. A Lewis, "Democrats Plan to Allow Confirmation of 2 Judges," *New York Times*, 13 November 2002.

36. Gabe Martinez, "Issue Kept Gaining Momentum," *CQ Weekly Report*, 4 January 2003, 24.

37. Maltese, *Selling of Supreme Court Nominees*, 5.

38. Mike Allen and Charles Lane, "President Set for Confirmation Fight over High Court Nominees," *Washington Post*, 18 January 2003.

39. Dana Milbank and Jonathan Weisman, "White House Maps Ambitious Plans," *Washington Post*, 6 November 2002.

CHAPTER 10

Cheney and Vice Presidential Power

PAUL KENGOR

As Americans everywhere went about their daily lives on the morning of September 11, 2001, so did first-year Vice President Richard B. Cheney. He was behind his desk in the White House, where he had just returned from a trip to Kentucky the previous day. President George W. Bush was in Florida. If crisis struck, Cheney would be the on-site commander at 1600 Pennsylvania Avenue.[1]

A few minutes before 9:00 A.M. the vice president was sitting next to a speechwriter discussing some upcoming speeches. His secretary walked in and announced that a plane had hit one of New York's Twin Towers. Cheney turned on the television and watched a second plane dash into the other tower. His thoughts immediately turned to terrorism. American commercial airplanes flown by suicide bombers had been converted into giant missiles.

Cheney convened a meeting of top staff. As he decided how to react, Secret Service agents burst into the room and grabbed him, literally hoisting him off the ground and whisking him out of the room and into the bunker below the White House. By Cheney's description, the agents moved him "very rapidly" down the hallway. The Secret Service had received a report from the Federal Aviation Administration that an airplane was headed for the White House. The plane was Flight 77 out of Dulles Airport, and indeed it was on a track headed toward the White House. For whatever reason, it turned away, flew in a circle, and ventured toward the Pentagon.

What happened on that day transformed America, a fact Cheney himself was quick to acknowledge. "I think the important thing . . . is for people to understand that things have changed since last Tuesday," he said five days later, on September 16. "The world shifted."[2] Proof of that was the location from which Cheney offered that summation. He was situated in what was only disclosed as "the shadows" of the presidential retreat at Camp David, where he was interviewed by NBC-TV's Tim Russert, who noted that it was the first time that a television program had originated from that spot.

Over the next few months, Cheney's precise location was a mystery outside of the White House. For security reasons, the site of the nation's second-in-command was not disclosed. He and Bush were rarely together, communicating by secure video link. He was oddly absent from the president's historic September 20, 2001, speech to a joint session of Congress, where the vice president is typically seated directly behind the president. His undisclosed location even became a source of much-needed levity for post-September 11 America, when *Saturday Night Live* fingered him armed in a cave in Afghanistan looking for Osama bin Laden. "Sometimes," joked the Cheney character, "if you want a job done right, you have to do it yourself."[3]

There should be little doubt that much in America changed that September day when the towers fell. Like many other aspects of government, Dick Cheney's vice presidency was transformed. Though he was already arguably the most influential vice president in history, the terrorist attacks added a new sense of enormity to the job. The administration's focus would shift to foreign policy and war—exactly Dick Cheney's expertise. This was a war that would go from Kabal to Baghdad.

Put more dramatically, and accurately, what happened on that day dropped the former secretary of defense smack in the middle of another war. This new battle has prominently featured his input, so much so that newspapers on both sides of the Atlantic, including the *New York Times*, have dubbed him "the war minister."[4]

There is one thing we can say of Cheney's vice presidency: from the outset, it has been a serious one and, at times since, a solemn one dealing with grave issues. That solemnity is not completely unusual. Other vice presidents have found themselves enveloped by somber times. Harry S. Truman served under Franklin Delano Roosevelt (FDR) in those trying days of 1944–45, when much of world civilization was at stake. The major difference, however, is that while both Truman and Cheney desired to play a substantive role in events of their times, only Cheney has been afforded that option. Truman's place in history had to await the death of FDR and his own ascendancy to the presidency itself.

This is decidedly not the case for Cheney, a man with apparently no presidential ambitions. He has served as one of Bush's most trusted and influential advisers, particularly in foreign policy. He has been an active vice president. Unlike some past vice presidents, he is not overshadowed by other administration members. To the contrary, as David Sirota, a spokesman for Representative David R. Obey (D-Wisc.), says of Cheney: "He's the heavy in the administration."[5]

In Cheney's case, "vice presidential power" is not an oxymoron. He wields real power and real influence in a difficult time. His ability to play such a role is a direct by-product of his rich policy background from the 1970s to the 1990s. What is that background and how has it translated into Cheney's vice presidential role in the administration of George W. Bush? What are Cheney's duties? What does vice presidential power mean in his case? How does Cheney's vice presidency compare historically? This chapter seeks to answer those questions.[6]

HISTORICAL CONTEXT

Before detailing what Cheney has done, it is important to consider what vice presidents have done historically. I focus here mainly on foreign policy, since that is the realm where modern vice presidents have made impressive strides and because that is the place (along with defense policy) where Cheney has been most involved.[7]

Prior to the post–World War II era, the role of the vice president in foreign policy was essentially nonexistent. That would change under the leadership of President Truman. Harry Truman became FDR's vice president in 1945. FDR kept his vice president completely in the dark on the critical issues facing the country in the 1944–45 period. Roosevelt has been credited by scholars for being remarkably proactive in many areas, but such was not the case when it came to his relationship with his vice president.

FDR died in April 1945. A stunned Truman had big shoes to fill. He must have looked like a deer caught in the headlights—a *clueless* deer in the headlights. FDR had told Truman nothing of his discussions with Winston Churchill and Joseph Stalin, including at Yalta, one of history's most important international conferences. This was especially irresponsible in light of the fact that the Potsdam conference was scheduled for July. Yalta and Potsdam decided not only the course for ending World War II but the literal postwar division of all of Europe. These were not trivial matters. FDR also told Truman nothing about the Manhattan Project and the atomic bomb development. Truman would have been an ideal vice president to be informed of this effort—as a senator he headed the Senate committee with oversight of such clandestine military efforts. Truman's dilemma was captured by General Harry Vaughan, a confidant of Truman who became his chief of staff in the White House:

> [Truman] talked to everybody that had been to Yalta; everybody that had been to Tehran and everybody that had been to Casablanca, to any of those conferences; he talked to Mrs. Roosevelt and even talked to Anna Roosevelt, the President's daughter, because she had accompanied the President. I'm sure she wasn't in any of the conferences but he thought she might have overheard some casual conversation that might give him some pointers. It was a terrific job to try to prepare himself because the Potsdam Conference was scheduled. . . . I can recall meetings at the Potsdam Conference where some item would come up and Mr. Churchill said, "Now, Mr. Roosevelt promised he would do so-and-so." Well, you don't want to doubt Mr. Churchill's word, but Mr. Churchill is a man who is dedicated to . . . the interests of the British Empire. I'm sure he demonstrated that sufficiently. Mr. Joe Stalin would say, "Now the President [Roosevelt] promised that he would. . . . " Everybody within the sound of his voice suspected that it was a lie from start to finish but how could you prove it?[8]

Others have spoken to this difficulty. "I discovered that he actually hadn't been informed of the vast bulk of the foreign policy decisions that were in progress," recalled Ambassador Robert D. Murphy, who accompanied Truman to Potsdam. "Nor did he really know the president's planning for the future. Thus when Mr. Roosevelt died on the eve of the conference, it was extremely difficult for the new president who had nothing to do with it before."[9]

What FDR did—or failed to do—was an act of shocking historical irresponsibility by a president, which, to this day, has not served as the adequate demerit on FDR's record that it deserves to be.

As a result, once Truman became president he saw to it that the vice president would never again be so ill-informed on the major foreign-policy events and decisions facing the nation. Among other things, he made the vice president a statutory member of the National Security Council (NSC), which meant the second-office holder would daily partake in the crucial meetings dealing with the nation's security and foreign policy. Through this change alone, Truman ensured that even if future presidents ignored their understudies and told them nothing, vice presidents would still at least be knowledgeable about key matters facing the United States.

Truman's changes began the evolution of the vice president's role in foreign policy. Other presidents would allow their vice presidents certain tasks that added to the portfolio. President Dwight D. Eisenhower delegated unprecedented tasks to his vice president, Richard M. Nixon, including consequential trips abroad to meet with foreign leaders, particularly Soviet Premier Nikita Khrushchev.

To be sure, not all subsequent presidents were as generous as Eisenhower and Truman. Some vice presidents simply were not of a foreign-policy bent, such as Spiro Agnew and Nelson Rockefeller, and thus were not tapped for noteworthy duties.

Yet, on the other hand, other presidents were generous—and innovative. President Jimmy Carter allowed Vice President Mondale to relocate his office to the West Wing. President Ronald Reagan permitted Vice President George H.W. Bush to chair task forces—an enormous leap forward for vice presidential responsibility—including leadership of the executive branch Anti-terrorism Task Force (later renamed the "Counter-terrorism Task Force"). Presidents George H.W. Bush and Bill Clinton assigned a host of impressive duties to their vice presidents, Dan Quayle and Al Gore, respectively. By the time Quayle was finished, he had been arguably history's most active vice president in foreign policy, especially in Latin America and during the Persian Gulf crisis, to be surpassed only by Gore.[10]

In short, the rise in vice presidential influence and responsibility in foreign policy is a historically new phenomenon, unique to the post–World War II era and particularly salient since 1977, picking up steam with Mondale and continuing upward through Gore. Thus, Cheney arrived naturally poised to ride this wave. The fact that his background made him a perfect fit for foreign-policy duties made it all the more likely that his president would so utilize him. That reality was amplified by the critical fact that Cheney's president, George W. Bush, was, like Clinton before him, a governor prior to the presidency, who brought little to no foreign-policy experience of his own. This meant that Bush, like Clinton, might look to his vice president for help in foreign affairs. He has done just that.

CHENEY'S PRE–VICE PRESIDENTIAL BACKGROUND

In the area of defense and foreign policy in particular, Cheney brings to the vice presidency credentials unseen among previous occupants. He first entered politics in the Nixon administration, before working as a deputy assistant to the president under President Gerald Ford and then as Ford's chief of staff. After serving in the executive branch, Cheney won election to the House of Representatives as a congressman from Wyoming; from there he went on to hold the position of chairman of the Republican Policy Committee and Minority Whip. In Congress, he also served on the House Intelligence Committee. He left Congress in 1989 to serve as secretary of defense under President George H.W. Bush.

Cheney is the first vice president in history who previously served as a secretary of defense. While at the Pentagon, he oversaw an extraordinarily smooth military operation to liberate Kuwait. The administration of George H.W. Bush had cautiously defined very limited objectives in the Gulf war and achieved all of them. (A critical point to keep in mind is that removing Saddam was *not* one of those expressed objectives.) Iraqi troops had been dislodged with an astonishingly low loss of life on the American side (roughly 120 killed in action), amid pre-invasion protests that U.S. losses could number in the thousands, even tens of thousands. So successful was the operation that it created a bizarre post-Vietnam syndrome new to the American public: the novel expectation that American soldiers could go to war with minimal to almost no loss of life.

In part because of the Gulf war, Cheney was widely heralded as an outstanding secretary of defense. Underappreciated is the fact that the Gulf war went so smoothly even while Cheney presided over one of the largest-ever reductions in the U.S. military budget. This slashing of defense was consistent with his assuming the job as the first post–Cold War secretary of defense. His equitable downsizing of the military budget and military bases nationwide won widespread acclaim.

Republican presidential candidate George W. Bush chose Cheney as his running mate in 2000. No one questioned Bush's sincerity when he said he selected his father's secretary of defense not for political reasons, or the opportunity to win a certain demographic, but instead because of Cheney's knowledge and experience. The catchword among the media's talking heads was that Cheney had *gravitas*—a certain respectability and seriousness that George W. Bush seemed to lack. The reaction in foreign media was much the same.

Writing in London's *Sunday Times*, for instance, Andrew Sullivan noted this sentiment when he said that by picking Cheney, the consensus was that

Bush had shown "that he is smart enough to know how dumb he is."[11] A writer in the *Sunday Telegraph* went so far as to insist: "[Cheney] ought to be President rather than his running-mate George W. Bush. The supporting actor outplays the star."[12] While insulting Bush as the "genial son" of a ruling Bush family "monarchy," *The Economist* elevated Cheney, claiming that, "the vice-presidency is being upgraded into a prime ministership."[13]

Much of this Cheney sentiment was intended to cast aspersions on Bush. Nonetheless, it is not a stretch to say that among all incoming vice presidents, Cheney brought with him one of the most impressive lists of credentials in defense and foreign policy. It is in fact difficult to identify a vice president better suited to provide insights in a war against a Middle East foe. He was tailor-made for the challenges the administration would face.

In those first days after hijacked planes crashed in New York, Pennsylvania, and near Washington, D.C., when President Bush looked to put together an international coalition to combat a Middle East threat, Cheney could say he had already been part of such an effort. In both crises, he helped assemble coalitions and was involved at all levels of policy and decision making. But there is even more to Cheney's recent background that could benefit him in dealing with current Middle East issues.

After he left the administration of number "41"—the first George Bush—Cheney worked in the oil and energy industry as cheif executive officer (CEO) for Halliburton, a prominent Texas oil company with corporate offices in the Beltway area. There he stayed before joining the campaign and then administration of number "43"—the second George Bush. During the 2000 campaign, his former job at Halliburton occasionally became a topic of discussion, including in the vice presidential debates.

Republicans generally praised his experience in the "real world" and his knowledge of the important energy sector of the economy. Democrats and some in the media, however, demurred. Questions were raised about the multinational oil company awarding Cheney a $20 million retirement package for less than five years of service. An overly excited British newspaper called Cheney's Halliburton dealings "a deadly business" (because it did business with Burma) and, thereby, compared him to Slobodan Milosevic.[14] Gore spokesman Chris Lehane charged that the Bush-Cheney ticket was the "Big-Oil ticket," and said, "They'll turn the Oval Office into the Oil Office."[15]

After Cheney became vice president, it appeared at one point that the critical view might win out. The Enron scandal rushed corporate corruption to the front pages with a salience unseen in America since perhaps the days of Teddy Roosevelt and the monster trusts. Private-sector management fell under the media gaze, and Cheney did not escape its glare. The events of September 11, 2001, however, changed everything. The Middle East and terrorism were ushered in with a vengeance and knocked the problems of corporate corruption and the bankruptcy of Enron off the front pages.

Cheney's background as secretary of defense during the Gulf war would be an invaluable credit on the résumé of any vice president under such circumstances. Ironically, however, the changed environment made even his private-sector experience in the oil industry a tremendous asset to the administration. His Halliburton experience made him quite knowledgeable about a crucial commodity that influences American foreign policy more than any other, especially as it relates to the Middle East. Of all the private industries he might have worked in, none seemed more relevant to Middle East turmoil than the oil sector.

CHENEY'S ROLE IN THE BUSH ADMINISTRATION

Speaking a decade earlier as secretary of defense, Dick Cheney commented on the nature of the vice presidency: "It's an uncomfortable position to be in. The vice president is there sort of as an overall generalist. . . . He's there as the president's understudy, in a sense."[16] While that is true of most vice presidents, it has not held true for Cheney. His background has made him more of a specialist than a generalist as vice president. He came, one could say, with a niche and Bush seemed to know where and how to deploy him.

Cheney's foreign-policy itinerary is evident in his daily routine. He begins each day at 8:00 A.M. in the Oval Office, where he sits for coffee with the president, the national security adviser, and the director of the Central Intelligence Agency (CIA) for a regular morning intelligence briefing. (On occasion he also heads to CIA headquarters at Langley, where he receives extensive briefings on terrorism.) After that, he meets with his chief of staff and from there, he heads to any number of NSC sessions.[17]

Cheney has been a regular and active participant in all NSC meetings, which usually take place each weekday morning at 10:00 A.M. He sits to the right of Bush. He also attends the so-called Principals Meeting, which takes place at the end of the day, almost every weekday evening. The Principals Meeting includes all top security staff with the exception of the president himself. He also takes part in numerous "pre-meetings," in which he helps coordinate issues to be raised at these other get-togethers. In addition, says Cheney, there are "lots of meetings in-between" all of these.[18]

Cheney has his own private meetings with Bush, and typically interacts with foreign leaders who visit, such as Britain's Tony Blair and Israel's Ariel Sharon. It is not unusual for Cheney to host lunches for leaders, as he did for the emir of Qatar in October 2001. It is a testimony to his background that Cheney can make such arrangements with someone like the emir of Qatar. "He's an old friend," Cheney explains, "and involved in this area [Middle East] and we've got bases in Qatar."[19]

Cheney has continued the recent role of vice presidents as administration spokesmen on key issues.[20] He has spoken on science and technology, freedom and democracy, human rights, environmental issues like the Kyoto Agreement, the federal budget, tax policy, and "economic security," and has even stumped for political candidates. He has delivered a number of speeches on oil and energy matters—an understandable extension of his

Halliburton years. His venues have been as diverse as the INTEL Science Talent Search Awards Gala (March 2001) and a luncheon for Texas Attorney General and U.S. Senate candidate John Cornyn (July 2002). His audiences have ranged from the Conservative Political Action Committee, to the National Association of Manufacturers, to undergraduates at Michigan State University, to Korean War veterans. He provided formal remarks or granted sit-down interviews on fifty-seven separate occasions between mid-February 2001 and late October 2002—a rate of almost three per month.[21]

One of Cheney's key duties as spokesman is to address defense and foreign-policy matters, where he offers an authoritative voice. Prior to September 11, he spoke frequently in support of a national missile-defense system, on the doctrine of deterrence, on the problem of nuclear proliferation and weapons of mass destruction, and a host of other issues.[22] Since then, he has spoken primarily on Bush policies on the war on terror, specifically those regarding Osama bin Laden, the campaign in Afghanistan, and Saddam Hussein's Iraq. After September 11, Cheney gave lengthy interviews to most of the major news shows and outlets, including NBC's *Meet the Press*, the PBS *Newshour*, CBS's *60 Minutes II*, the BBC, ABC's Diane Sawyer, *Fox News Sunday*, ABC's *This Week*, NBC News, CNN's *Late Edition*, and CBS's *Face the Nation*. He has given notable foreign-policy talks before groups like the Council on Foreign Relations, the U.S. Naval Academy, and the Council of the Americas.

THE "SEPTEMBER 11 VICE PRESIDENT"

This brings us back to September 11. Seeing the situation unfolding in New York, Cheney sprung into action at the White House. When the attack began, President Bush was visiting an elementary school in Florida. Cheney immediately assembled top staff, including National Security Assistant Condoleezza Rice, his Chief of Staff, I. Lewis "Scooter" Libby, and his advisor Mary Matalin. At the same time, he got the Counter-terrorism Task Force "up and operating" and instructed the office of Bush's Chief of Staff Andrew Card to get him in contact with Bush as soon as possible. In effect, until that contact was made, Cheney was running the show at the White House.[23]

He and Bush eventually established contact, and they worked together to make a string of crucial decisions. In their first conversation by secure telephone, while Bush was still on the ground in Florida, the two discussed the statement Bush would make later that day and, according to Cheney, "the first statement he made describing this as an act of apparent terrorism flowed from that conversation." Then, before the two finished, Secret Service agents burst into Cheney's office after receiving word that a plane might be headed to the White House. He was lifted out of the room and propelled down the hall with his feet only occasionally touching ground. "They don't ask politely," recalled Cheney, with a smile, in reference to his transporters. He was carried off to the underground facility beneath the White House.[24]

Once in the bunker, Cheney again used a secure phone to reestablish communication with the president. He told Bush, "Delay your return. We don't know what's going on here, but it looks like we've been targeted." In keeping with his constitutional duties, and the few that apply to the vice president, Cheney had concerned himself, first and foremost, with the line of succession. He later explained his thinking:

> My basic role as vice president is to worry about presidential succession. And my job, above all other things, is to be prepared to take over if something happens to the president. But over the years from my time with President Ford, as secretary of defense, on the [House] Intel Committee and so forth, I've been involved in a number of programs that were aimed at ensuring presidential succession. We did a lot of planning during the Cold War . . . with respect to the possibility of a nuclear incident. And one of the key requirements always is to protect the presidency. It's not about George Bush or Dick Cheney. It's about the occupant in the office.[25]

At first Bush took Cheney's advice and spent the day flying in undisclosed patterns to undisclosed military bases in Louisiana and Nebraska before deciding to return to the White House that evening.

Immediately after talking to the president, Cheney ordered the evacuation of Speaker of the House Dennis Hastert, next in line to the presidency behind Cheney, other members of the congressional leadership, and three Cabinet members, also in the line of succession, to secure facilities outside Washington, D.C. At the same time, Cheney refused requests by the Secret Service that he leave the White House. "I didn't want to leave the mode that we'd established there, in terms of having all this capability tied together by communications where we could, in fact, make the decisions and act." "And if I'd have left, gotten on a helicopter and launched out of the White House," Cheney said, "all of that would have been broken down." Cheney, having moved to the Presidential Emergency Operations Center, had National Security Assistant Condoleezza Rice and Secretary of Transportation Norm Mineta at his side, along with video links to Secretary of Defense Donald Rumsfeld, the State Department, the Central Intelligence Agency, and the Justice Department.[26]

From the very beginning, Cheney gathered and evaluated information and advised the president. He had a role in one particularly difficult decision in those earliest minutes, a decision nobody wanted to make. He advised the president to order the Air Force to shoot down any threatening civilian airplane. Bush agreed and gave the order. Cheney revealed those details in an interview with NBC's Tim Russert on September 16:

CHENEY: [T]he toughest decision was this question of whether or not we would intercept incoming commercial aircraft.

RUSSERT: And you decided?

CHENEY: We decided to do it. We'd, in effect, put a flying combat air patrol up over the city; F-16s with an AWACS, which is an airborne radar system, and tanker support so they could stay up a long time. It doesn't do any good to put up a combat air patrol if you don't give them instructions to act, if, in fact, they feel it's appropriate.

RUSSERT: So if the United States government became aware that a hijacked commercial airline was destined for the White House or the Capitol, we would take the plane down?

CHENEY: Yes. The president made the decision on my recommendation. . . . [I]f the plane would not divert, if they wouldn't pay any attention to instructions to move away from the city, as a last resort, our pilots were authorized to take them out.

The decision to shoot down passenger aircraft was probably the most difficult order given on September 11.

One of the most important early statements made by the Bush administration in the immediate aftermath of September 11 was this particular September 16 *Meet the Press* interview between Cheney and Russert. To this day, it was Cheney's highest profile moment since the start of the administration. He was thrust into the limelight, a spot few vice presidents have shared. His interview was watched by millions and received news coverage throughout the world.[27]

In this interview, Cheney became the first administration official to state categorically that the United States would in fact hunt down Osama bin Laden. "It looks as though the responsible organization was a group called Al-Qaida," asserted Cheney, beginning the education process. "It's Arabic for 'The Base.' " He continued: "I have no doubt that he [Bin Laden] and his organization played a significant role in this. . . . What we are going to do is go after Mr. Bin Laden and all of his associates." Asked if there were any international law prohibiting the United States from hunting down and "killing" bin Laden, Cheney replied: "Not in my estimation."[28]

Prior to this interview, President Bush, who had been quite bellicose in his words, had said only that bin Laden was, at that point, a prime suspect. Cheney, in his talk with Russert, was the first to state that the United States would flat-out pursue bin Laden.

Cheney went further. He made clear that the Bush administration was embarking on a major change in U.S. policy by not simply going after terrorists but nations that lend support to terrorists as well:

CHENEY: If you've got a nation out there that has provided a base, training facilities, a sanctuary, as has been true, for example, in this case, probably with Afghanistan, then they have to understand, and others like them around the world have to understand, that if you provide sanctuary to terrorists, you face the full wrath of the United States of America. And that we will, in fact, aggressively go after these nations to make certain that they cease and desist from providing support to these kinds of organizations.

RUSSERT: "Full wrath." That's a very strong statement to the Afghans this morning.

CHENEY: It is, indeed. It is, indeed.

Above all, this was a warning to the Taliban regime in Afghanistan.

Also in this interview were traces of two dominant themes in the Bush response and war on terror in general. The first was the notion that Americans must ready themselves for the long haul in this new war. Cheney stated:

It's also important for people to understand that this is a long-term proposition. It's not like even Desert Storm where we had a buildup for a few months, four days of combat, and it was over with. . . . There's not going to be an end date that we say, "There, it's all over with." It's going to require constant vigilance on our part to avoid problems in the future, but it's also going to require a major effort and, obviously, quite possibly use of military force.

A second dominant theme, carried by Bush especially in the months after September 11, was that Islam was not responsible for the tragedy but, rather, a few radical individuals who had twisted Islam for their political purposes. "This is a perversion, if you will, of some of these religious beliefs by an extremist group," said Cheney in the September 16 interview. "We have extremists associated with . . . every imaginable religion in the world. But this is by no means a war against Islam."

Cheney also emphasized the need for the CIA to once again dig into dirty corners to find the people and intelligence it needs, a method of intelligence gathering that had long fallen into disrepute, especially since the Church hearings held by a suspicious Congress in the 1970s:

We also have to work, though, sort of the dark side, if you will. We've got to spend time in the shadows in the intelligence world. A lot of what needs to be done here will have to be done quietly, without any discussion, using sources and methods that are available to our intelligence agencies, if we're going to be successful. That's the world these folks operate in, and so it's going to be vital for us to use any means at our disposal, basically, to achieve our objective.

This meant that the nation's intelligence agencies would need to deal with some shady characters, and perhaps even criminals, to find the bad guys. Bad guys interact with other bad guys. Cheney was issuing a warning: To be successful, the intelligence community will be forced to rub shoulders with bad guys. When these unpleasant connections are later unveiled and disclosed, they may look unseemly. Americans may feel uncomfortable. But when Americans learn of these encounters, they must understand why they were pursued—to get the bad guys, to get the terrorists. This is what Cheney was trying to convey to the American people.

There was more. In the same interview, Cheney was asked about the possible involvement of Saddam Hussein and what it would mean. He was asked pointedly: "If we determine that Saddam Hussein is also harboring terrorists, and there's a track record there, would we have any reluctance in going after Saddam Hussein?" Cheney replied tersely: "No."[29] It was a harbinger of times to come.

Overall, that Sunday, September 16 appearance on NBC was effective. In fact, he may have done too well. Eric Schmitt of the *New York Times* reported:

> The television appearance the Sunday after the attacks may have left the impression that the vice president was the man in command at the White House. . . . In fact, some prominent Republicans said, the interview with the program's host, Tim Russert, was just a bit too commanding for senior White House aides like Karl Rove and Karen P. Hughes. In allowing Cheney to describe his role, the aides walked a fine line between affirming the vice president's stature and having him overshadow the president.[30]

Much of the acclaim for Cheney came, once again, at Bush's expense, reminding one of the public's reaction when Bush picked Cheney as his running mate in 2000. Yet, this time, the problem vanished as Bush appeared forceful and strong in the days after September 11. Ironically, ever since that dreadful day, Bush faced little question about his stature—a fact not due strictly to a rally-around-the-flag phenomenon but mainly, as Gary Gregg points out in his contribution to this volume, to his performance during that time of crisis. Since then, Bush no longer faces a stature gap when measured next to his vice president. This is a testimony more to Bush's leadership than to any shortcoming on Cheney's part.

As noted, Cheney gave the September 16 interview from Camp David, the presidential retreat in Maryland. When Cheney arrived at Camp David on the Friday after the attacks (September 14), he chaired a meeting of the president's war cabinet—Secretary of State Powell, Secretary of Defense Rumsfeld, National Security Assistant Rice, and himself. Under Cheney's guidance, the group set the agenda for Bush's discussions the next day, deciding how best to respond.[31] In short, Cheney, seasoned in war planning, helped give structure to a new presidency faced with crisis; this is precisely the sort of action that prompted Bush to choose him as vice president. Cheney knew whom the president needed to see and what needed to be discussed.

Cheney assisted the president with more than just structure at Camp David. He recommended that Bush create the mammoth Office of Homeland Security, which would become the largest overhaul of the federal government in decades, and carried with it a fundamental change in defense thinking. America's defense focus would become more domestic-oriented than it had been in many years, arguably since the Civil War. He also advised that Pennsylvania Governor Tom Ridge fill the post as new head of the executive-level office, another suggestion Bush accepted. Cheney also stressed to Bush "the importance of building coalitions," one of the keys to success during the Gulf war.[32] Cheney certainly gave additional recommendations about the pending war on terrorism that the public may never know.

After working with the president at Camp David that weekend, however, Cheney seemed to disappear. Some speculated that he had had another heart attack while others said he had gone on a secret mission to meet with Middle East leaders.[33] Neither theory was true. He spent much of his time at "secure locations" in order to guarantee the line of succession in the event of another attack. Though he was not often at the president's side after the attacks, he remained in constant communication with the president. Besides talking with Bush several times each day, for the first few months after September 11 he participated in NSC meetings by secure video teleconference and a giant screen. According to *Washington Post* reporter Mike Allen, who was surely guilty of hyperbole, Cheney's video image loomed over those sessions "like the omnipotent figure that Cheney had become in Washington legend even when he was there in the flesh."[34]

Aside from advising the president, Cheney also went to work as a diplomat-emissary. This, too, has become a common role for recent vice presidents.[35] Vice presidents carry the stamp of second highest-ranking individual in the U.S. government. They have the president's ear. For these and other reasons, foreign leaders take them seriously, and they can serve as effective diplomats and information collectors.

Cheney has been no exception. In fact, he is an ideal candidate as a diplomat, considering that a decade ago he met many of these same foreign officials and began a personal relationship with them. He already has the respect of many foreign officials.

Shortly after the September 11 attack, Cheney met with the emir of Qatar, Sheik Hamad Bin Khalifa, as well as Eduard Shevardnadze, the president of the nation of Georgia. He also held meetings with the foreign ministers of China and Italy and the Saudi ambassador to discuss their roles in the war on terrorism. Though Secretary of Defense Rumsfeld "loathes traveling abroad," the vice president, harkening back to his role during the Gulf war, insisted Rumsfeld travel to Saudi Arabia, Uzbekistan, Oman, Turkey, and Egypt to work out military logistics and meet defense ministers in the region.[36] Recalling his own actions in 1990–91, Cheney believed Rumsfeld should make these contacts, deeming them necessary to wage a successful war.

Cheney continues to play a key role in the president's anti-terrorism agenda. One could track his impact merely by headlines. "Terrorists Will Face Justice, Cheney Vows," read the headline across the October 19, 2001, *Washington Post*, reporting on the vice president's first visit to Ground Zero, emerging after weeks at an unannounced "undisclosed location." On February 15, 2002, *CBS News*, in its on-line Web site, reported, "Cheney Rattles Saber against Iraq."

At the six-month anniversary of the September 11 attacks, Cheney undertook his first overseas mission, fully seizing his role as a diplomat-emissary abroad. In a ten-day tour that began in London, he visited twelve nations, including eleven Muslim countries. His goal was to marshal support for the war on terror, gauge interest in military action to unseat Saddam, solidify relationships, discuss the issue of weapons of mass destruction, and gather input on the Arab-Israeli conflict and peace process. His role was rightly described in the press as a "diplomatic mission."

By August 2002, reflective of the direction of the administration as a whole, Cheney turned his attention to Iraq, as the Bush team pursued United Nations' support and a global coalition to remove the Iraqi dictator. He was once again a spokesman, making the case for the use of force against Iraq. He returned to the Sunday morning talk-show circuit and gave more speeches and statements.

This continued through the months and then days leading up to the coalition invasion of Iraq. On January 30, 2003, Cheney spoke at the Conservative Political Action Conference in Washington, D.C. He echoed a theme laid out by President Bush two days earlier. The vice president warned, "We will not permit a brutal dictator with ties to terror and a record of reckless aggression to dominate the Middle East and to threaten the United States." His talk that day was described by *The New York Times* as the start of a public relations offensive by the vice president, designed to sell the nation on action against Saddam.[37]

On Sunday, March 16, Cheney returned to Meet the Press with Tim Russert. He remained for the full hour. Russert began the interview by openly informing his viewers: "We know things are very serious when we hear from this man." Cheney fielded tough questions from Russert, such as: How close are we to war? What could Saddam do to stop war? Must Saddam disarm completely and leave the country? Why is it acceptable for the United States to lead a military attack against a nation that arguably has not attacked American soil?[38]

In a nationally televised prime-time speech the next day, President Bush himself provided some of those answers. He told the world that Saddam Hussein had 48 hours to get out of Iraq. Two evenings later, on March 19, the strike on Iraq began with a cruise missile and bunker-buster blast on a Baghdad compound believed to hold Saddam Hussein, his sons, and other high-level Iraqi officials.

Overall, Cheney's role in the war on terror has not gone unnoticed. As noted, some papers have referred to him as "the war minister." Abroad, the London *Daily Telegraph* wrote, "Before the attacks, Gen. Powell appeared to have emerged as the most influential foreign policy figure in Washington. That mantle may now have been taken by Mr. Cheney."[39] In the opinion of *Time*, "He was an authoritative, reassuring leader in a time of national crisis."[40] When *The London Times* asked Cheney if he was chosen for a time like this, Cheney responded, "I wasn't chosen for my sex appeal."[41]

He was not. Bush chose Cheney for substantive reasons. As Bush said often, with sincerity no one doubted, he picked someone to help him govern, not win an election. The fruits of that decision were evident in the ashes of September 11.

CONCLUSION

Cheney's role in the administration of George W. Bush shows how far the vice presidency has come. Vice President Lyndon B. Johnson once recalled that, "every time I came into [President] John Kennedy's presence, I felt like a goddamn raven hovering over his shoulder."[42] Johnson felt it would take the president's death for him to have any meaningful role in the administration. He was right. And yet, once president himself, LBJ similarly slighted his vice president, Hubert H. Humphrey.[43]

Watching Johnson and Humphrey, it looked as though the vice presidency had improved little in two centuries, when the nation's first vice president, John Adams, wrote, "I am Vice President. In this I am nothing." Vice President Adams sarcastically called himself "His Superfluous Excellency." He lamented: "My country has in its wisdom contrived for me the most insignificant office that ever the invention of man contrived or his imagination conceived. . . . I can do neither good nor evil."[44] It was hardly a position of power or influence.

For many years, the extent of vice presidential "power" seemed to extend only to trips abroad, faking tears and laying wreaths at the funerals of foreign dignitaries. That has changed in recent decades, beginning with the Presidency of Truman, then with the vice presidency of Richard Nixon, and picking up again with the substantive vice presidencies of Walter Mondale, George H.W. Bush, Dan Quayle, and Al Gore.

Dick Cheney is a part and even an extension of that more recent tradition. For Cheney, vice presidential power is a substantive, serious power. It is real power; the type Johnson and Humphrey longed for as they languished without impact in their administrations.

Cheney is not a wreath layer; he is a policy player. Indeed, if ever there were a "wartime vice president," Cheney fits the bill. His executive branch experience has been forged by war, war emanating from the Middle East. It began for him as a secretary of defense. It has continued into the vice presidency. By the time Cheney leaves public office for good, he will have played a significant role—perhaps greater than any other single individual[45]—in the two largest U.S. military endeavors of the post–Cold War era. That is a critical reality that has not been appreciated.

Cheney has no reason to complain to staff and reporters about a lack of weighty duties. And he does not. Sparked by events, as well as his own background, abilities, and the president's confidence, in only two years Cheney has become one of history's most active vice presidents, certainly in regard to defense and foreign policy matters. His only concern might be the gravity of his daily tasks in light of the ongoing struggle he and his country now face in the post-September 11 environment. Purely from the standpoint of duty, for an office long accustomed to being marginalized, such a concern is, at long last, a good problem for a vice president to have.

NOTES

1. Cheney described these details in an interview with Tim Russert on 16 September 2001. See also Helen Kennedy and Thomas M. DeFrank, "Prez Gave Shootdown Order," *New York Daily News*, 17 September 2001, p. 10.

2. "The Vice President Appears on *Meet the Press* with Tim Russert," 16 September 2001.

3. On the speculation at the time, see Mike Allen, "Cheney's Vanishing Act Sparks Curiosity," *Washington Post*, 13 October 2001, p. A4; and Earl Lane, "More Than Security Driving Cheney's Low Profile?" *Newsday*, 12 October 2001.

4. See "Dick Cheney: 'The War Minister,' " *The Scotsman*, 19 September 2001, p. 5; and Eric Schmitt, "A Nation Challenged: The Vice President; Out Front or Low Profile, Cheney Keeps Powerful Role," *New York Times*, 7 October 2001, p. A4.

5. Schmitt, "A Nation Challenged: The Vice President; Out Front or Low Profile," p. A4.

6. I would like to thank Matt Divelbiss and Nick Emery for their research assistance in collecting information for this chapter.

7. For an extensive treatment of the material in this section, see Paul Kengor, *Wreath Layer or Policy Player? The Vice President's Role in Foreign Policy* (Lanham, Md.: Lexington Books, 2000).

8. Harry Vaughan, Oral History Interview, Harry S. Truman Library, Independence, Missouri, p. 36, as cited by Marie D. Natoli, "Harry S. Truman and the Contemporary Vice Presidency," *Presidential Studies Quarterly* vol. 28, no. 1, (1988), 82.

9. As quoted in R. Gordon Hoxie, *Command Decision and the Presidency* (New York: Reader's Digest Press, 1977), 337.

10. On the roles of Quayle and Gore, see Paul Kengor, "The Vice President, Secretary of State, and Foreign Policy," *Political Science Quarterly*, 115, no. 2, (2000), 175–200; Paul Kengor, "The Foreign Policy Role of Vice President Al Gore," *Presidential Studies Quarterly* 27, no. 4, (1997), 14–38; and Paul Kengor, "The Role of the Vice President during the Crisis in the Persian Gulf," *Presidential Studies Quarterly* vol. 24, no. 3, (1994), 783–808.

11. Andrew Sullivan, "It's the Cleverest Dumb Show in Town," *London Sunday Times*, 30 July 2000.

12. Nigel Nicolson, "Cheney for President!" *Sunday Telegraph*, 15 October 2000, p. 2.

13. "The Power behind the Throne," *Economist*, 23 December 2000.

14. "A Deadly Business," *Manchester Guardian Weekly*, 9 August 2000, p. 12.

15. Quoted in Martin Kettle, "Cheney Gets Dollars 20m Company Pay-off," *The Guardian*, 14 August 2000, p. 10.

16. David S. Broder and Bob Woodward, "Facing Limitations in an 'Awkward Job,' " *Washington Post*, 8 January 1992, p. A14.

17. Sources: Cheney interview with Jim Lehrer of PBS's *The Newshour with Jim Lehrer*, 12 October 2001; and Schmitt, "A Nation Challenged: The Vice President; Out Front or Low Profile," p. A4.

18. Cheney interview with Jim Lehrer; and Schmitt, "A Nation Challenged: The Vice President; Out Front or Low Profile," p. A4.

19. Cheney interview with Jim Lehrer.

20. On this, see Kengor, *Wreath Layer or Policy Player?* 271–76.

21. This figure is based on my own calculations, with material provided by the Office of the Vice Presidency.

22. As of the writing of this chapter, he appeared forty-four times over fifty-two weeks between September 16, 2001, and October 25, 2002.

23. Cheney has described this situation in interviews with NBC's Tim Russert on September 16, 2001, and PBS's Jim Lehrer on September 9, 2002. The following information is taken from transcripts of those two interviews.

24. Quote from "The Vice President Appears on *Meet the Press* with Tim Russert," p. 11.

25. Cheney interview with Russert, p. 9.

26. Cheney interview with Russert, p. 12.

27. Among others, see Eric Schmitt, "After the Attacks: The Vice President," *New York Times*, 17 September 2001, p. A2; and Vicky Collins, "Cheney Set to 'Work the Dark Side,' " *Herald* (Glasgow), 17 September 2001, p. 2.

28. Cheney interview with Russert, pp. 1–4.

29. Cheney interview with Russert, p. 9.

30. Schmitt, "A Nation Challenged: The Vice President; Out Front or Low Profile," p. A4.

31. Barton Gellman and Mike Allen, "The Week That Redefined the Bush Presidency: President Sets Nation on New Course," *Washington Post*, 23 September 2001.

32. See Schmitt, "A Nation Challenged: The Vice President; Out Front or Low Profile," p. A4; and Susan Page, "Cheney Takes 'Backseat' in a Strong Way," *USA Today*, 16 November 2001, p. 13A.

33. Earl Lane, "The War on Terror: More Than Security Driving Cheney's Low Profile? White House Asserts Role Not Diminished by Public Absence," *Newsday*, 12 October 2001.

34. Mike Allen, "Cheney's Vanishing Act Sparks Curiosity," *Washington Post*, 13 October 2001, p. A4.

35. For more on this, see Kengor, *Wreath Layer or Policy Player?*, 271–76.

36. Schmitt, "A Nation Challenged: The Vice President; Out Front or Low Profile," p. A4; and Page, "Cheney Takes 'Backseat,' " p. 13A.

37. Elisabeth Bumiller and Eric Schmitt, "Cheney, Little Seen by Public, Plays a Visible Role for Bush," *The New York Times*, 31 January 2003.

38. "The Vice President Appears on Meet the Press with Tim Russert," March 16, 2003.

39. Tony Harnden, "The President is the President but Everyone Looks to Cheney," *Daily Telegraph*, 18 September 2001.

40. James Carney and John F. Dickerson, "Where's Dick?" *Time*, 15 October 2001.

41. Roland Watson, "Cheney Stays out of Sight but He Is Still Calling the Shots," *London Times*, 9 October 2001.

42. Quoted in Doris Kearns, *Lyndon Johnson and the American Dream* (New York: Harper and Row, 1976), 164.

43. Among others on the LBJ-Humphrey relationship, see Jules Witcover, *Crapshoot: Rolling the Dice on the Vice Presidency* (New York: Crown Publishers, 1992), p. 197.

44. C. F. Adams, ed., *The Works of John Adams*, 10 vols. (Boston, 1850–1856), 1: 460.

45. The only rival in that respect would be Colin Powell, who was chairman of the Joint Chiefs of Staff during the Gulf war and is currently secretary of state amid the war on terrorism.

CHAPTER 11

On the Edge

The Electoral Career of George W. Bush

ANDREW E. BUSCH

The electoral career of George W. Bush has been marked, above all, by a political environment characterized by an unsettled issue arena and an extremely close partisan division in the country. This translated into a near-death experience for Bush during the 2000 Republican primaries, one of the narrowest presidential election victories in the history of the United States, and, in 2002, a hard-fought congressional campaign in which control of both houses of Congress hinged on the outcome of a handful of competitive races.

The very closeness of the presidential result lent itself to two opposing interpretations which competed for dominance during Bush's first two years in office and which corresponded with rival interpretations of his presidency. One emphasized the picture of Bush the inarticulate, Bush the unambitious, and Bush the shallow—altogether, Bush the accidental. In this view, the Republican nomination of 2000 and the general election versus Al Gore were his to lose, and he nearly did. The other emphasized the picture of Bush the instinctive strategist, Bush the persistent, and Bush the leader. In this interpretation, Bush successfully refashioned his campaign to defeat a strong challenge from John McCain, then found the right message and the right tone to snatch the presidency from Al Gore, who began with most of the fundamental advantages. In the aftermath of the stunning Republican midterm election win of 2002, the debate seemed settled, at least for the time being, in favor of the more generous interpretation of Bush.

THE TEXAS GUBERNATORIAL RACES

After a brief foray into politics as an unsuccessful congressional candidate in 1978, George W. Bush did not reenter the political fray until he ran for governor of Texas in the big Republican year of 1994. Running against a relatively popular incumbent, Ann Richards, Bush was widely assumed to be the underdog. He was also often compared unfavorably with his brother Jeb, who was simultaneously running for governor of Florida against incumbent Lawton Chiles. However, George ran a disciplined campaign, was not rattled when Richards baited him, and won with 53.5 percent of the vote. Jeb, on the other hand, made a crucial mistake in the final days of the campaign and lost narrowly to Chiles.

In the ensuing four years, Governor Bush pushed through a conservative program of tax cuts and education reforms tied to testing and accountability. He also stressed bipartisanship and reached out to constituencies, particularly Hispanics, whom Republicans had long conceded to the Democratic Party. In 1998, an otherwise bad Republican year on the national stage, Bush won an overwhelming reelection landslide, gaining nearly one half of the Hispanic vote and over one quarter of the black vote on a platform of "compassionate conservatism." Indeed, Bush's political record in Texas was one of persistence and a steady growth in popular support. As veteran political correspondent David Broder described it, Bush methodically converted his narrow 1994 win "into a broader and more lasting victory for the Republican Party."[1] By 2000, Texas was a solid Republican state up and down the ballot.

Bush's trademark "compassionate conservatism," focusing on a combination of limited but active government and ethnic inclusion, provoked consternation from right and left. Liberals considered it oxymoronic and conservatives insultingly redundant, but it appealed to Texans and to many Republicans searching for new leadership outside of Washington. The midterm elections of 1998 thus played a critical role in his nomination. House Republicans suffered a five-seat loss, representing the first time since 1934 that a president's party had gained House seats in a midterm year. Speaker Newt Gingrich resigned, and the entire congressional wing of the Republican Party was under a cloud. In the wake of his big win—juxtaposed with Republican losses elsewhere—Bush immediately became the clear frontrunner for the 2000 Republican nomination.[2]

The environment into which his campaign was launched was one of stalemate. For the last six years of the Clinton administration, a Democratic President had butted heads with a Republican Congress, leading to consistent bitterness, two government shutdowns, the impeachment and trial of Bill Clinton, and the inability of either party to move its agenda forward decisively. America was what political analyst Michael Barone called "the 49 percent nation," in which neither party could boast even a simple majority, let alone a breakthrough.[3] In certain respects, this stalemate was traceable to the election of Ronald Reagan, who brought the Republicans to a position of near parity with the Democrats. From the elections of 1960 to 1980, Republicans had held the presidency, House, or Senate for a combined 13 percent of the time and were shut out completely for twelve years; from 1980–2000, they controlled the institutions for a combined 50 percent of the time, and were shut out completely for only two years. Reagan had formed a new coalition and stopped Democrats from expanding the welfare state; Clinton had stopped Republicans from contracting it. Neither side had succeeded in winning the majorities needed to move much beyond the status quo. It was clearly the goal of Bush and his chief strategist, Karl Rove, to achieve not just a victory but a long-term realignment of the electorate.[4]

THE PRESIDENTIAL RACE OF 2000

The 2000 presidential election[5] was framed by several key features. One was the issue of character and the fallout of impeachment for both Republicans and Democrats, including the radioactive status of Bill Clinton among voters in the middle and the perception of hyper-partisanship in Washington. Another was the strength of the economy. A third was the apparent onset of a period of federal budget surpluses, which elicited the obvious question of what to do with them. A fourth was an ongoing assumption, only briefly interrupted in October 2000 by renewed Palestinian violence and the Al Qaeda attack on the U.S.S. *Cole* in Yemen, that foreign policy was and would remain a non-issue. Finally, a series of "micro-issues" like prescription drugs and health maintenance organization (HMO) reform promised to be left over from the outgoing Clinton administration. There were five essential stages to the 2000 campaign, which will be examined in turn. George W. Bush became President of the United States because he won each of the five stages.

The Invisible Primary

The invisible primary is the term used to describe the period before the actual primaries begin during which candidates jockey for support. The importance of this period has been demonstrated by William G. Mayer, who pointed out that the candidate who has started the election year with a lead in two areas—fund-raising and national poll numbers—has won his party's contested nomination eight out of nine times since 1980.[6] Of course, money and poll numbers are indicators of a single factor which is decisive to victory—deep and broad support within the party.

George W. Bush took a commanding lead in both of these areas, and a host of others. In national polls, he led over McCain, his nearest competitor, by up to 50 percentage points in January 2000. He had outraised McCain by $70 million to $15 million, and the other Republican candidates by even more. Bush received the endorsements of 39 of 55 Republican senators, 175 of 227 representatives, 26 governors, and the Republican Governors Association, which had not been so unified and influential since supporting Eisenhower in 1952. McCain had been endorsed by four senators, seven representatives, and no governors.[7] Bush's organizational strength had also been displayed in the Iowa straw poll in August 1999, which he won over Steve Forbes by a three to two margin. And Bush spent most of the invisible primary routinely lionized by the media as a "new kind of Republican" and the presumptive front-runner.

He achieved this front-running status in a variety of ways. First, as mentioned, he was a popular governor of a large state at a time when Republicans were looking for leadership from outside of Congress. Bush also parlayed his family name into fund-raising, endorsements, and national poll numbers. (Indeed, there was some evidence that his high poll ratings in early head-to-head contests with competing Republicans and with Al Gore was partly due to poll respondents confusing him with his father.[8]) At the same time, however, he had to be careful not to identify himself too closely with his father, especially among Republican activists, many of whom believed that George H.W. Bush had squandered the Reagan legacy with his tax increase and other compromises.

Not least, Bush became the front-runner by assuming the posture of a front-runner. Much of his campaign in 1999 consisted of receiving visitors in Austin much in the style of the front-porch campaigns of the 1800s. His campaign largely succeeded in establishing an aura of invincibility around his nomination, an aura that contributed to his advantages as much as it was derived from them.

Consequently, by the end of 1999, more than half of the putative Republican presidential candidates—seven out of thirteen—had dropped out of the race without a real vote ever having been cast. These dropouts included such big names as Dan Quayle, Elizabeth Dole, Lamar Alexander, and John Ashcroft, as well as Pat Buchanan (who left to run for the Reform Party nomination), John Kasich (former chairman of the House Budget Committee), and Senator Bob Smith of New Hampshire.

The Primaries and Caucuses

While Bush won the invisible primary and headed into the primary season with a sizable lead, by early 2000 John McCain had established himself—in finance, in the polls, and in the press—as his main challenger, and had even opened up a lead in New Hampshire. When McCain not only won New Hampshire but blew out Bush by 18 percentage points, the race entered a five-week phase during which it seemed possible that Bush would lose it all, despite his advantages. He struggled to come back with a win in South Carolina, savored his success for three days, and then lost Arizona (predictably) and Michigan (not so predictably). He turned the tide again in Virginia and Washington at the end of February, then delivered the *coup de grace* with wins in New York, California, Ohio, and nine of fourteen states overall on "titanic Tuesday," March 7. McCain withdrew from the race on March 9.

McCain's stronger-than-expected challenge to Bush and Bill Bradley's parallel weaker-than-expected challenge to Al Gore were both the result of the third, unofficial primary contest of 2000: the interparty competition between McCain and Bradley to see which one would carry the standard of "reform." This competition was very real, as thousands of Independent and potential crossover votes were at stake in open primary states. John McCain won that contest to be the "reform" candidate, and reaped enormous numbers of Independent and Democratic crossover votes in states like New Hampshire and Michigan.[9]

This set up a challenge for Bush. The front-runner had to simultaneously dent McCain's advantage as the "reform" candidate and reap more fully the benefits of being the candidate of Republican regularity. In New Hampshire, McCain had not only won big with Independents, but had run neck-and-neck with Bush among Republicans. In South Carolina, Bush retooled his message and his tactics. Without contradicting any of his previous stands, Bush emphasized the "conservative" half of the "compassionate conservatism" formula and adopted a new theme: "A reformer with results," pointing to his accomplishments on education reform, tort reform, and other such issues. The once-aloof front-runner also became a more engaged candidate, using town hall formats with audience interaction. While he came under criticism by some commentators for swinging too far to the right, the formula worked. By primary day in South Carolina, more voters rated Bush a "reformer" than McCain. Perhaps more importantly, Bush won solidly among Republican voters by forging an alliance between the "very conservative" and "somewhat conservative" voters that had eluded him in New Hampshire.[10] Despite the ups and downs of the race, from that moment forward McCain was never able to dislodge the right and center-right coalition which had united behind Bush.

An important moment in this development was hardly noticed by the media in the wake of McCain's New Hampshire triumph. Bush's otherwise disastrous showing obscured an important victory won by Bush against conservative publisher Steve Forbes. Knocking Forbes out of the race, thus ending the threat of a "two-front war," had long been a central strategic objective of the Bush campaign. Success cleared the way for the consolidation of the conservatives behind Bush that ultimately proved decisive.

A final crucial factor—one which had first appeared in Texas in 1994— was that Bush appeared to wear well with voters over time. While McCain seemed more exciting, he was also testy and mercurial, and Bush's temperament compared favorably. A focus group assembled by Republican pollster Frank Luntz for *U.S. News and World Report* and MSNBC reported that they liked Bush better the more they saw him.[11]

The Interregnum

When both parties' nomination races effectively ended on March 7, Bush was clinging to a bare lead against Gore. It is clear that Bush did a much better job of utilizing the four-month preconvention "interregnum" than did Gore. After the election, Bush and Gore advisors agreed that this period was crucial to the final outcome.[12]

Bush gradually rebuilt his lead as he came forward with innovative proposals on missile defense, Social Security, and other major issues. Gore was forced into reactive mode, often reduced to decrying the "riskiness" of the

Texan's latest "scheme." Indeed, Gore was unable to settle on a strategy, shifting his approach among at least four distinct "faces." In succession, the vice president became "Gore the Reformer," "Gore the Attacker," "Gore the Affirmer," and "Gore the Populist."[13] Bush's relative constancy was beneficial to him not only by strengthening the force of his argument, but also by demonstrating an important difference between him and Al Gore: Bush seemed to know who he was and what he wanted.

The General Election Campaign

When Bush came out of the Republican national convention, he led Gore by 17 percentage points in the Gallup polls. When Gore came out of his convention a few weeks later, he had pulled even, and within another two weeks had moved into a modest lead. The vice president's surge resulted from a variety of factors, including his vice presidential selection (Joseph Lieberman), a strong convention speech touting the theme of "the people versus the powerful," and a much-remarked-upon kiss planted on his wife Tipper as the speech ended, which served the dual purpose of humanizing Gore and emphasizing that he was not Bill Clinton. For his part, Bush stumbled several times. Consequently, for most of September, Bush trailed Gore after having led in every head-to-head poll for the previous two years. Media pundits began circling, and anonymous Republican Party operatives questioned whether Bush could reverse his fortunes. Political scientists added their voices to the chorus; at the American Political Science Association convention, seven mathematical models unanimously predicted a Gore win with anywhere from 54 to 60 percent of the vote.[14]

Bush turned the tide beginning in late September when he put forward the argument that while Gore trusted government, he trusted the people on issues from Social Security to Medicare to education to tax cuts. This thrust proved ingenious. First, it used the issue of trust, on which Gore was already vulnerable, in an effective but subtle way ("Why trust him if he won't trust you?"). Second, it established a theme out of otherwise disparate issues, providing greater coherence to the Bush candidacy. Third, it refocused attention away from particular programs, where Gore seemed to have an advantage, toward the philosophical question of big government versus limited government, where Bush could more than hold his own.

Having established the foundation for a comeback, Bush moved ahead of Gore on the strength of the presidential debates. In the first debate, Gore made a number of exaggerations that were quickly pounced on by the media. He also appeared unpresidential to many viewers—too aggressive and too condescending. In the second debate, Gore overcompensated, appearing altogether too agreeable. In the third, he found a better balance, but still hurt himself by presenting three distinct Al Gores to the nation in three debates. Bush used the debates to demonstrate that he had the steadiness to govern; Gore's missteps persuaded many Americans that he did not.

Thus the campaign entered a period of stasis, with Bush leading by about five points. Rove predicted 320 electoral votes. The final weekend, however, caught the Bush camp by surprise. While the Texan seemed to wind down, Gore ran a high-octane last-minute campaign. He and Lieberman ratcheted up their rhetoric to new levels of intensity in a successful drive to maximize the turnout of the Democratic base. At the same time, revelations of a 1976 Bush "driving under the influence" (DUI) citation put the Republican on the defensive, as did a verbal slip-up when Bush implied that Social Security was not a federal program.[15] Altogether, a late surge of support for Gore carried the vice president into what amounted to an Election Day tie with George W. Bush. One half of a percentage point separated them in the nationally aggregated popular vote—with Gore in the lead—and the decisive electoral college vote hung in the balance, with only hundreds of votes dividing them in Florida.

A slight shift in either direction would have produced a decisive outcome. Bush narrowly lost states like Wisconsin, Iowa, Oregon, and New Mexico that his campaign had counted in his column; even his losses in megastates like Pennsylvania and Michigan were relatively close (both decided by 51 percent to 46 percent). Had Gore only won his own home state (Tennessee) or Bill Clinton's (Arkansas), Florida would not have mattered.

In the end, neither Bush nor Gore succeeded in seriously penetrating each other's bases: 86 percent of Democrats and 91 percent of Republicans voted for their party's nominee. Despite considerable Republican efforts to lure black voters, Gore also won 90 percent of the black vote. The final vote count was evidence of the close partisan division of the nation and the striking regional concentrations that undergirded that division. Gore won every Pacific state but Alaska, every New England state but New Hampshire, and every state in the industrial upper Midwest. Bush won every Southern state, every state of the prairie Midwest, and every Rocky Mountain state but New Mexico, which he lost by fewer than 500 votes. Gore could have flown from Dulles Airport to San Francisco without ever crossing a state he won until reaching the border of California. All in all, Bush won thirty of fifty states and about 78 percent of the counties in the United States, while Gore won the urban centers. Bush's philosophical conservatism and Gore's operational liberalism balanced each other out, as did Bush's temperament and Gore's experience, Clinton's (apparent) economy and Clinton's morals. Bush had been the tortoise, Gore the hare, with the verdict not yet rendered.

The national pattern evidenced in the presidential race—very close partisan division, striking regional and urban versus rural dichotomies—appeared at the congressional level as well. Democratic strength in the urban centers helped Democrats pick up four seats to gain a 50-50 split in the Senate, but since that strength was so locally concentrated, it was not translated into significant House gains (only a net Democratic pickup of four, not enough to regain House control). Bush had no national coattails, a performance consistent with a norm going back three decades, during which time only Ronald Reagan in 1980 had significant congressional coattails.

The Postelection Campaign

Two broad points about George Bush in this intense roller-coaster period merit elaboration. First, Bush was more relaxed, more comfortable with himself, and less driven than was Gore. This may have been in part because he knew that he held many of the high cards in the game, but something else was also probably at work. Gore, for both political and psychological reasons, had to win. Bush, less ambitious than Gore and with the governorship of Texas to fall back on, did not. In the words of Gore, "I'm not like George Bush. If he wins or loses, life goes on. I'll do anything to win."[16] As the postelection campaign proceeded, it became clear that Bush had instinctively adopted the right tone for the situation. By early December, 56 percent of Americans had a positive view of Bush to only 40 percent negative, while Gore was seen negatively by a 52 percent to 46 percent margin.[17]

Second, the circumstances of Bush's ultimate victory clearly put him in a more difficult position as he took office. Despite the controversy, most Americans—83 percent in Gallup polls, including 68 percent of Gore voters—stated a willingness to accept Bush as the legitimate president.[18] Some questions were also resolved over the next year, as numerous media organizations conducted their own recounts of the Florida ballots which almost uniformly confirmed Bush as the winner.[19] Nevertheless, the cloud hanging over Bush was one that could only be fully lifted by another election. This made the midterm elections all the more important.

MIDTERM ELECTIONS OF 2002–02

The electoral environment in America was radically transformed as a result of the terrorist attacks of September 11, 2001, and the Bush administration's response to those attacks. Two effects were obvious, and two more loomed in the background, difficult to quantify but impossible to ignore. First, national security issues were vaulted to the top of the list of Americans' concerns and also underwent an important qualitative change: national security became a matter of personal security.[20] Second, Bush's stature increased considerably, and with it his approval ratings, which started the crisis at about 90 percent and held steady in the mid-60s for most of 2002. Third, less obviously, the attacks placed a premium on stability and made Americans less likely to seek drastic change at the ballot box.[21] Finally, the terrorist attacks activated a diffused but potentially decisive set of interlocking attitudes among Americans. Patriotism was strengthened considerably, there was some revival of religious sentiment, and Americans grew more hardheaded about a variety of ancillary issues ranging from gun control (arming pilots) to racial profiling (of potential terrorists) to missile defense. This subterranean attitudinal shift did not bode well for liberals.

While the midterm elections of 2002 loomed largest on the horizon, there were a handful of key races in November 2001. Democrats took over governorships in New Jersey and Virginia, and lost the New York mayoral election to replace Rudolph Giuliani. However, the political season was almost completely overshadowed by the aftermath of September 11 and the ongoing war in Afghanistan. George Bush himself resisted calls to campaign for the Republican gubernatorial candidate in Virginia, whose narrow loss might have been averted by presidential assistance. By 2002, Bush no longer felt constrained from campaigning.

As Republicans prepared for the midterm elections of 2002, they were faced with a decidedly complicated picture. On one hand, the midterm election pattern has been one of the most firmly established features of American electoral politics. In the twenty-seven midterm elections from 1894 through 1998, the president's party had suffered net seat losses twenty-five times in the House and eighteen times in the Senate. This pattern has endured even with popular wartime presidents: Franklin D. Roosevelt's Democrats lost fifty-five House and nine Senate seats in the World War II midterm election of 1942. Given that Democrats could control the House with a net gain of only six seats and already controlled the Senate, the historical prognosis was disturbing for Republicans. On the other hand, there were several reasons for Bush to hope that his party might hold its own in 2002. To understand why, one must sort through the explanations that political scientists have offered for the midterm pattern.

Coattails

In the presidential year, the winning candidate's party gains seats in Congress as a result of the "coattails" effect. In the midterm years, that help at the top of the ticket is removed and the weakest winners from two years before lose their congressional races. However, Bush had no national coattails in 2000, as Republicans lost four House seats.

Surge and Decline

The typical decline in midterm voter turnout comes disproportionately at the expense of weak partisans or Independents who were stirred to vote for the winning presidential candidate (and his congressional copartisans) but who lose interest in the lower-profile midterm year.[22] However, Gore obtained more popular votes nationally than Bush, and attained his small plurality on the basis of last-minute decisions by undecided and marginal voters—exactly the sort of voters the surge-and-decline model would expect to drop out of the electorate in the next midterm election.

Exposure

The more seats the president's party holds, either absolutely or relative to a past average, the more seats it is likely to lose in the next midterm election.[23]

Yet the congressional parties were very close to even in both chambers and neither was far from the baseline of rough equilibrium established in 1994, so it was difficult to argue that Republicans were exposed in 2002. Indeed, Republicans had lost House seats in the previous three elections, leaving fewer vulnerable seats; not since the realignment of 1930–36 had any party lost congressional seats in four consecutive elections.

National Conditions (or "Referendum")

Key indicators of national political conditions, most notably measures of economic well-being and/or presidential popularity, determine midterm election results. This can happen either directly, through voter calculation, or indirectly, through the strategic calculations of potential candidates, parties, and contributors.[24] The worse the national conditions in the year of the midterm election, the bigger one can expect the presidential party's losses to be. From the standpoint of early 2002, the national conditions model militated against large Democratic gains, as presidential approval ratings remained stratospheric by historical standards. Even at election time, Bush's approval rating was higher than 60 percent (the midterm average is below 50 percent). The economic picture was mixed, and the big question of 2002 was how voters would perceive it, what priority they would place on it, and who they would blame for the problems. There were many signs of trouble, including a continued decline in the stock market, increased unemployment, and an abrupt return of the federal budget deficit. At the same time, however, the economy was growing at 3 percent a year, income was growing at 2 percent a year, and the pre-election unemployment rate stood at 5.7 percent, lower than the average in Bill Clinton's first term (6.0 percent). In November 2002, 55 percent of Americans approved of Bush's handling of the economy.[25]

Presidential Penalty

Voters seek to punish the president's party simply because they want to hurt the president.[26] This desire may be driven by an attempt to balance the government, or simply because negative appraisals are a more powerful motive than positive appraisals.[27] This presidential penalty effect, which might have been given greater force by the anger of Democratic partisans over the outcome of the 2000 election, was mitigated by post September 11 bipartisanship.

Partisan strategists, who are generally not thoroughly versed in arcane political science theories, tended to focus on the economic and presidential approval factors, as well as a few additional facts. First, the new focus on national security was assumed to work to the benefit of the Republicans. Indeed, Karl Rove stepped into some controversy early in the election season when he advised Republican candidates to "run on the war." Second, the potential for large House gains for either party was limited by the relative lack of competitive seats. Most analysts put the number at thirty to fifty

House districts that were really in play, in comparison to approximately 150 a decade before. Third, analysts believed that Republicans would net a gain of three to six seats due to the post-2000 redistricting alone. In the Senate, while twenty of the thirty-four seats up for election were held by the GOP, Republicans identified several relatively vulnerable Democratic incumbents facing reelection in states Bush won handily in 2000, giving them hope of regaining control of the Senate.

This situation set up the paradox of a highly competitive national environment which pivoted around only a handful of competitive seats. The battle for those seats was largely carried out locally and hinged on the particular strengths and weaknesses of the candidates and their campaigns. Nevertheless, Bush played a central role in the midterm election campaign. Agreeing to an aggressive campaign plan, Bush made a decision to put his prestige on the line by heavily engaging on behalf of Republican candidates. This was a choice made by few presidents, and made to work by fewer still. The potential benefits were enormous, but the risks were great.

1. As early as mid-2001, Bush, working with Rove and national Republican leaders, began personally recruiting strong candidates and clearing the primary fields for key challenges and open seats. These candidates included Elizabeth Dole in North Carolina, Norm Coleman in Minnesota, Saxby Chambliss in Georgia, and John Thune in South Dakota.[28]

2. Bush was an active and massively successful fundraiser for Republican candidates and the Republican Party. He was featured in 70 different Republican fundraisers—an average of one every four days—and raised $140–$150 million. This figure far outpaced the previous record for presidential fundraising set by Bill Clinton, who pulled in $50 million in his first midterm year of 1994 and $105 million in 2000. This meant that the Republican National Committee had $30 million on hand at the beginning of October to only $5 million for the Democrats.[29]

3. Bush translated his popularity into votes for Republican candidates, both by mobilizing the Republican base and by swaying some percentage of undecided voters in close races. After concluding his fundraising efforts in late October, he continued visiting states with crucial House and Senate races such as those in Colorado, Georgia, Minnesota, Missouri, and North Carolina. Altogether, Bush made ninety campaign visits to key congressional races.[30] In the last five days of the campaign, he traveled ten thousand miles on a fifteen-state, seventeen-city blitz, easily the most extensive and intense campaigning by a president for his party in recent memory.[31] One Bush rally in Georgia three days before the election produced five hundred volunteers who proceeded to knock on thirty thousand doors.[32]

4. Bush governed with the upcoming elections in mind. For example, early in 2002, Bush announced higher steel tariffs. This position was inconsistent with his general free-trade principles but gave an edge to Republican candidates in key steel states like West Virginia, Pennsylvania, and Ohio. Similarly, when Bush signed the bloated $180 billion multiyear farm bill, it was apparent that he did not want to saddle Republicans in important farm state races with the burden of defending a presidential veto. As corporate corruption came to the fore in the summer of 2002, Bush signed on to the Senate reform measure, which then passed ninety-seven to zero. Republicans thus gained a large measure of inoculation against Democratic attempts to link them to the scandals. In late summer the president convened an economic summit, presenting a stark contrast with his father's apparent inaction on the economic front in 1991–92. Some observers also accused Bush of devising policy to aid his brother's reelection prospects in Florida.[33] (Bush, however, passed up the opportunity to turn the congressional debate over the economic stimulus package and renewal of welfare reform to partisan advantage.)

More importantly, Bush adeptly capitalized on his party's natural edge on national security issues. As the bill to create a Homeland Security department stalled in the Democratic-controlled Senate, Bush turned up the heat. At one point, while campaigning for New Jersey Republican Senate candidate Douglas Forrester, he accused the Senate of putting special interests ahead of national security, a charge which led Senate Majority Leader Tom Daschle to demand a presidential apology. This issue became intertwined with debate over the prospect of war in Iraq; indeed, Daschle, by accident or design, treated Bush's comments as if they were directed at the pending Iraq resolution rather than the Homeland Security bill. Bush came under a great deal of criticism, open from protestors and veiled from congressional Democrats, that he was manipulating the Iraq situation for purely electoral purposes. However, there were many reasons to believe such a charge was spurious. For one thing, Bush acceded to a congressional debate only after being pressured by Democrats and some Republicans to allow one. It was the Democrats who preferred that the debate come earlier rather than later, in hopes that it would allow them to put national security issues behind them well before Election Day. The timing was also influenced by U.S. war planners, who reportedly preferred to initiate war in January or February and needed congressional authorization to come in the previous fall to allow for the requisite buildup of forces. To whatever degree the Iraq resolution and the midterm elections were connected, the connection was mostly the reverse of what critics feared: rather than using the resolution to affect the elections, the Bush administration used the elections as leverage to gain support for the resolution.[34]

For their part, Democrats found themselves boxed in and outmaneuvered by Bush in three crucial areas, including Iraq. There, they could neither uniformly oppose the president for fear of appearing weak on security, nor embrace him whole-heartedly for fear of alienating their base on the left. Consequently, the Democratic leadership dithered but signed on at the end;

a majority of Senate Democrats supported the Iraq resolution, while a majority of House Democrats (mostly from safe seats) opposed it. Just as Democratic leaders seemed to be signaling accommodation with the administration's tough stand, an ill-advised trip to Baghdad by three House Democrats revived the ghosts of McGovernism and Jane Fonda cavorting in Hanoi. On the economy, the origin of the slowdown in the final months of the Clinton administration and the obstruction of Senate Democrats mitigated the party's appeal. On the Bush administration's signature economic policy—the tax cut of 2001—Democrats again sounded an uncertain trumpet. While most opposed it, few were willing to call for its repeal, an act of political (and probably economic) foolhardiness in a slow economy. Finally, while Democrats counted on the corporate corruption issue, it simply did not stick. Bush led Republicans in embracing reform, and Democrats were saddled with a tarnished image of their own, including ties to Global Crossing and the shady financial record of their own national chairman, Terry McAuliffe. While House Minority Leader Richard Gephardt declared in July that Democrats could gain thirty to forty seats in the House on the strength of corporate corruption, it was obvious by late September that no such thing was going to happen.

Democrats also found it rough-going on other traditional staples like health care, education, and even Social Security. Passage by House Republicans of a prescription drug program and HMO reform largely neutralized those issues. Congressional enactment of Bush's education plan in 2001 erased the Democratic edge there. And Social Security, which wound up becoming the centerpiece of many Democratic campaigns around the country, did not cut as deeply as Democrats had hoped, partly due to aggressive Republican efforts to redefine themselves as favoring "personal accounts" rather than "privatization." On these issues, prodded by Bush, Republicans seized both the political center and the mantle of action.

5. Bush became a magnet which exerted his unseen force on Republicans and Democrats alike. Republican campaigns around the country sought to emulate the White House's Hispanic outreach program, contesting seriously for that bloc of voters.[35] Likewise, a number of Republican congressional candidates adopted Bush's "compassionate conservative" theme. While Bush has not yet established himself as the philosophical leader of the Republican Party in the way Ronald Reagan did, he clearly was well on his way. "Bushism" was not yet as well-defined as "Reaganism," and did not define Republicans as thoroughly, but the outlines were emerging, and many Republican candidates signed on. At the same time, many Democrats in close races around the country became, at least for the moment, "Bush Democrats." In Montana, Georgia, Texas, Iowa, Louisiana, and Missouri, Democratic Senate candidates ran television ads touting their cooperation with Bush. As one conservative analyst argued, "In this year's competitive races, Bush Democrats are far more plentiful than Daschle Democrats."[36]

As the race drew to a close, Democrats were left with little but an appeal for divided government. Tacitly conceding they were not going to regain the House, liberal groups like People for the American Way began running ads in key Senate races arguing for a vote against Republicans to prevent domination of government by "the far right." In some ways, this was a plausible strategy, as a plurality (46 percent) of Americans indicated a preference for divided government.[37] It nevertheless lacked substantive content. It may also have inflamed Republican voters, who were reminded of the obstruction of Senate Democrats against Bush's legislative priorities and judicial appointments (itself a potent issue in some states). It also collided directly with the efforts by many Democrats mentioned earlier to tie themselves to Bush's popularity.

In the end, Republicans gained two seats in the Senate and six in the House. Almost every close race broke the Republicans' way, except for South Dakota, where incumbent Democrat Tim Johnson held off John Thune by a mere 527 votes. Democrats looked to the states for some consolation; they gained four governorships, but it was fewer than expected and still left a majority of governorships in Republican hands. Jeb Bush, gubernatorial target number one of national Democrats, won by 13 percentage points, and Republicans won governorships in Democratic strongholds like Massachusetts, Vermont, Maryland, and Hawaii. Republicans also made a net gain of about 225 state legislative seats, compared to an average midterm loss of 350—putting them into the national lead for the first time since 1952—and went from an eighteen to seventeen deficit in legislative chambers to a twenty-one to sixteen lead.[38] It was both a narrow victory and a victory of historic magnitude: the first time a Republican president had gained seats in the House and the Senate in a midterm election since the Civil War, and the first time control of the Senate had shifted to a president's party in a midterm election since popular election of Senators began in 1914.

The Republicans beat Democrats in the nationally aggregated House vote by 52 percent to 46 percent, much improved over the 49 percent to 48 percent margin they held in 1996, 1998, and 2000.[39] To be sure, local circumstances were often important, nowhere more than in Minnesota, where Democratic Senator Paul Wellstone died in an airplane crash twelve days before Election Day. When his memorial service turned into a partisan rally that offended swing voters, Walter Mondale's replacement campaign was dealt a blow from which it did not recover. Most analysts agreed, however, that the key to broad Republican success was the "nationalizing" of the elections behind Bush's themes of national security and tax cuts.[40] Solid majorities of Americans supported the Republican position on the key issues: national security and Iraq, permanent tax cuts, judicial appointments, and even Social Security.[41] Voters also placed security issues higher than the economy, and viewed Democrats as "too weak" on security by a 57 percent to 34 percent margin.[42] Indeed, national security turned out to be the powerful undertow that shaped the election by its force even when it was not visible. While there was little movement in particular races or in nationwide generic congressional preference polls that was directly traceable to the Iraq debate, it dominated the news for weeks during which Democrats had hoped to make their case on the economy and increased social spending. Four dramatic events also helped keep the war on terrorism a pressing issue: the assassination in Jordan of U.S. diplomat Laurence Foley, a bloody Al Qaeda bombing of a club in Bali, the takeover of a Moscow theater by Chechen terrorists, and the American missile attack that killed a key Al Qaeda leader and five cohorts in Yemen two days before Election Day. In the end, at least two Democratic Senate candidates—Max Cleland of Georgia and Jean Carnahan of Missouri—lost primarily and explicitly on the basis of the national security issue, and the national Democratic defeat was generally traceable to it directly or indirectly.

In addition, Bush and Republicans were rated decisively higher than Democrats on most leadership qualities and for having a clear plan to deal with problems.[43] Finally, Republicans were much more motivated and more successful at turning out their vote (by a projected rate of 43 percent to 36 percent of Democrats).[44] This was not an accident, but the product of an intense and well-planned get out the vote drive (the "72 Hour Plan"). In the end, Republicans solidified their hold on the South, made surprising gains in New England, extended their lead among men, whites, and the married, and cut their deficit among women, Catholics, Hispanics, and union households, groups targeted by Bush for inclusion in a new coalition. Indeed, while the "gender gap" persisted, Republicans nearly erased their disadvantage among women, who were actually more likely than men to cite terrorism as a key concern. They also won seniors, despite the Social Security scare.[45]

The day after, it was clear that Washington was a different place. Previous presidential party victories in midterm elections have been portrayed by the winners and much of the media as a mandate for the president. In 1934, Democratic gains were heralded as "an overwhelming popular endorsement" of Roosevelt,[46] who used his bigger majorities and new momentum to push through Social Security and other key programs. In 1962, when John F. Kennedy gained four Senate seats and lost a meager four seats in the House, analysts compared his win to that of FDR. Within a short time, Congress moved on many of his stalled legislative priorities. Thus, presidential midterm election success was integral to the New Deal and New Frontier/Great Society policy eras and arguably to the presidential landslides of 1936 and 1964.[47]

On November 6, 2002, the question was raised in regard to Bush: Will his unexpected midterm victory be translated into legislative successes? And did it foreshadow the coming of a new long-term majority coalition? As to the first question, several things could be said without too much hesitation. First, his judicial and executive appointments would get an expedited and more favorable hearing in the Senate. Second, some long-stalled items like the Homeland Security bill and even a partial birth abortion ban, which passed in 1996 but was vetoed by Bill Clinton, had renewed hope of enactment. Indeed, the logjam on both judicial appointments and Homeland Security were broken in the 2002 lame-duck session of Congress, before Senate Republicans even took the reins of majority power. Third, Bush's strengthened domestic position translated almost immediately into a strengthened position abroad. Within hours of the election results, France relented in its opposition to a tough new Security Council resolution on Iraq. Altogether, the debate over the two interpretations of the electoral Bush subsided in favor of a new consensus that this was a president to be reckoned with. The corollary was that claims of Bush's illegitimacy were set aside by almost everyone but Al Gore, who renewed that argument in public interviews shortly after Election Day.

Bush's improved position should not be exaggerated. For one thing, the rules of the Senate do not allow a party with a small majority to run roughshod over the minority, as in the House. Holds, filibusters, and right of senators to attach nongermane amendments to bills on the floor all give the Senate a more fluid and more consensual character, in which a minority or even an individual can still wield tremendous influence. Much of the time, one needs sixty votes, not fifty-one, to prevail, and Republicans after 2002 were still far from that standard. Nevertheless, the political leverage offered by the new pro-Bush consensus in Washington was potentially far-reaching.

The second question cannot be answered until 2004 or later. Michael Barone, who coined the term "49% nation," explicitly compared 2002 to 1962, declared "No more 49% nation," and argued that Bush was well positioned for the future.[48] Others were more skeptical, arguing that Republicans won because the election played to their preexisting strength on national security, not because they grew fundamentally stronger.[49] For his part, Rove detected the makings of a "fundamental" shift toward the GOP.[50]

In any case, Democrats immediately began a search for the guilty, opening up a fierce debate over the future direction of the party. Democratic National Committee Chairman Terry McAuliffe—who had taunted that "George Bush has never had coattails. . . . We hope George Bush goes to all our highly contested races"[51]—came under attack. Richard Gephardt resigned as House Minority Leader, just as Newt Gingrich had done under similar circumstances in 1998. On one side of this debate were moderate and conservative Democrats who pointed to Clinton's success as a model and argued that Senate obstructionism and the party's emphasis on abortion had hurt in some key races. On the other side, liberals contended that Democrats had defeated themselves through failure to draw distinctions over Iraq and tax cuts. In this view, "me-tooism"—once an epithet used by conservative Republicans to describe moderates like Dwight D. Eisenhower—has become the curse of the Democratic Party.[52] This battle came first to the House, where liberal Nancy Pelosi of San Francisco won Gephardt's position over the opposition of moderates Harold Ford of Tennessee and Martin Frost of Texas. Pelosi's election represented a lurch to the left by House Democrats, who had chafed for years under Clinton's pragmatism, yet only two in five Democratic voters called for their party to be more liberal or more confrontational with Bush.[53] This shift meant that Bush would be faced with a more focused, possibly more articulate, and probably harsher minority opposition, but it also meant that Republicans might have more frequent opportunities to paint Democrats as extremists. Sharp distinctions are a prerequisite for partisan realignment, a fact understood by Clinton, who forestalled Republican gains after 1994 by fuzzying distinctions.

LOOKING AHEAD TO 2004

Assuming that George W. Bush runs for reelection, there are several factors that will decide the result. These will be examined in order from the most fixed to the most variable, in the context of the aftermath of the 2002 elections.

George W. Bush

Bush himself will be the greatest known quantity. Based on his electoral career, one can make several predictions. He will likely approach the election with a consistent, focused message, well-pitched tone, and a steady pace. He will continue wearing well with voters; his even temper will benefit him, as will his reputation for sincerity. Bush will be a prolific fund-raiser for himself and his party. He will use his office effectively, understanding as his predecessor did (and as his father did not) the inherent connection between politics and governing. He will learn from his mistakes, just as in 2002 he forcefully corrected the two greatest flaws of his 2000 campaign: relaxing at the end and being beaten at the turnout game. If in trouble, Bush will return to his conservative roots to define the race, as he did against McCain and Gore. And he will not be afraid to take calculated risks.

Institutional Structure of the 2004 Presidential Election

The nominating system will be more front-loaded than any primary calendar in previous history, probably giving Bush a big advantage in the unlikely event he faces a primary challenge. The electoral college will also continue working in Bush's favor. In 2004, the electoral college map will change to account for population movements. Most of the shifted electoral votes have migrated from states that voted for Gore in 2000 to states that voted for Bush. Had the 2000 popular vote distribution been aligned with the 2004 electoral vote distribution, Bush would have gained a net of seven additional electoral votes.

Finally, the 2004 presidential election will be the first conducted under the provisions of the McCain-Feingold Act passed in early 2002. It banned soft money to the parties but raised the individual contribution limit from

$1,000 to $2,000 per person per election. In 2000, Bush eschewed federal matching funds and federal spending limits in order to retain the freedom of raising and spending money in the months prior to the national conventions. He raised $70 million, by far a new record for a presidential candidate, all in "hard money" subject to the $1,000 limit. With a $2,000 limit and the advantages of incumbency, it is conceivable that he could raise twice that amount or more in 2004. At the same time, Democrats would be unable to counter his campaign with soft money donated to the party. (It bears noting that in 2002, Democrats raised about as much soft money as Republicans but were outraised in hard money by more than two to one[54]). Of course, campaign finance reforms often have the effect of simply redirecting campaign money rather than stopping its flow. Thus, the campaign finance act of 2002 will undoubtedly have many unintended consequences. Furthermore, portions of the act may well be voided by the Supreme Court before 2004. It is, however, difficult to imagine a scenario in which Bush would not gain from an increase in the individual giving limit.

Field of Candidates

Bush's opponent will be a key variable. When Al Gore removed himself from contention in December 2002, the Democratic race became wide open. There will be two key dimensions to that race: inside versus outside, and centrist versus liberal.[55] On the inside-outside dimension, the elections of 2002 arguably damaged congressional Democrats as a whole, and especially leaders like Gephardt and Daschle. As in 1998, when Republicans looked beyond Congress, there seemed to be an opening for a Democrat from outside the Beltway. Gray Davis of California, the most obvious Democratic governor, was hurt by his weak win against inept challenger Bill Simon and chose not to run. However, before the 108th Congress was even convened, Democratic governors as a group demanded a stronger voice in the party, and got it: they were guaranteed the right to deliver the response to Bush's January 2003 State of the Union address. This struggle in the nomination battle will pit Democratic congressional figures—perhaps including Gephardt, Daschle, John Kerry, Joseph Lieberman, and John Edwards—against Democratic governors or former governors (like Howard Dean of Vermont) and other dark horses (even General Wesley Clark and Gary Hart were mentioned by some).

The liberal-centrist dimension will test the question of whether Democrats will choose to resume the Democratic Leadership Council/Bill Clinton presidential strategy or to revert to ideological form, as they seemed already to be doing in the House. Along this line, centrists (perhaps represented by Edwards and Lieberman) will fight with liberals (Kerry and Dean, among others) for the "soul of the Democratic Party." The fact that candidates will have to run somewhere on both of these dimensions will complicate the race, as will the fact that it is far from clear which dimension or which choice within each dimension Democratic primary voters are going to prefer. The apparent vacuum at the end of 2002 also probably increased pressure on Hillary Clinton to run, though she steadfastly said she would not. If she changes her mind, the Democratic race would be turned upside down yet again. Finally, the third-party plans of Ralph Nader and the Greens were both potentially crucial and indecipherable. Those plans will also undoubtedly be influenced the direction of the Democratic nomination race. For example, Nader might be more likely to stand aside if Democrats go "liberal and outside" than if they go "centrist and inside."

Coalition Building

In 2002, Republicans made a special effort to crack the Democratic base by appealing to three groups long taken for granted by Democrats: non-Cuban Hispanics, the fastest-growing immigrant group in America; blacks, the most solidly Democratic group in America; and Jews, whom the GOP considered newly approachable on the basis of antiterrorism and Middle East policy. Due to a breakdown in exit polling, it was unclear to what degree Republicans made inroads with these groups and with Catholics, long a targeted swing group. There was scattered evidence that there was some pro-GOP movement among Hispanics and Catholics. Black turnout also seemed lower than in 1998 or 2000, a fact attributed by Democrats to apathy and by Republicans to their campaigning in black communities; not voting for Democrats was in this view a first step toward voting for Republicans.[56] It was also unclear whether 2002 signaled the start of a broader and longer-term shift, like the first almost imperceptible cracks of tectonic plates moving beneath the earth's surface. On the other hand, focusing on women, minority groups, and professionals, authors John B. Judis and Ruy Texeira argued that the long-term coalitional picture was brighter for Democrats than for Republicans.[57] Much for both parties, in 2004 and beyond, will ride on the answers to those questions.

Events

At once the most important and most unpredictable variable of all will be the course of events. The condition of the economy, as always, will loom large. War, peace, and terrorism will also be crucial. Finally, the degree of success Bush and congressional Republicans have in proving themselves competent at governing with unified government will be important. Responsibility will be unified, even though power—given the close margin in the Senate—will not. Republicans will have to deliver without overreaching, and divide without seeming to. The 2004 election will be, more than anything else, a referendum on the Bush presidency and the state of the nation.

CONCLUSION

George W. Bush has spent his electoral career on the edge, as befits a man seeking to govern a nation on the edge between Republican and Democrat,

conservative and liberal, heartland and coastal metropolis. In the "49% nation" that he inherited Bush has, as a matter of course, seen victory or defeat, triumph or disaster separated by the smallest of margins.

In that environment, he has sought to remake the Republican Party and
in so doing end the long stalemate of American politics in favor of the GOP.
The decisive breakthrough that he and strategists like Karl Rove have sought
did not come in 2000 or 2002. But the election of 2002 opened for the first
time the concrete possibility that Bush was in a position to make that breakthrough in the future, especially if abetted by a sharp shift to the left by
Democrats. Bush rolled the dice, staked his reputation on the outcome, and
won. Was the man on the edge—the nation on the edge—about to come off?

In politics, two years can be a lifetime, a fact made obvious from the Republican sweep of 1994 to the Clinton reelection of 1996, from the surprising Democratic midterm win of 1998 to the Bush win of 2000, and again
from the muddled and bitter Bush win of 2000 to the clearer win of 2002.
Events and the responses of both parties to those events will determine 2004
more than any other factor. What did become more clear two years after
Florida chads and *Bush v. Gore* is that George W. Bush has been consistently
underestimated by his opponents. He may be the tortoise—steady, unas-
suming—but as Jay Ambrose pointed out after the midterm election, Bush
"somehow measures up to what he confronts."[58] After November 2002,
Bush's electoral career seemed less the result of accident than of skill.
Whether that skill carries him to a second term and Republicans to a new
majority status will be the story of 2004.

NOTES

1. David Broder, "Dems Should Take Hard Look at Bush's Political Career,"
Denver Post, 17 November 2002, p. 4E.

2. See, for example, "Can Bush Save the GOP?" *U.S. News and World Report*, 16
November 1998.

3. Michael Barone, "The 49 Percent Nation," *U.S. News and World Report*, 25
December 2000–1 January 2001, 43.

4. Rove was, for example, well-versed in the history of the McKinley administration, the leader of the last unambiguous Republican realignment in 1896–1900.

5. For a more detailed academic discussion of the 2000 election, see James W.
Ceaser and Andrew E. Busch, *The Perfect Tie: The True Story of the 2000 Presidential
Election* (Lanham, Md.: Rowman & Littlefield, 2001); Michael Nelson, ed., *The Elec-
tions of 2000* (Washington, D.C.: CQ Press, 2001); Gerald M. Pomper, ed., *The Elec-
tion of 2000* (Chatham, N.J.: Chatham House Publishers, 2001); Paul R. Abramson,
John H. Aldrich, and David W. Rohde, *Change and Continuity in the 2000 Elections*
(Washington, D.C.: CQ Press, 2001).

6. William G. Mayer, "Forecasting Presidential Nominations" in William G.
Mayer, ed., *In Pursuit of the White House: How We Choose Our Presidential Nominees*
(Chatham, N.J.: Chatham House, 1996), 44–71. When Mayer made this observation,

the number was five of six; all three subsequent contested nominations (Dole, Bush, and Gore) fit the same pattern.

7. See Harold W. Stanley, "The Nominations: The Return of the Party Leaders" in Michael Nelson, ed., *The Elections of 2000*, 32.

8. Adam Nagourney, "Wins of the Father are Visited on the Son," *New York Times*, 14 July 1998, Section IV, p. 1.

9. For example, in New Hampshire, the best estimates are that McCain outpolled Bradley by about 35,000 votes (or a two to one margin) among Independents and party-crossers; Bradley only lost to Gore by 7,000 votes. See Ceaser and Busch, *The Perfect Tie*, chapter 3.

10. Voter News Service, "GOP Primary: South Carolina; Exit Poll: Republicans," retrieved from http://www.cnn.com/ELECTION/2000/primaries/SC/poll.rep.html.

11. Kenneth T. Walsh, "A Bloody Battle," *U.S. News and World Report*, 13 March 2000, pp. 16–18.

12. Kathleen Hall Jamieson and Paul Waldman, *Electing the President 2000: The Insiders' View* (Philadelphia: University of Pennsylvania Press, 2001), pp. 19, 21, 69, 178.

13. Ceaser and Busch, *The Perfect Tie*, chap. 4.

14. Robert G. Kaiser, "Academics Say It's Elementary: Gore Wins," *Washington Post*, 31 August 2000, p. A12.

15. A Gallup poll indicated that 10 percent of undecided voters might have been influenced against Bush by the DUI revelation, a number at once small and pivotal, given the closeness of the race, retrieved from http//:www.gallup.com/poll/releases/001105/asp.

16. Evan Thomas, "What a Long, Strange Trip," *Newsweek*, 20 November 2000, 30.

17. Gallup poll of December 2–4, 2000, retrieved from http://www.gallup.com/poll/releases/pr001206.asp.

18. Paul J. Quirk and Sean C. Matheson, "The Presidency: The Election and Prospects for Leadership," in Michael Nelson, ed., *The Elections of 2000*, 178.

19. See Clay Lambert, "Paper's Count," *Denver Rocky Mountain News*, 14 January 2001, p. 56A; "Analysis of Florida Ballots Proves Favorable to Bush," *New York Times*, 4 April 2001, p. A18; Amy Driscoll, "Bush Would Have Won Florida Recount, Review Shows," *Columbus Dispatch*, 26 February 2001, p. 4A; Damian Whitworth, "Miami Recount Shows Gore Was Still the Loser," *Times of London*, 16 January 2001; "Florida Recount Study: Bush Still Wins," retrieved from http://www.cnn.com/SPECIALS/2001/florida.ballots/stories/main.html.

20. Wirthlin Worldwide, 7 November 2002.

21. By Election Day 2002, that possibility was confirmed by polls showing higher approval ratings for Congress and no desire by the public for a wholesale cleaning out of incumbents. See "Voters in No Mood to 'Throw the Bums Out,'" Gallup News Service, (e-mail publication) 6 November 2002, retrieved from http://www.gallup.com/poll/releases/pr021106.asp.

22. Angus Campbell, "Surge and Decline: A Study of Electoral Change," *Public Opinion Quarterly* 24 (1960), 387–419; James E. Campbell, *The Presidential Pulse of Congressional Elections* (Lexington: University Press of Kentucky, 1993).

23. Bruce I. Oppenheimer, James A. Stimson, and Richard W. Waterman, "Interpreting U.S. Congressional Elections: The Exposure Thesis," *Legislative Studies Quarterly* 11 (1986), 227–47.

24. Gerald H. Kramer, Short-term Fluctuation in U.S. Voting Behavior," *American Political Science Review* 65 (1971), 131–43; Howard S. Bloom and Douglas H. Price, "Voter Response to Short-Run Economic Conditions: The Asymmetric Effect of Prosperity and Recession," *American Political Science Review* 69 (1975), 1240–55; James E. Piereson, "Presidential Popularity and Midterm Voting at Different Electoral Levels," *American Journal of Political Science* 19 (1975), 683–702; Edward R. Tufte, *Political Control of the Economy* (Princeton, N.J.: Princeton University Press, 1978); Gary C. Jacobson and Samuel Kernell, *Strategy and Choice in Congressional Elections* (Boston: Little, Brown, 1981); Gary C. Jacobson, *The Politics of Congressional Elections*, 3rd ed. (New York: HarperCollins, 1992).

25. David W. Moore, "Bush Approval at 68%," Gallup News Service, retrieved from http://www.gallup.com/poll/releases/021115.asp.

26. Robert S. Erikson, "The Puzzle of Midterm Loss," *Journal of Politics* 50 (1988), 1011–29.

27. Alberto Alesina and Howard Rosenthal, *Partisan Politics, Divided Government, and the Economy* (Cambridge: Cambridge University Press, 1995); Samuel Kernell, "Presidential Popularity and Negative Voting: An Alternative Explanation to the Midterm Decline of the President's Party," *American Political Science Review* 71 (1977), 44–66.

28. See Howard Fineman, "How Bush Did It," *Newsweek*, 18 November 2002, 28.

29. See "Bush in Campaign Mode," CNN Allpolitics, 22 October 2002, retrieved from http://www.cnn.com/2002/ALLPOLITICS/10/22/elec02.bush.campaigning.ap/index.html.

30. Wirthlin Worldwide, November 7, 2002.

31. Elisabeth Bumiller and David E. Sanger, "Republicans Say Rove Was Mastermind of Big Victory," *New York Times*, 7 November 2002, p. B1.

32. David M. Halbfinger, "Bush's Push, Eager Volunteers, and Big Turnout Led to Georgia's Sweep," *New York Times*, 10 November 2002, p. A24.

33. See Richard A. Oppel Jr., "President's Help for His Governor Brother Includes More Than Campaign Stops," *New York Times*, 18 October 2002, p. A18.

34. It also bears pointing out that his father was attacked by Democrats in late 1990 when he waited until *after* the midterm elections to begin a build-up in Saudi Arabia of the armored forces needed for offensive operations to free Kuwait. The timing of the decision, it was argued, did not give Americans an opportunity to fully take war into account in their midterm vote.

35. As an indication of the fact that Hispanics were suddenly "in play," 2002 saw a massive increase in political ads on Spanish-language television. By one estimate, $8 million was spent on 12,000 such ads touting Senate, House, or gubernatorial candidates. Lizette Alvarez, "Latinos Are Focus of New Brand of Ads," *New York Times*, 28 October 2002, p. A20.

36. Kate O'Beirne, "They're All Bushies Now?" *National Review*, 11 November 2002, 20–22. An extreme form of this phenomenon could be seen in Louisiana, where incumbent Democrat Mary Landrieu narrowly held on to her seat in a December runoff only by completely shunning the national Democratic Party and boasting that she supported Bush "75 percent of the time."

37. See Wirthlin Worldwide, 7 November 2002; Cokie and Steven V. Roberts, "Democrats Hope Desire for Balance Garners Votes," *Rocky Mountain News*, 1 November 2002, p. 43A.

38. See Fineman, "How Bush Did It"; and Timothy Noah, "Democrats 36,000: Where's That Emerging Democratic Majority?" *Slate*, 11 November 2002, retrieved from http://www.slate.msn.com/?id=2073779&device=.

39. Michael Barone, "No More 49% Nation," *U.S. News and World Report*, 18 November 2002, 33.

40. Todd S. Pardum and David E. Rosenbaum, "Bush's Stumping for Candidates Is Seen as a Critical Factor in Republican Victory," *New York Times*, 7 November 2002, p. B4.

41. Frank Newport, "New Poll Measures Support for Issues on GOP Legislative Agenda," Gallup News Service, 13 November 2002, retrieved from http://gallup.com/poll/releases/pr021113.asp.

42. On security vs. economy, see Wirthlin Worldwide, 7 November 2002; and Jeffrey M. Jones, "Economy, Terrorism Continue to Top List of Most Important Problems," Gallup News Service, 18 November 2002, retrieved from http://www.gallup.com/poll/releases/pr021118.asp. On Democrats, see Lydia Saad, "Democratic Party Image Takes a Post-Election Hit," Gallup News Service, 14 November 2002, retrieved from http://www.gallup.com/poll/releases/pr021114.asp.

43. Wirthlin Worldwide, 7 November 2002; Moore, "Bush Approval at 68%."

44. David W. Moore and Jeffrey M. Jones, "Higher Turnout among Republicans Key to Victory," Gallup News Service, 7 November 2002, retrieved from http://www.gallup.com/poll/releases/021107.asp.

45. Steven Thomma, "Survey Tells How GOP Triumphed," *Denver Post*, 14 November 2002, p. A1.

46. "Mr. Roosevelt's New Responsibility," *New York Times*, 8 November 1934, p. 22.

47. See Andrew E. Busch, *Horses in Midstream: U.S. Midterm Elections and Their Consequences 1894–1998* (Pittsburgh: University of Pittsburgh Press, 1999), chap. 6.

48. Barone, "No more 49% nation"; and Michael Barone, "Party Like It's 1962," *Wall Street Journal Opinion Journal*, 9 November 2002, retrieved from http://www.opinionjournal.com/editorial/feature.html?id=110002599.

49. For example, see Donald Green and Eric Schickler, "Winning a Battle, Not a War," *New York Times*, 12 November 2002, p. A31.

50. Michael Janofsky, "Rove Declares Nation Is Tilting to Republicans," *New York Times*, 14 November 2002, p. A27.

51. Todd S. Purdum, "Stung by Losses, Party Buzzes about Its Leader," *New York Times*, 12 November 2002, p. A18.

52. See David S. Broder, "Tipping Left toward 2004," *Washington Post*, 13 November 2002, retrieved from http://www.washingtonpost.com/wp-dyn/articles/A46162-2002Nov12.html; Robert D. Novak, "Rocky Road for Democrats," *Denver Post*, 4 December 2002, p. 7B; Tom Freedman and Bill Knapp, "How Republicans Usurped the Center," *New York Times*, 8 November 2002, p. A33; Jesse Jackson, "Clueless Candidates Failed to Address Issues That Inspire Minorities to Vote," *Chicago Sun-Times*, 12 November 2002, retrieved from http://www.suntimes.com/output/jesse/cst-edt-jesse12.html. The latter argument echoes Ralph Nader's 2000 critique of the Democratic Party. See Nader, *Crashing the Party* (New York: St. Martin's Press, 2002).

53. Saad, "Democratic Party Image."

54. "Fund Raising for Midterm Races Sets Record," CNN Allpolitics, 3 November 2002, retrieved from http://www.cnn.com/2002/ALLPOLITICS/11/03/elections.money/index.html.

55. This kind of two-dimensional political grid was last obvious in 1992, when Bill Clinton benefited from being both ideologically centrist and a centrist—standing between George Bush and Ross Perot—on the inside-outside dimension. See James Ceaser and Andrew Busch, *Upside Down and Inside Out: The 1992 Elections and American Politics* (Lanham, Md.: Rowman & Littlefield, 1993).

56. Fred Barnes, "The Emerging 9/11 Majority," *Weekly Standard*, 18 November 2002; Michael Barone, "Whose Majority?" *National Review*, 9 December 2002; John Berlau, "GOP Makes Gains with Minorities," *WorldNet Daily*, 27 November 2002, retrieved from http://www.worldnetdaily.com/article.asp?ARTICLE_ID=29794; for a more cautious view, see Steve Sailer, "The Color of Election 2002," *National Review Online*, 15 November 2002, retrieved from http://www.nationalreview.com/comment/comment-sailer111502.asp.

57. John B. Judis and Ruy Texeira, *The Emerging Democratic Majority* (New York: Scribner, 2002).

58. Jay Ambrose, "Missing the Boat on Bush," *Rocky Mountain News*, 7 November 2002, p. 52A.

Index